Alexander Stuart's novel *The War Zone* caused some controversy with the Whitbread Prize committee. They voiced no objections to his second novel *Tribes*, his two children's books or *Five and a Half Times Three*, the book written with Ann Totterdell about the life and death from cancer of their young son, Joe Buffalo. In 1990 Stuart went to Miami to interview the boxer Nigel Benn – and never quite left. The executive producer of Nicolas Roeg's film *Insignificance*, Stuart teaches screenwriting at the University of Miami, when not enjoying the more meaningful pleasures of the beach.

CRITICAL ACCLAIM FOR *LIFE ON MARS*:

'*Life on Mars* is simply the most stunning read of the year. Alexander Stuart's wit is like clear glass – under it the exotic and lurid blooms of Florida flower, fluoresce and flourish with the most hilarious ripeness and crackling richness. Between laughter and gasps of astonishment there is little time to breathe. Never has the approach of a final page caused such pangs. This is the kind of writing that drives people into bookshops. Brilliant'
Stephen Fry

'A really original book about an amazing place. Alexander Stuart is far more interested in people than geography. The story of John Hood alone (a sort of real-

life Travolta gangster) makes *Life on Mars* hilarious, moving and bizarre'
Danny Boyle, film director, *Trainspotting* and *Shallow Grave*

'Like a melancholy, uplifting night on the beach at the end of the world. Miami is where the crazy seek sanity and the sane seek madness. Alex has found both'
Robert Elms

'A vibrant but tender tour of Florida low-life that seeks a human touch behind drugs, drag and Disney'
New Statesman & Society

'In fizzling lines of addictive prose which can almost be sniffed off the page, he upturns the glass-fibre stones of travel-poster Florida. Stuart's reality is much funnier and strangely more optimistic than any theme park'
The Times

'You will not find a better social biopsy of Miami than this'
Carl Hiaasen, *Guardian*

'There's much diverting anecdotage here, but also a disconcerting sense that this is a real work of escapism in which it's not the reader who is trying to escape'
GQ

'A firework of a book – all the strange human fauna of Florida. His personal exploration of Miami in all its eccentric extravagance is hilarious. Stuart's unrivalled gift for appreciating the quirky, the tragic and the terrible all at once comes into play'
Daily Express

LIFE ON MARS

Alexander Stuart

BLACK SWAN

LIFE ON MARS
A BLACK SWAN BOOK: 0 552 99617 3

Originally published in Great Britain by Doubleday,
a division of Transworld Publishers Ltd.

PRINTING HISTORY
Doubleday edition published 1996
Black Swan edition published 1997

Set in 11 on 12¾ pt Melior by Falcon Oast Graphic Art

Black Swan books are published by Transworld Publishers Ltd,
61–63 Uxbridge Road, London W5 5SA,
in Australia by Transworld Publishers (Australia) Pty Ltd,
15–25 Helles Avenue, Moorebank, NSW 2170
and in New Zealand by Transworld Publishers (NZ) Ltd,
3 William Pickering Drive, Albany, Auckland.

Reproduced, printed and bound in Great Britain by
Cox & Wyman Ltd, Reading, Berks.

To Charong

Wor ai ni.

1

AMERICA IS A VIRUS

Strange thoughts, in the dead of night: America is a
virus, invading my soul, destroying my Britishness,
my faith in humanity, my quiet calm and natural
reserve. Florida is a swamp, sucking me under,
seducing me with its heat, its soft, moist air and
expanses of human flesh, draining me of all but my
most immediate sensual needs: sex, food, sleep . . .

And yet I love it. Who wouldn't? I can step outside
right now, at almost midnight, and feel the June heat
of Miami Beach wrap itself around me, making me
sweat even in a T-shirt. I can walk four blocks and
find a sea warm enough, at this time of night, to
swim in. I can listen to the crickets or the beat of a
conga drum from the park up the road. Or, in a
different mood, drive around, past million-dollar
homes, past Madonna's house and Gianni Versace's
and Sylvester Stallone's, then venture downtown,
across the causeways, beneath Miami's web of
elevated freeways, just north of the urban ghetto
of Overtown and south of the crack neighbourhood of
Liberty City, to the local public hospital, Jackson
Memorial, where every day in their trauma centre
they perform two craniotomies due to gunshot
wounds to the head.

There are times – even with this violent edge, of

which I have seen very little in five years – there are times when Miami seems so perfect that I truly feel at peace. And others when this sticky little sand trap feels like the arse-end of the universe, when intelligent conversation seems a lifetime away, and the relentless heat and humidity offer a perverse torture to a fugitive from the chill nights and unreliable days of British summertime.

So why am I here? And why, when I try to think of a single image that will capture how I feel about my surroundings, do I come back to this – my friend, Jason, a Brooklyn-born plumber turned model, who knelt on the punishingly hot sand of Miami Beach one Saturday afternoon and, with a surprisingly vulnerable light in his New York-hoodlum eyes, said something which struck a chord in me:

'When I first came here, I thought this was a spiritual place.'

It was an odd remark to make, given the popular view of Florida as a mix of vice, violence and Mickey Mouse, but he had just returned from travelling in Thailand, and the calmer perspective of the East had focused his feelings about Miami.

Perhaps his words are lodged in my memory because he was such a part of my first months here, one of a group of fashion models I hung out with after meeting two ridiculously attractive nineteen-year-olds, Shana and Stephanie, in a laundromat one night. There was Billie, a college-educated woman in her mid-twenties, keen to work behind the scenes in film production; Chris, a cheerleader-type with an appetite for large diamond rings; Elissa, the youngest of the group at seventeen, already well travelled and a little too worldly; and Tom, a dark, brooding figure, whose quiet, family-directed anger would on occasion surface without warning – usually when drunk.

They all shared the same overcrowded house, a few blocks from my newly rented apartment on Miami Beach, and I quickly found myself caught up in their tireless cycle of parties, castings and personal crises. They were my introduction to Florida, and if fashion models don't immediately prompt thoughts of spirituality, I had my own reasons for seeking some kind of reaffirmation, and they more than provided it with their friendship.

I came here following the death from cancer of my five-year-old son, Joe Buffalo, and my separation from his mother, Ann, wanting to unload the past and find a new future, and this group of five or six young people made me welcome in a town where I knew no-one. More than anything, they made me feel that life would get better again.

Then one day Jason left, followed soon after by Chris, then Stephanie and Shana, and like so many people who have been for a time close friends in Miami, I lost contact with them entirely. The city is like that: both a place to stay or even to stop – the end of the line – and a switching point, where people change course or change identities, then move on.

2

PARADISE WITH A LOBOTOMY

At the airport there is no-one to meet me when I touch down in Miami for the first time in October 1990. I search aimlessly for Nick, the photographer from *GQ*, whom I've never met but who is supposed to help me concoct a story for the magazine about the British boxer, Nigel Benn. Benn is training in Miami and is the reason I've flown across the Atlantic from a pleasantly autumnal Britain to this dank hothouse of (so far as I could judge from the air) sand bars and tract homes and great swathes of glistening turquoise ocean.

Accustomed to airport arrival cock-ups, I climb into a beat-up maroon taxi and give the driver the name of an hotel where the magazine has hopefully arranged a reservation. As we ride Route 836, following signposts promising Miami Beach, he asks in a thick New York accent why I'm here, and I wonder: 'Yes, why? What do I know about boxing? Or Miami, for that matter?'

And the answer is: not much. Virtually my only sense of Florida comes from a story my sister told me about landing in a seaplane in Key West during a flood. Having expected perfect weather for their holiday, she and her husband instead found the streets submerged, but with the help of sandbags the bars and restaurants had managed to stay open, and my sister had a good time.

But that was Key West. Miami is a blank to me. Even *Miami Vice* didn't register, beyond key images burned into my memory from its opening title sequence: flamingoes in flight, speedboats, grids of light and water, walls of tropical pastel. As far as I know, Miami is simply a retirement heaven, especially popular with New York Jews and with an average age situated in the low nineties.

Only as we roll across the MacArthur Causeway, past the Port of Miami, past the vast but somehow tawdry ocean liners, the *Fantasy* and the *Ecstasy*, waiting to cruise the Caribbean, do I appreciate that Miami Beach is not just mainland Miami's deckchair ghetto but in fact an island – and, in the American way of making things greater than they are (baseball's World Series is a case in point), a city in its own right.

And only as my taxi driver points out the nondescript but evidently historic Fifth Street Boxing Gym, next to a parking-lot between Washington and Collins Avenues, do I understand that Miami has a rightful place in boxing's past, and remember that this is where middleweight champ Jake LaMotta (as played by Robert De Niro in the unforgettable *Raging Bull*, the source of much of my meagre knowledge of boxing), retired to, running his own seedy nightclub and encountering a critical run-in with the law over underage drinking.

An hour later, I'm sitting at a table on the hotel patio, rejoicing in my luck.

I've already dumped my bags, crossed the road for a swim in the seductively warm sea, and now here I

11

am, margarita in hand, gazing at the human traffic on Ocean Drive and wondering how there can be so many startlingly attractive, model-thin women in one town – and why they're all wearing the same life-threateningly short sundress?

The pool beside me has a painted mermaid beckoning enticingly from beneath its Hockney-blue water, but I fail to recognize the signs: my life is being lured towards a reef; I am about to be shipwrecked on what one British friend will later call, 'Paradise with a lobotomy.'

The next morning, I kick into gear. I have a meeting set with Nigel Benn and his British trainer, Vic Andretti, at the Fifth Street Gym, but first there's time for breakfast.

As I walk down Collins Avenue with the sun on my neck and sweat inching down my vertebrae, I feel that I am in a city unlike any I've visited. This is America, yet it doesn't feel like America. Flies buzz in the heat. A *salsa* tune plays on a radio. The buildings are low-rise, people-sized and, for a square mile which has been designated an historic district, mostly Art Deco – or more accurately a 1930s and 1940s American interpretation of the style known as *moderne*, with curves, lips and mouldings distinguishing what would otherwise be fairly basic boxes.

The colours are faded pastel: sun-bleached pinks, blues and yellows, peeling in the salt air. This is 1990, so the much vaunted revival of South Beach has only just begun. The streets have a run-down, neglected air to them, and the ethnic accent of this end of the Beach (as the whole area is called, not

12

just the strip of sand by the sea) is not Jewish but Hispanic, as evidenced by the intriguing Cuban laundry-cum-*cafetería* opposite me now, with its fake-brick exterior and wrought-iron window grilles – or the newspapers in the corner stores: *Diario Las Américas* and *El Nuevo Herald* (the Spanish-language sister to the *Miami Herald*, usually included free inside the English-language edition, but here displayed on its own).

And when I hunt down my eggs, toast and steaming *café con leche* at Puerto Sagua, the restaurant recommended by my hotel's desk clerk, I feel as though I've left America altogether and entered some sort of space-time continuum. For the restaurant is entirely staffed by non-English-speaking (or nominally bilingual) Cubans, dressed in white shirts or *guayaberas* and black trousers, and the whole feel of the place is dark-wood 1950s, with a large breakfast counter and a three-dimensional mural on the wall of the restaurant's Havana namesake.

But despite Miami's Cuban dominance (44 per cent of the population is Hispanic, mostly Cuban, as compared to 35 per cent Anglo and 21 per cent African-American), when I step outside, back onto Collins and the short walk to the Fifth Street Gym, I have less a sense of Cuba and its island glories than of some Central American backwater, beaten into submission by relentless heat and dust.

I feel dislocated, in an interesting way, as if I'm caught somewhere between the First World (CNN, high technology, the great American hinterland beyond) and Third World (Spanish boxing handbills pasted to the lampposts, faded *ferreterías* and *fruterías*, hardware stores and fruit shops, spilling out onto the sidewalks). Miami does not feel like America or Cuba, and certainly like none of the clichéd images the souvenir manufacturers tend to promote: plastic flamingoes, wind-surfing snow scenes (!), swizzle-sticks shaped like palm trees. It's stranger than that – like Frank Sinatra crossed with Luis Buñuel, or Flipper trapped in a labyrinthine fiction by Borges.

On this particular morning, my first in Miami, Roosevelt Ivory's Fifth Street Boxing Gym stands proudly next to the parking-lot of a supermarket named Pantry Pride.

Due to some sick, infantile perversion of my mind, this registers repeatedly – every time I care to think of it, in fact – as *Panty* Pride, but even this felicitous image cannot distract me from my surprise, as I mount the narrow flight of stairs leading to the gym, where Nigel Benn, current (1990) WBO world middleweight champion, is training in a grimy pink stucco building in a low-rent neighbourhood, its existence marked only by a modest, hand-painted sign over the door.

As I step inside the magical squalor of the gym itself, I'm met by Vic Andretti, Benn's trainer, with whom, truth to tell, I shared a drink at my hotel bar the night before. Andretti is a character straight out of a Martin Amis novel. Short, stocky, with a voice and even a face a little like Bob Hoskins's, his amiability can't mask the fact that he's the kind of man you wouldn't want to rub up the wrong way in an East End pub – or anywhere else, for that matter. Forty-nine and a former British junior welterweight champion himself, he's the owner, with his wife, Brenda, of a restaurant in Shoreditch called The Ringside.

'Nigel's just warming up,' he tells me, in gruff tones which transport me straight back to a London street market. 'I'll introduce you in a minute.'

And so I watch the reason I'm here, thousands of miles from Brighton and home: Nigel Benn, twenty-six-year-old Dark Destroyer and Mean Machine, working up a sweat in front of a full-length mirror in this picture-perfect setting of trenchantly seedy Americana.

Look at this place, the Fifth Street Boxing Gym, while you still can, because even as you read this the whole building has been reduced to a flat patch of tarmac: a parking-lot. But, for the present, the air inside is so thick with dust floating in the few shafts of sunlight to penetrate the gloom that you could almost slice through to the past with a knife, peel away the layers to reveal the gym's forty years of boxing history. Worn red theatre seats line one side of the ring — whose canvas floor has a rip in one corner. Boxing paintings and sun-bleached posters adorn the walls, while everywhere is the smell of boxing itself: a miasma of stale sweat and saliva, dried blood and damp towels, that is no different here than in the Albert Hall or a spangled Las Vegas arena.

Benn comes over. He looks me up and down. He shakes my hand. I feel as if my ignorance of boxing is advertised by a pulsing neon sign above my head. He quite possibly thinks I'm an idiot. Equally he might wonder if I think the same of him.

But he's no idiot, Nigel Benn. He has sharp eyes,

the whites of which pierce through the shadows of the gym with a searching intelligence, an intelligence which seems twinned with his aggression, as if they are born of the same root – as if he's endured much abuse at some distant point in his past and still expects, or is at least prepared for, the same from you.

He looks slightly rougher in the flesh than in his photographs (though who doesn't?), but still sharp enough with his gangsta rap image and lean muscularity to make Andretti's job, sparring in the ring with him, less than enviable.

'I have to train now,' Benn apologizes. 'We'll talk over lunch . . .'

And as he continues to work out and I continue to watch, I'm struck by a rush of conflicting thoughts and emotions. I know nothing about boxing, but I want to know, partly because I'm in the middle of writing a novel about tenderness and aggression, and I think it might be useful to look at culturally sanctioned violence – but also for vaguer, more personal reasons: boxing's earthiness and animalism, the fact that it's rooted in physicality, the way I would like my life and work to be.

Still more than this, I sense a peculiar nostalgia – for my childhood and memories of my father watching fights on our old black-and-white TV; and for boxing itself, as if, at the end of the twentieth century, we know that boxing can't go on much longer: it's out of date, it's both too brutal and perhaps not brutal enough in a world of ear-amputation movies, serial murders and domestic beatings.

Over the next two weeks, I spend time with Benn,

here on Fifth Street and at the far fancier health spa of the Fontainebleau Hilton on Forty-fourth and Collins, as he trains for a fight in England against Chris Eubank and for a proposed five-million-dollar Las Vegas contest against Thomas 'Hit Man' Hearns.

I notice that Benn talks often and loudly about winning:

'We're second-class citizens in sport in England. Like, Eddie the Eagle flying off that slope and coming last, and everyone cheering so that it all becomes a joke. If it was me, I'd shoot the motherfucker out of the sky! I'm being serious, because he comes last, you know, I can't handle that. I'm a winner, I'm not no frigging loser or second-class citizen. Hey, I am a winner and I will remain a winner.'

But his mask of arrogance and bravado sometimes slips and I'm impressed by a throw-away remark about Las Vegas, where he beat Iran Barkley:

'When I went to Las Vegas, I was scared just seeing my name in lights. Because you always think about Mike Tyson or Sugar Ray Leonard there – or Frank Sinatra. You don't think, "*Nigel Benn*"! You can't get no higher than Vegas. My heart was just going.'

I have my photograph taken with Nigel and his girlfriend, Sharon, at a health food restaurant near the Fontainebleau, then take my life in my hands, as I see it, when I put training pads on my arms and venture into the ring with him, to test the force of his blows. Only as he throws a punch at my forehead, seemingly at the speed of light, his gloved fist miraculously halting within a hair's breadth of my brow, do I recall a cautionary item by the great

17

Hunter S. Thompson, wherein, for the purpose of a story, he entered the ring with Muhammad Ali, then realized: 'What if he *forgets* we're only fooling around? What if he suffers some kind of mental lapse and suddenly thinks this is *serious*?'

And later, over cocktails – juice cocktails, in Benn's case – we talk about whether, as a black fighter, he finds more racism in Miami than in England.

'Over here,' he says, 'it seems like everybody's got an attitude problem with blacks. Some I can understand, because they've got this problem with crime. But what it is, it seems that when a black guy does something, it always gets blown out of fucking proportion. Not only blacks do it – whites do it as well! But when a black guy does it, it's in big bloody black letters all over the place. And I think to myself, "Don't just do it to us. If you're going to do it, do it to everyone."

'You see, in England, we was watching a programme, me and Sharon, and there was adverts with black guys in there, modelling and being the top part – in England. I ain't seen an advert with a black model here.'

He glances at Sharon, the mother of two of his three children, a woman who seems very rooted – perhaps the anchor to his raw energy? The tip of his tongue plays over his upper front teeth in an engagingly mischievous grin.

'To me, it's not even like America in Miami. It's more like Puerto Rico. And it's not just racism. They've got this attitude problem with everything. It's not like you're in England and your fight's coming up and it's, "Come on, mate, let's have a beer."

Here, it's, "OK, motherfucker, I'll get you."

'It's not like you're in England, you have a street fight and that's it. Over here, you hurt someone and they say, "Yeah, I'll be back to fuck you up." And you think, "Who's laughing now?" Because suddenly you've got a double-barrel in your face!

'So I think to myself, "Well, it's not really worth it. I'll just keep my nose clean." I come here to train, I don't really come here to party. England's my home, England's pleasure. This is business here.'

Now comes the hard part: turning this into a story. With my deadline looming and a trip to Cuba for another article two days away, I lock myself in my cell at my comfortably refurbished Deco hotel, the Edison, and try to figure out what the hell I'm going to write for *GQ*. We've done the photos and Nigel Benn will smile glossily out from the cover of the January issue, so I'm expected to come up with something big, but the problem is, every time I start to write I'm distracted by the noise and bustle a few metres outside my window on Ocean Drive.

It's Saturday afternoon and the ritual weekend march of massed humanity up and down the strip has begun. Men and women in micro-skirts, micro-shorts and tank tops glide on their rollerblades among the groups of Latinos, Anglos and tourists cruising the sidewalks and cycle-path which run parallel to the beach. Models, hustlers and hangers-on negotiate the common obstacles of any town: a hairy man with an iguana on a leash, a bikini-clad woman draped with a lithe, tongue-flicking python, a drag queen on stilts.

Cars crawl at showcase speed, their vast sound

systems pounding the pavement, vibrating even the wood floors of my hotel room with their heavy bass – no-one going anywhere, just driving to look and be looked at: boys watching girls watching boys holding hands.

And everywhere human flesh on display. Not quite so much perhaps as across the road on one of America's rare topless beaches where almost anything goes, but still plenty of people sufficiently fried by the heat to parade in their crack bikinis, their strings and thongs, asses hanging out, mostly toned to perfection, but occasionally a little cellulite squeezing by to ripple criminally in the sun.

My gaze shifts distractedly from window to typewriter and back again, and I find myself bewitched by this rolling carpet of excess outside, this confusion of amber skin, money and shiny objects, its huge collective shark-jaws wide open and moving forward, ever forward, devouring all in its path, then constantly demanding, *'More!'*

And I am filled with wonder and envy and fear. I feel much like Woody Allen at the start of *Stardust Memories*, when he is on the train bound for the junk-heap of human despair, while on the other train – the train he can glimpse so tantalizingly through his carriage window – everyone is gaily dressed and beautiful, champagne glasses in hand, balloons in the air, as they celebrate the party that life (other people's lives, never yours) can be.

But I press on with work, feeling righteous, feeling moral, dealing swiftly and professionally with the latest problem to arise – a deafening reggae party alongside the pool below my window – by switching rooms to the other side of the hotel.

The only flaw in this arrangement is that the Clevelander, the hotel across the street from my new location, also has a party in progress, this one playing hormone-thrashing white rock and roll, and both events are set to finish, I'm assured when I enquire politely by telephone, at around four a.m.

So I close my mind to the music and concentrate solely on Nigel Benn, convincing myself that somehow I will fax the story through to the magazine before I leave for Cuba early Monday morning.

I dredge up everything I know about boxing, reflecting again on Muhammad Ali, a luminous figure from my childhood not simply for his matchless skills as a fighter, his grace and gentle-voiced poetry, but as a man who epitomized integrity at least twice in his life – once when he put his Muslim faith on the line and changed his name from Cassius Clay, and again when he was jailed for refusing to fight in Vietnam, throwing his race's history back in the face of America when he argued, 'No Viet Cong ever called me "nigger".'

I am transported back to being eight years old and coming home from swimming with my father in Plumstead, and going into a tobacconist's to buy his cigarettes, to be told by a tearful shopkeeper that President Kennedy had been shot. I barely knew who Kennedy was, but the gravity of the event was unmistakable and its violence seemed linked in my mind with images of Ali and far-distant ringsides (but Ali as a potential *victim* of violence, from the Klan or whomever, not as a perpetrator), creating a disturbing sense of profound aggression somewhere out there, in America, beyond the TV's window.

21

I remember my surprise at the first Benn fight I attended at the Albert Hall in 1988 (which was also the first boxing match I had ever gone to), that half the sweat-drenched audience seemed to be on Ecstasy – a suspicion confirmed, to my mind at least, by the almost musical, pre-fight cries which issued from the crowd of an enquiry common enough in those heady days of acid house: 'CAN – YOU – FEEL – IT?'

I trace the meat-and-potatoes of the story: the arc of Benn's career; his contentious split from former manager, Frank Warren (later injured in a controversial East End shooting); Benn's sole professional defeat – at this point in time – by Michael Watson; his family background; his preparation for the upcoming fights against Eubank and Hearns.

And around five a.m., exhausted but relieved that silence now reigns outside by the pool, I find a quote from Benn which seems nicely to wrap things up:

'If I can encourage some kids out there to achieve something, to let them know the pitfalls, and I can bring them through with me, then that's a bonus. Because things are getting better. Here's a black guy driving around in a Bentley at twenty-six and owning a Porsche 911 Turbo, and his missus has got two BMW 325i's, and we've bought a big five-bedroom house in Manor Road, Chigwell – *the* road! Hey, things are changing! Me and Sharon, we're going to have a wicked life. We're going to have a laugh. We're laughing now.'

I turn off the typewriter, brush my teeth and fall into bed, thinking: 'The beach this afternoon! Get some sleep, check through the piece, then hit the sand! Sun, surf and . . .'

Beside my ear, the telephone rings. It's six a.m. I listen, groggy from the promise of sleep.

'Hey, Alex, right?' A man's voice, deep and slightly scratchy. 'It's James. We met Friday in the hotel bar – you bought me a beer, remember?' I do, vaguely: a tired-faced black guy with a warm smile and a string of minor arrests to his name. 'I'm downstairs in the lobby, man. I've got cocaine and two beautiful women. We were thinking, we could come up to your room and party.' A low chuckle. 'Party time, *amigo*!'

'James,' I grunt, wondering who on the desk gave him my room number at this time in the morning. 'I've been working all night. I'm tired. I just want to sleep.'

'Hey, two beautiful girls, man.' He sounds crestfallen. I almost feel guilty. 'It's six a.m. Where we gonna go?'

But this is the Devil's voice – the Devil on my shoulder, the Devil of Miami. And it's just too late an hour, and I'm too wrecked, seriously to consider entertaining the Devil right now.

'No,' I tell him. 'No, no, no, no, no . . .'

And of course there's irony to all this. There's always irony.

Even with all that talk of winning, Nigel must have entertained in the deep recesses of his heart (as I, in my innocence, did not) the possibility of *losing*. Or more significantly from my point of view, of losing a fight and his title before my article about him could appear.

23

Which is what happened. One month later, in November 1990 at the Birmingham NEC Arena, Benn battled against Chris Eubank in a fight which would become legend. By this time I had already rented an Art Deco apartment on Miami Beach, five blocks from the ocean, opposite a park watched over by spindly palms perhaps fifty feet tall, but I was back in England for the fight and I screamed myself hoarse as Eubank simply refused to be bested by Benn. The match was long and brutal – even as the victor, Eubank required stitches in his tongue – but after it, Benn's WBO world middleweight belt passed to Eubank.

Next morning, my editor at *GQ* called to say that we had no story. My profile of Benn as Britain's hippest, most aggressive, unbeatable fighter simply made no sense any more. His Las Vegas contest against Thomas Hearns, for which Benn was to have received five million dollars, would not take place. (By way of consolation Benn reputedly received one million pounds for the Eubank fight.) Eighty thousand colour covers of the January *GQ* had already been printed and would have to be scrapped.

I would be paid, I had made a major decision to shift, temporarily at least, the core of my life thousands of miles overseas – but as far as Miami as a place of transformation was concerned (and this was a theme I had been exploring: Miami as a springboard from which Benn would propel himself further into the major league of American boxing), its magic had not exactly worked on Benn. How would it work for me?

3

THE THREE-MINUTE BELL

My interest in the Fifth Street Gym did not end there. Even with Benn gone, I paid occasional visits to the gym, to drink in its atmosphere and watch wiry young Latinos and sweat-sheened Blacks train in the hope of making the leap from obscurity to celebrity. It became part of the texture of South Beach for me, somewhere I passed every time I came off the MacArthur Causeway from downtown. I loved its smell, its echoing gloom, the pounding of the punchbags and the ringing bell dividing the hours into three-minute dramas. But most of all, I loved Beau Jack, the legendary old black fighter who acted as caretaker, commentator and unofficial oral historian.

Sixty-nine years old when I first met him, Beau's frail frame and soft southern tones gave little hint of the fact that he was twice world lightweight champion, or that during the Second World War he drew Madison Square Garden's highest box-office gross in history. The fight raised thirty-five million dollars for US War Bonds – and paid Beau a nominal one dollar.

In a sense that equation reflected his life story, for he certainly wasn't rich now, living alone in a single room not far from the gym. But it would be insulting to see him as a tragic figure. There was something

25

inspiring in his undeterred passion for boxing, and you had to put into perspective his struggle as a black man in what until remarkably recently was entirely a white man's world – in Florida, as late as the 1960s, Blacks and Jews could be refused entry to hotels, stores and other public places; Blacks, in particular, were not allowed on Miami Beach after sundown.

For Beau, who started his career as a shoeshine boy, and whose personal history (I was told by a storeowner who had known him for years) encompassed six marriages and a whole clutch of children, life still had dignity. You didn't ask him anything nearly so intimate as his current marital status – the man had an aura, a quiet reserve, which would make such a question a gross intrusion on his privacy.

What he would talk about was boxing and the gym of which he seemed such a part. First opened in 1943, and the longest-surviving establishment of its kind in the US, the gym was owned by the magically named Roosevelt Ivory, who took it over from his more famous predecessors, trainer-owners Angelo and Chris Dundee.

'Every great fighter has walked through this building at one time or another,' Beau told me proudly. 'Joe Louis, Rocky Marciano, Sugar Ray Robinson, Muhammad Ali, Thomas Hearns . . . They come to Miami because it's got the beach to run on and the ring to train in. One day, this place will be a monument.'

I can still hear in my head his mumbled southern vowels, the way he truncated 'Co-Cola', as he responded to a young fighter's complaint that he lost a hundred dollars in a bet over a Buster Douglas/Evander Holyfield championship bout.

'I don't bet money,' Beau said. 'Douglas was never going to win. Co-Cola, that's all I bet. A can of Co-Cola.'

Time shifts. A year passes, maybe more. I go back to the gym and find Beau gone, sick with stomach cancer. Although he is someone I barely know, I feel it as a blow to my own stomach.

Months pass. I pay a return visit and find him back, frailer and more difficult to understand than ever, but still breathing.

'It got me all of a sudden,' he says, when I ask about his tumour. 'I don't know what happened. I know I'm pretty strong, but it was all of a sudden, *boom*!'

Fortunately the tumour proved non-malignant. But although he's fighting back, Beau is a changed man – seventy-one now and a figure hard to imagine ever having entered a boxing ring, let alone drawn record crowds at Madison Square Garden.

We talk briefly about Ali, whom Beau recently met for the first time at a ceremony dedicating a hall of the Miami Beach Convention Centre in Ali's honour. 'Ali', Beau says, 'was the greatest boxer in one hundred years.' His condition now, due to Parkinson's disease, clearly touched Beau – perhaps all the more so, given Beau's shadow-bout with mortality.

'When I see Ali,' Beau says, in his own soft, slurred voice, 'he's talking a bit slow, but he's the same guy that likes to talk a lot! And I had a lot of fun with him, I was glad to see him anyway. And whatever sickness that he has, I hope he gets over it. I hope they find a cure for it – I hope they find a cure for a lot of things!'

And now the Fifth Street Gym is gone, levelled and replaced by an asphalt parking-lot. I feel a loss every time I pass it. In a town where the Deco District has long had its champions, where the historical status of many buildings is officially recognized (but still given scant legal protection from the more aggressive developers), I remember no placards, no posters, no protests concerning the fate of the gym.

I've lost touch with Beau Jack, but I still recall his quietly restrained pride, the last time we talked of his career. 'I fought twenty-one times at Madison Square Garden,' he told me, 'and sold out every time. No-one in history had done that. If I was still fighting today, I'd be rich. But I just wanted to please my fans. I'd hear them hollering – they made me fight on. And when I'd done that, I knowed they was happy.'

The three-minute bell rings.

4

INTO THE JUNGLE

In Miami, even the simple act of finding furniture somehow draws me into unknown territory.

Having rented, with no great foresight, an unfurnished apartment, I find myself sleeping for my first few nights on a Moroccan rug I have brought with me and eating cross-legged on the floor. Money is tight, and although I have budgeted for a desk and a mattress, I intend buying other furniture only as I need it.

Then, on a Tuesday evening less than a week after my arrival, as I pick up my model friend, Shana, for dinner, one of her neighbours introduces me to Laura, a slightly blowzy career woman in her thirties, who is moving in with her boyfriend and who wishes to sell practically every piece of furniture she owns. After a swift visit to Laura's apartment, I confirm that I will happily relieve her of two tables, some chairs, a sofa and a small but rather pleasing black Deco cabinet – all for only two hundred dollars.

The next morning, when I return to collect these items in my rented red convertible (not perhaps the ideal removal vehicle, but surprisingly adaptable), I find Laura in the corridor of her West Avenue highrise, shut out of her apartment, the landlord having changed the locks in some dispute over unpaid rent.

As I greet her, Laura is already in a state of some anxiety and anger, brandishing a small handgun she always carries in her bag – with which she threatens to shoot off the locks.

Despite the gun, she seems a likeable enough person: self-possessed, funny, simply trying to steer her life past the obstacles – aggrieved landlords, locked doors – fate has placed in her way.

I offer to help, suggesting first that I try to pick the locks, then, when that fails, encouraging her to call the landlord to try to work something out, which she does.

The landlord gives her twenty-four hours to get everything out of her apartment. Since Laura's boyfriend is working all day, she asks if I will help her move. In return, she will pay a day's rental on my car, I can take virtually anything I want of her furniture for our agreed price of two hundred bucks – and she will provide at the end of the day a gram of cocaine for our shared relaxation.

It is not merely this last offer which suggests, in terms of furniture moving arrangements, a city whose everyday currency is perhaps a little different from London's or Brighton's; nor even the fact that I shift the heaviest pieces in my red LeBaron with the help of three of my most attractive model friends. Rather it is the detail Laura points out about five feet up one of the white walls of her apartment, and the explanation she offers to go with it.

There in the plaster, circled by a pencil mark, are two bullet holes of about a centimetre in diameter, with an arrow pointing to them and these words delicately written in lead:

'As seen on Miami Vice.'

When I ask Laura about them, she laughs and tells me that one night, on the telephone to her boyfriend, they got into an argument and he started shouting at her. Laura lost her temper, too, and grabbed the gun from her purse. '*You feel like that?*' she yelled down the phone at him. '*Then listen to this!*' And she fired twice at the wall.

'Afterwards,' she confesses, 'I realized how stupid I'd been. The walls are thin and I could have shot someone in the next apartment . . .'

She seems contrite. But the gun is still there in her handbag and she's about to start living right on top of the same boyfriend. As I drive home that evening, I have the uneasy feeling that if it comes to it, she will shoot – at the walls or who knows what else – again.

It is the people I meet in my early weeks in Miami who bind me to the place. There is such a mix: Cubans and Haitians, Venezuelans, Chileans, Jamaicans, Peruvians, Italians, Russians, Canadians – even a few Americans. Their backgrounds are so unlike my own or my friends' in England: this is Marquez territory, magical realism or maybe gangster realism, or a Bob Marley song.

Take Carlos. Carlos, I met in a bar one afternoon in Coconut Grove, south of downtown Miami. I have gone there with an English friend, Michaela, and Jodi, who happens to be Carlos's young American wife. Carlos is in his late thirties, from Honduras. He is tending this bar now, but mostly he has worked on cruise ships. He met Jodi, twenty-two, petite, diamond-sharp, while they were both working at sea.

We don't talk very much this first afternoon. Carlos is dark, with classically Latin good looks. His soft face has perhaps an ounce too much flesh on it, which makes him seem vulnerable rather than predatory as he might otherwise be. He's very charming and makes us laugh, but at times an oddly puzzled expression haunts his eyes and a tension draws at his lips, to suggest some fear or remembered pain that is out of keeping with his easy exterior.

When Carlos finishes his shift, we negotiate a path through the two shopping malls that have come to dominate the centre of the Grove – the fake Spanish plaza of Cocowalk, like a destitute man's Alhambra realized on a tiny scale by Disney; and the more upscale, Gaudi-influenced Mayfair, a mall which apparently flourished in the 1980s amidst Miami's wash of Latin American drug money, but has now achieved a sort of recessionary tranquillity, cooled by the gentle play of fountains and host to chic designer boutiques next to unrented stores.

We drive through the surrounding residential streets, a jungle maze shaded by sprawling ficus trees, their aerial roots snaking in tangles to the ground. Here vastly expensive waterfront homes on private roads nestle only a few streets away from the poverty of the brightly painted wooden shacks which make up the Grove's Afro-Caribbean section – one of the poorest neighbourhoods of Miami and also one of its oldest, originally settled early this century by immigrants from the Bahamas.

Then at Carlos and Jodi's apartment, in a rented house with an overgrown garden, somewhere between the masters and the slaves (or so it seems), we drink beer, slap mosquitoes and shoot not the walls but the breeze.

But it is only later, perhaps months later, that I really get to know Carlos, when he comes calling at my apartment one night – literally yelling out my name to attract my attention, since I live on the first floor (which in America is the second) and lack, in this high-tech society, such a thing as a doorbell.

At the top of the stairs, he looks sad, his face like a lost dog's, his bearing awkward, as if his body has no more enthusiasm for movement. He and Jodi have split up after four years together, and Carlos can't for the moment come to terms with the shock.

It is dinner time. Carlos, who among many other things has been a chef, insists on cooking an omelette for me – perhaps the lightest, most fragrantly spiced omelette I have tasted.

We start to drink and to talk. Carlos does not want to think about Jodi, but of course can talk of nothing else. He tells me he misses her, then says he doesn't, he doesn't need her. He gets angry, clutching a sharp kitchen knife he has picked up and I wonder for a moment how well I know this man. He asks how Jodi could be with him for four years and not learn Spanish?

'She didn't want to learn. She wanted to know parrot-fashion what is the word for sofa, for shoe. I'm not interested in what the word is,' he says, getting hot under the collar. 'It's the function. If you know Latin and Greek, you see the function.'

He stands up and points with the knife to where I'm sitting. 'This may be a sofa, but a sofa can be anything, a sofa can be four legs and boards and a blanket on top.' He starts to pace. 'A person can be a table if

33

she gets on all fours and I say she's a table.' His movements now match the speed of his thoughts. 'Shoe is from French: *chaussure*. The function? What is a shoe? Is it a foot covering or something to walk in, to give support?' He waves the knife as he paces. 'Sandal is from the Greek – from soldiers. Sandal was a military shoe.' Finally he slows and turns to me. 'But she wanted to know: *"Carlos, how do you ask what is the time?"* '

He sits down again. The knife is back in the kitchen, to my relief. We drink some more; it's late. He starts to talk about his childhood, far removed from mine:

'When I was a child, I used to catch my breakfast. My mother would cook it, but she would say, "You want to eat? Go find food." So I would fish for breakfast with my brothers, and she would clean and skin it for us. I love my mother. We didn't have toys, instead of play we would go into the jungle, three or four days at a time, into the jungle with the animals, hunting and sleeping. When it rained we would have only a scrap of sack or plastic to cover us. The animals would come and shelter beneath us – when it's raining hard they have no fear – right under our feet!'

He pauses and I realize that I do have a point of reference from my youth, when I would devour every book of Gerald Durrell's that I could lay my hands on, often sitting inside my wardrobe, pretending I was in my own jungle, while reading his sometimes bizarre descriptions of exotic animals in their natural habitat.

'At night,' Carlos resumes, 'the jungle comes alive. That is when the animals eat, except for the birds.

34

We may sleep, but night is feeding time. It's like Ocean Drive, everyone comes out! The cries at night are strange, powerful. You do not know the jungle until you know the night. Weird cries, shrieks, cats killing monkeys. Three or four nights we would spend there, huddled together for warmth, shivering in the wet.

'We didn't have problems with our teeth, with our feet. We wouldn't clean our teeth in the jungle – at home I would have to, my mother would say, *"I'm going to kick your ass!"* But in the jungle we ate only what grows naturally and we had no problems with our teeth. When I first knew Jodi, she had everything in cans. She said, "Let me cook for you." I said, "I'm not eating this, these cans. Let's get some real food." So we went out to the store and bought everything fresh. And what you don't use, you throw away. But here in America, everything is artificial, chemical. Even the juice – Jodi didn't like fresh orange juice when she first had it, she was used to orange juice from a can, like when she was a child.

'I want to buy some jungle,' Carlos goes on. 'I want to go back to Honduras and buy some jungle to grow old in. The jungle is the only place that's going to be safe, safe from destruction, from nuclear power. I can survive in the jungle, but the people here wouldn't know how to survive without shops to go to for their food. No electricity, no power, and they'd be lost.'

I sit listening to him, understanding perhaps more clearly than before that the bizarre occurrences, powerful family ties and seductive, heat-soaked detail that Gabriel Garcia Marquez transforms into fiction have their roots in a reality which is simply different from that of Europe or northern America. Carlos will hear no ill spoken of Marquez (we have discussed the book I would most have liked to have written, *Love in the Time of Cholera*: 'You should read it in Spanish, his language has a beautiful, classical rhythm – like the slow tolling of an ancient bell'), but other Hispanic friends have told me that at times Marquez can read like soap opera, like the everyday experiences of their own lives.

Carlos is winding down. He is tired; so am I. But before he leaves, we touch on writing, on the history of ideas.

'You have to know something,' he says. 'You have to know yourself, to have a belief system before you can know anything. They only teach you what they want you to know – not the heretics, only the philosophers who saw things the way they want you to see things now. "One way, there is only one way," they tell you. But there are many. The Mayans, like the ancient Greeks, had a matriarchy. Then the whites came with their Christ. But there are stars of David on some of the ruins! You have to know history, I love history. I studied anthropology, the study of man. Anthropology believes man is transcendent, history is the history of ideas. It's all cyclical, everything comes in cycles.'

Later, after we have hugged goodbye, as I am clearing up and preparing for bed, I think about Carlos. He has worked for many years as a barman, both on cruise liners and on land, yet he has two degrees, including one in architecture from Mexico City. When he wears a white shirt and the smile of convenience, in Coconut Grove or afloat in the

36

Caribbean, he acquires a degree of perhaps desired invisibility. But when you look at your barman, do you wonder what he knows?

5

SAFE SEX

Six months pass. I have signed a year's lease on my apartment, but as far as I am concerned, everything is movable, negotiable. My novel is coming along, but my life is in some confusion: it is still only two years since my son's death; sometimes I wake at night, wander through to my living room and lie on the floor, crying.

I make a trip to England, where my friends are all depressed by the recession and planning, if possible, to spend time abroad. I stare at the Thames and wonder where I belong. London is sunny and the chop of the river seems a lifeline to Conrad, to Dickens, and more: great music, intelligent newspapers, the bustling, fruit-trodden streets of Soho, where I lived for nine years.

Back in Miami Beach, a different energy is in the air. While the rattle of dusty palms or a swim in the sea is reward enough for my being here, it's impossible to deny that there is an excitement building about South Beach as a mecca for the trendy – especially the trendy from New York. Everywhere, crumbling Art Deco apartments and hotels, badly scarred by neglect in the 1970s and by the crime wave which followed the *Mariel* boatlift of 1980 (see the Al Pacino movie, *Scarface*, for a fast education in the impact a combination of cocaine and 125,000 new Cuban refugees had on Miami in the following decade), are being stripped bare, renovated and repainted in ever brighter pastel colours.

Madonna has bought a house on the water downtown, close to a gay cruising park and the thirty-four room, mock-Renaissance and baroque winter retreat, *Vizcaya*, built by industrialist fat cat John Deering in 1916, and more recently home to a meeting between Ronald Reagan and Pope John Paul II. Apparently Madonna parted with almost five million dollars for her shack, the most anyone so far has paid for a house in Miami – but what is more remarkable is the degree of fascination, even obsession, she sparks. She really is America's Holey Virgin, an icon of the nation's true religion – celebrity and wealth – as marvelled at as John Paul himself. People want to see Madonna, to touch her, to eat in the same restaurant, breathe the same air, as if she has the answers, as if her own hardly ideal life is not bound by the same gravity of loneliness and time that afflicts us all.

And Madonna is not alone in securing a base here. On South Beach, fashion magnate Gianni Versace snaps up one of my favourite buildings, the Casa Casuarina (more popularly known as the Amsterdam), a 1930s Spanish/Moorish re-creation of the sixteenth-century home of Viceroy Diego Columbus of Santo Domingo, complete with bronze-domed tower, red-tiled roof and a brick from Columbus's original house in what is now the Dominican Republic.

The property, bang on Ocean Drive, seeps soul from every crack and pore. I know – I looked at a six-hundred-dollar-a-month apartment there when I first arrived, but it was a little *too* soulful, a little too dark. Houdini's mother lived and died somewhere inside, and her ghost is present at the eviction party virtually every waif on the Beach attends before Versace takes possession. A sound system has been set up on the balcony running round the internal courtyard – open to the heavens, in true Spanish style – and as pounding dance music plays, the now trademark South Beach throng of models and ravers, druggies and developers, thrusts flesh against flesh in the struggle for a drink or a place to dance.

It is a magical evening: the prick of stars overhead in the balmy night sky; the white wash of the black ocean opposite. Soon, however, the property will be off-limits to all but Versace's friends. Versace – who has dubbed South Beach 'America's Riviera' (a slightly less eloquent description than Hemingway's of Key West in the 1920s: 'the St Tropez of the poor') – will in the next three years completely remodel the building in keeping with his notably under-stated taste. The absence of a garden and pool will not faze him: to create both he will simply buy the Revere, the 1950s hotel next door, demolish it and landscape the space, throwing up a high wall around it all to keep the curious and indigent out and, perhaps, his millions or minions in. By the end he will have spent a reputed fifteen million dollars erasing every blemish, every trace of character from the original property – and for what? An obscenely expensive home on one of the noisiest weekend strips in the world, whose greatest convenience is the unparalleled view it affords from the roof terrace when Luciano Pavarotti performs one of his free public concerts diametrically opposite on the sand at Tenth Street.

As the momentum builds, there is an ongoing carnival atmosphere on South Beach, seven days a week. Valiantly I trek from new bar to new restaurant to new club, as each throws an opening party and forces free alcohol and food upon its willing guests. Every night I drive myself to a frenzy till five a.m. when the clubs close (some don't even get going until three a.m.), mingling with models and photographers, high fliers from New York, Los Angeles, Latin America and – the great collective put-down of an entire continent, *my* continent – the dread Eurotrash, flashing their Gaultier sunglasses even after dark, speaking their clipped English, their German, their French, loving and loathing Miami in the same breath, and generously distributing, as locals see it, snot-nosed, tight-assed *attitude*.

Celebrities come to town for the 'season', roughly the six months of the year between October and March when, while the rest of the known world languishes in winter, the sun here reminds you that Miami is south of Cairo, Baghdad and Delhi in latitude. An evening out, or a perusal of Miami Beach's many free, gossip-driven magazines, is an education in name-dropping: Cindy Crawford, Sylvester Stallone, Michael Caine, Sharon Stone and her unrelated namesake, Oliver.

Chris Blackwell, the head of Island Records, buys up half of South Beach and opens a renovated Deco hotel, the Marlin, redesigned by Barbara Hulanicki, once famed as the creator of London's Biba store, and including a Jamaican 'cookshack' restaurant and a recording studio attracting the likes of U2 and Grace Jones. Ultrahip New York hotelier Ian Schrager unveils an even more stylish hotel, the two hundred and thirty-eight room Delano, remodelled (at a cost rumoured to be as high as forty-two million dollars) by designer Philippe Starck as a grand, almost *Alice in Wonderland* fantasy, and featuring a restaurant co-owned by Madonna. Mickey Rourke and Sean Penn each buy a share in their own trendy-for-a-time nightclubs, while The Artist Formerly Known As . . . (Prince) buys his – Glam Slam – outright.

On every corner, every stretch of sand, photo shoots and film and TV production units block your path, so much so that sometimes it seems as if Miami Beach is one big studio backlot and the Deco buildings are just there for effect. I have dinner one night with Charles Sturridge, an English film director friend, at a sidewalk table of the News Cafe on Ocean Drive, and right in front of our salad bowls, arc lights burn and actors fire guns and run about for a new TV series. Charles is here to shoot a TV commercial himself, and is amused to watch other people work for once – but the sense endures that, as with Madonna, something is being sold that promises more than it can possibly deliver.

Friends who come – male friends – can't believe how many beautiful women stalk the streets, but after a while the accent on youth and perfection begins to pale and I find myself yearning for different physical types: big fat Cuban *mamás*, sunbathing topless, their watermelon breasts and golden rolls of flesh glistening in the sun; old people with the grace and character of unadulterated years: deep-etched lines, hollowed cheeks, telling eyes; or just someone plain ugly – a Fellini freak, a John Major look-alike.

And the party goes on. Barriers erode: night merges with day, play seems indistinguishable from work, everything blurs under the democratizing and sensualizing influence of extreme heat, and gender means as little or as much as you want it to. Nothing is fixed. In a town where for many people their main project in life is themselves – reinventing their history, their sexuality, or, in the case of so many models and work-out junkies, their bodies – a party is less an entertainment than an opportunity to try out a new role, to test-drive a transformation. Dressing up and dancing in a giant penis costume, as someone does one night at one of the main gay clubs, Paragon, is as much a statement of intent as wearing a suit to the office.

After a time, gender-bending seems almost the rule, rather than the exception. The 'pink dollar' – the purchasing power of gays and lesbians – is suddenly a major factor for South Beach businesses, many of which in turn are gay and lesbian owned and want to take advantage of the estimated seventeen billion dollars a year gays spend on travel.

Gay clubs, such as Warsaw, and movable one-night lesbian feasts, such as the 'Girls in the Night' parties, offer even arrow-straight customers the best music and most interesting crowds in town, while a glance at the classifieds in *New Times*, Miami's weekly listings and news magazine, captures something of the flavour of relationships out there:

(Men Seeking Men) LOOKING FOR EUROPEAN HEAT.

Brazilian 5'11", dark hair and eyes, HIV-. Seeking gay or bi Italian 20–30 or descendent of. Must be Masculine and private, to share hot evenings.

(Women Seeking Women) VOLLEYBALL/ TENNIS ANYONE?

Hi there, this fun, outgoing, androgynous girl is ready to party again. Looking for cool friends who can handle a fun-filled itinerary this summer.

This democracy of sexuality throws up its own styles, its own stars – none brighter or more fabulous than Adora, drag queen extraordinaire, dazzling host of local 'tea dances' and block parties, of one restaurant's regular Monday drag night and another's gay, onstage versions of straight American TV game shows.

With her extravagant blond bouffant hairstyle, glitter lipstick and slim figure always adorned in a high-camp elegance befitting Imelda Marcos, it is Adora's wit, her exaggerated broken English and the balletic precision of her movements that mark her out as special.

When I see her for the first time, bewitching the crowd at Washington Avenue's Barrio restaurant, running between the tables, taking fast, funny, measured steps in her tight sequined dress and extreme high heels, the illusion that she is in fact a very glamorous woman is almost complete.

'Lay-dies and gen-tle-men! *Chi-cos y chi-cas!*'

Her sing-songy vowels and spangled English-Spanish mix resound across the PA system, delighting the audience inside the restaurant and drawing more faces to the window from the sidewalk, where a small crowd has gathered, peering in. She cools herself coyly for a moment with a wave of an ornamental fan, then announces that she will perform a Spanish version of the jazz classic, 'Fever', by La Lupe – a Cuban singer of the 1960s and 1970s, with a voice pitched somewhere between Nina Simone, Shirley Bassey and Frank Sinatra.

Amidst the amplified hiss that even a CD cannot disguise, the music begins. Adora teeters on her heels, the glitter in her lipstick catches the light, then she laughs along with La Lupe in the manic opening to the song, before lipsyncing the lyrics with perfect timing.

Later, intrigued by Adora's theatrics, her sharp humour and whiplash character, I arrange to meet her true – or other – persona, Danilo de la Torre, for a talk one Sunday morning.

It's a shock when I arrive at his modest apartment, overlooking Flamingo Park, to find a slight, attractive man, much shorter than Adora without the heels, casually dressed in a tank top and sweatpants, and with a shaved head and a quiet, obliging manner far removed from Adora's extravagance. It takes a moment to adjust to the reality, and I am grateful for the time alone, while Danilo makes coffee, to gaze around at the magazines on his tables and the strangely coloured oil portraits on his walls.

'Those are by Carlos,' Danilo tells me sadly as he returns with steaming black Cuban coffee. 'Carlos was my best friend for almost fifteen years, and he pass away like two years ago, three years ago. We were like twins, we were not lovers, we were just verygoodfriends.' The words seem to tumble from his lips. 'Roommates and everything. He was super-cool with me and nice, very smart. A party person, but he had a brain, he had culture. He study a lot, he went to art school, so we could talk together about things that we knew in Cuba, things that we liked, like music. . .'

Danilo is Cuban and thirty years old. When he was younger, he studied ballet in Havana, then spent eight years in Paris, where a problem with his back forced him to abandon dance for hairdressing, which is still the mainstay of his income.

Adora was born, he says, not as a drag act, but in play, when Danilo came to Miami from Paris in 1989 and found Carlos – his best friend from Cuba – living here. Together they became the Adora Sisters, and started dressing up to dance at the gay clubs. Donning drag for the first time was nothing strange, because he had been training as a dancer, often in costume and make-up, since he was seventeen:

'When you put make-up on, your face change a little bit and your personality change a little bit. I mean, you're Danilo, but you dress up as a dancer. It's like a mask, you can do whatever you want. Then, when you start to be a club kid, you dress up to go out and you start having fun *before* you go out, putting things together – "*Oh, look at this!*" You laugh at the shoes, you laugh at your outfit. So you put some make-up on, eyelashes, whatever, maybe a flower, and it's a mask. So I don't think it was really a drastic change, it was more a progressive change. I never really feel like it was something very different – but once I'm on, I'm changed completely. I'm somebody else!'

Then Carlos died. 'It was very sad, it was the worst time. And now, still, I miss him all the time, all the time.' Danilo pauses and looks around his apartment, at the paintings, the chairs, as if he expects to see Carlos sitting here now. 'But right away,' he says, 'somebody propose me to work and ask, "What's your name?" I say, "Adora." And everything start going better and better.'

When I ask Danilo to describe Adora, his face changes, his whole manner becomes more emphatic, more commanding, and his voice falls and rises with Adora's musical intonation.

'Adora is *Cuban*, absolutely, but she's like a very *rich* Cuban, who fled Castro and come to Miami very, very early. So she's still very *class*, but she's Cuban, you know, so she's got the roots – if the music is a *salsa* rhythm, she want to *move* and she *can't*! She want to move so much, but she can't because she's too *chic*!'

La Lupe, who was a major Cuban star, but virtually unknown to non-Hispanics, is a major inspiration.

'You know,' Danilo smiles darkly, 'La Lupe used to *beat* her pianist and drink on stage – and *pee*?'

'Pee?' I echo. 'On stage?'

A confirming nod of Danilo's head. 'On stage!'

I stare at him. 'This was when she was in Miami?' La Lupe, rather like Adora, fled the revolution and came to Miami and New York.

'Yes.' Danilo is beaming now. 'And she would *scream* and pull her necklace and earrings off, her shoes, *everything*! I mean, craziness, total craziness . . .'

'Did you ever see her in concert?' I ask. 'On film?'

'Nothing.' His voice tumbles out in a crazy, Cuban-accented flood. '*Never-never-never-never!* I found out things about her, little by little. Once I come here and I talk about her, somebody tell me, "Oh, I have a lot of things from her, La Lupe." And I thought, "Fine, I like her as a singer and everything." Then one day, I start doing Adora, and Adora went from being a club kid to a performer, and I say, "If I have to do a number one day, I do La Lupe!" And I did it.'

I ask Danilo if he has ever felt jealous of Adora.

'At the beginning, maybe, because she was getting the whole attention. Everywhere she go, it was, "*Aaaaah!*", everybody around her. If I go out as a boy, nobody look at me – or if they look, they say, "Oh my God, it's *you*!"' Danilo's voice falls, mimicking disappointment. 'Some people, only one or two people, prefer me as Adora. They say, "Where's your blond wig?" You know, I'm wearing overalls and combat boots and it's, "Where's your blond wig?" I say, "Here, in my pocket. You want to wear it?"

'But ninety-nine per cent of the people, they always say, "Oh my God, you're very nice. I like you as a man and I like you as Adora. You are a beautiful man and you are a beautiful woman." And that is – you cannot understand. Whatever I tell you is nothing, compared to what it makes me feel. It's big, it's very big when people say that to you.'

'But what would happen,' I ask, watching Danilo

48

drink coffee on his sofa, 'if someone wanted to make
love to you as Adora? Has anyone ever suggested it,
and would it feel different, if you did?'

Danilo pauses, stares at his coffee, frowns at me.

'Sex is a fantasy,' he says. 'To don't get boring, you
have to have some fantasies. And this never happen
to me until one day. It was a beautiful guy, and he
was straight and everything, and I didn't know how
to act. I don't think that I had to tell him that I'm not
a woman – because Adora is not *that* much of a
woman! I was thinking, "What do I do? Should I go
with him? Is he going to be wild?" '

'You met him as Adora?'

'Yes. And the first time, I say, "Oh my God! Well,
OK, let's see what happens . . ." And he's so crazy,
really crazy. I mean, it's safe sex, but the whole thing
that happened was wild. I don't know. I say, "How
this guy can like me with this glitter on my lips,
these clown eyelashes, and this hair and the whole
thing?" So, the first time, I was uncomfortable, but I
did it maybe four times in the whole of Adora's life,
and it's fine.'

'When you made love, were you Adora for yourself or just for him?'

'Oh no, just for him. You know, he want to enjoy
– and I enjoyed *making* him enjoy it. I had fun, too.
Because sometime, you just have to laugh at the
whole thing. You have to laugh because, "*How can
I be doing this with these platform shoes on and my
wig?*"

'But you have to separate your life,' Danilo says as
I stand to go. 'I don't criticize people who live drag
twenty-four hours a day. They have to be happy and
if they're happy that way – perfect. But I can't. I

49

have to take my make-up off and see my face and my body and everything. Adora is in that closet over there, that's *her* closet, but she's not taking over *my* closet!'

He looks at me almost wistfully and I wonder about the balance Danilo says he has found. South Beach is hardly lacking in drag queens, which must in part make it a reassuring environment, but also means it's extraordinarily competitive and perhaps only feeds insecurity.

'I'm very comfortable with myself,' Danilo insists. 'I have a lover now for eleven years – he's not here, he's in France, I get to see him maybe three or four times a year. I'm very happy. Danilo is happy, thank God! I'm very happy with me – with my mind, what I do, with my friends. And I'm happy with Adora, too, because I do with Adora what I want to do. If you like it, fine. If not, just, *"Goodbye!"* '

6

THE FREON SITUATION

'Hey, Alex!'
    'Yo, Alex!'
    'Whassup?'
    It's one a.m. and I'm at the entrance to a hotel garden and pool somewhere between Collins Avenue and the ocean, where a one-night club has been set up under the stars – sound system, stage and lights, the music pounding out now, putting a charge in the air and rocking the ground beneath my feet with its solid boom-bass. Here on the door, the promoters, who collectively call themselves Zeal, are as young as their audience, some of them still in their teens – the beautiful Macarina, for instance, selling tickets at the makeshift desk – not old enough to legally buy or drink alcohol until they're twenty-one, yet perversely entitled to own or work in a bar or club as soon as they're eighteen.
    'Where you been, nigger?' Juan, one of my young Hispanic friends, greets me with a slap of his palm, a squeezed handshake. 'I don't see you around no more . . .'
    'I've been here,' I tell him. 'Working. I don't go out so much.'
    'Yeah,' he grins. The standard lament: 'There's nothing to do on the Beach any more . . .'
    This is another night-time Miami, one which

intersects with Adora's but is different: a younger world of hard-core club kids who will, when it comes to having a good time, meet any challenge placed before them, who will expend vast and largely unsung reserves of energy and initiative obtaining alcohol and cigarettes, locating drugs, negotiating a way into clubs and other off-limits pleasure zones, or organizing their own events such as this, built around a holy trinity of mind-altering chemicals, liquor and loud, fast dance music.

The names of these one-nighters say much about what is sought – Energy, the Id, Mayday, Beyond Therapy – but what many adults fail to recognize when they learn of parties and raves and teenage drug-taking from their Sunday newspapers, or from their own teenagers, is that there is a whole *culture* involved, that it isn't simply about drugs or music or wantonness or escape – that it is also about innocence and camaraderie, that it is about partying with your schoolfriends, pushing life to the limits, venting your frustration and disillusionment with the betrayals and double-dealings of the adult world and having something that is yours: *your* domain, *your* language, *your* identity which outsiders cannot freely comprehend or appropriate.

I say hello to Macky and press through the crush of people waiting to get inside, then on past the pool, where groups of teenagers are gathered, sipping beer and talking, one or two even swimming in their T-shirts and shorts – past the stage, where the DJ is playing, to the crowd dancing on the raised wooden floor which has been set up over the sand at the edge of the beach, inside the fence that separates non-ticket-holding late-night passers-by (and the ocean beyond them) from what is going on in here.

The music is largely a mix of house, trance, ambient and hip-hop, less focused and not so insanely fast as the jungle beats of English clubs, but still quite sufficient to stir the body's adrenalin and drive limbs and muscles into a frenzy. The night is hot, the darkness over the ocean alive with the silent flickerings of an electrical storm, but moving like this will make you sweat whether you're outside or in the bowels of an air-conditioned club, and at least here there's the pool to cool off in.

As I dance, I'm surrounded by people I know perhaps only slightly, through clubs, but who communicate a real warmth with their enthusiastic greetings. They are all much younger than me – some less than half my age – but I have got to know them over a period of time, and even attended a high school graduation in south Miami (a formal affair here, complete with mortar boards and gowns), at which, it turned out, I knew practically half the graduating year.

What draws me to them, I think, is what has always drawn people to America: a dream of beginning – in my case, of beginning again. I find them mostly easier to relate to than the Americans I know in their late twenties and thirties, whose optimism takes on a depressingly materialistic edge. But also, perhaps due to a combination of my son's death and some personal denial as I confront my fortieth birthday (the words 'mid-life crisis' come to mind), I find myself fascinated and moved more by the conflicts of youth than those of middle age.

53

***

After a time, I break away from the tangle of bodies on the dance floor and retreat with some of my youngest friends – a collection of club kids, part-time drug dealers and runaways – to the beach, to relax and talk. To them, the international allure of Miami Beach means little. They grew up here, so there's no fantasy in the palm trees, no glitz to the neon. If Miami is a place of transformation, for them it is the universal one, from child into adult. South Beach is where you party each weekend, just as Disney World is where you go after high school graduation to drop acid and unwind.

And if clubs such as this offer a brighter glimpse of racial integration than elsewhere in Miami, with their Anglo/Hispanic/Black mix, it seems it's still not possible for all colours to come together without comment.

'The Spanish still call the Blacks "nigger" and the Blacks call the Spanish "spics",' says Lorraine, her long dark hair framing startling green eyes and Latin features. Recently turned seventeen, she has one parent from Ecuador, one from Puerto Rico. 'There's all this talk about unity. Why can't we just love each other?'

Soon the conversation turns, as it always does, to clubs and drugs, family and individual adventures.

'I stole money from my parents, I was like the fuck-up all the time,' says Diana, who is Chilean and fourteen, though she looks older dressed in black shorts and bra, under a black chiffon shirt. Charismatic and persuasive, 'Diana the One and Only Dominator' can talk her way into virtually any club, even though ID is usually required to prove

54

you're eighteen or twenty-one. (Many clubs admit eighteen-year-olds, allowing only over-twenty-ones with valid ID – and often an identifying armband – to drink.)

Her sister, Paulina, two years older, quieter, thinner and seemingly the younger of the pair, laughs.

'She got the bank card!'

I smile. 'Did you know the number?'

'Yeah!'

More laughter as Jennifer, a bright-eyed seventeen-year-old, takes up the story. Blonde, with a healthy plumpness to her body, Jennifer has always tested with a high IQ, but has had problems in school, insufficiently motivated by the lotus-eating torpor of South Florida.

'We'd just come back from a club,' she says, 'and we were like, "God, oh, we're so hungry!" *Drooom!* A bank card! So we went to the thing, the cash machine, and we're like, "OK, twenty bucks. Twenty bucks only . . ." '

Paulina grins. 'We ate the twenty bucks!'

Jennifer looks at me. 'We're like, "Shit, man! Twenty bucks? OK, fuck it . . . forty! Forty? OK, fuck it . . . sixty! Sixty? OK, eighty! OK, a hundred!" '

'So I spend a hundred,' Diana says. 'I got a hundred out and I went to Tampa, to rave. I bought two pills of Ecstasy – that's fifty dollars – and the rest I would spend on the rave. I got back, my parents were crying, because I was only fourteen, you know. And I still am fourteen.'

As she says this, a silent arc of lightning burns across the sky and illuminates her face, and it's weird, because although she's only fourteen, I see her face at forty, as it might look in a photograph, her features a little sterner, her jet-black hair more formally styled; and I see her as a mother, coping with her life and with her own children, maybe her own daughter who's out all night.

We shift around a little where we are gathered on plastic beach chairs, some distance from the back entrance to the fenced-in dance area. There is movement as a group of people leave and others try to get in, and a sampled phrase from a dance track hangs in the sullen night air.

I stare for a moment at three Hispanic boys struggling to light a joint as they sit on the sand. Their lighter is out of fuel and ignites only a tiny spark at each attempt.

'Why you such a pussy, bitch?' one of the boys says to another.

On a stool by the club's entrance, the doorman, a spiffily suited thug by the name of John Hood, shakes his head sadly.

'I've done some crazy shit,' Jennifer says, touching my arm and fixing me with her mischievous smile. 'I stole my parents' car. They were out of town, I stole their car!'

She picks up a plastic cup, supposedly filled with cranberry juice but spiked with a shot of Absolut. She tugs at her cut-off blue denim shorts and rips out a thread.

'I went with all my best friends, like four of us, and we ripped off a drug dealer! We ripped off a sheet of acid. He didn't notice because one of my friends was having sex with him at the time. And while she was having sex, she threw his pants over to us and we took the box with all of his stuff in it, and took the sheet out . . .'

'I heard about that!' Diana shrieks.

'There's no way you heard it, because—'

'I heard it, I heard it.'

'You did?'

Jennifer looks at her and reaches for a cigarette. Before she can continue, Diana finishes the story for her, and I have the strangest sense that these are universal tales, that they might be rites of passage stories told in a village in Thailand or Guatemala, except that the village is Miami, and cars and drugs and late-twentieth-century playthings have replaced simpler details: perhaps a water buffalo or some coveted possession.

'And then you went to Disney World and you tripped like crazy,' Diana prompts, glancing triumphantly from Jennifer to her sister, enjoying the authority of her knowledge.

Jennifer draws deeply on her cigarette. 'We had a pound of marijuana on us, we had—'

'He didn't come after you with a gun or a knife or anything?' I ask.

'No, because he's like a friend of ours.' She frowns. 'I feel bad about it. No, he has no idea it was us. He thought it was the guys at the party, so, you know, I don't care. Now it's long gone, it happened a year ago, so it doesn't matter. But we went to Disney World and we were popping acid, and every ride we kept popping another hit, another hit, another hit. We probably did about fifteen each – white blotter – and I drove there and back. I had tunnel vision, I could only see out of two little pinholes.'

A little later, we hook up with some other friends

and decide to leave. It's about four a.m. and the club is still going strong, but Jennifer has some grass where she's staying – in Kendall, a suburb sixteen miles south – and everyone wants a break before returning for an 'after-hours' party which starts at dawn.

We bundle into two cars and cruise around the Beach for a while, laughing and joking at the strands of people leaving other clubs to go home. At a stop light on Washington, outside Prince's club, we spot a woman walking almost naked on the sidewalk, but for high heels and strategically placed strips of black tape covering her nipples and vagina. A crowd of Hispanic boys is trailing her, shouting, 'Madonna! Hey, Madonna!'

'She's scary,' says Diana.

But in fact she looks sad, as if she has come this far but is not confident of her role now – or doubts her director (the black boyfriend walking two paces in front), or merely wonders what kind of night she is having.

We drive west and then south on a deserted elevated highway which rings downtown Miami's compact, silent skyline of well-designed modern towers – two by Miami-based, internationally famous Arquitectonica; another, by I. M. Pei, a graceful, three-tiered slab bathed each night in as many as three different colours of light, though tonight washed simply with white. Even the elevated track of the Metrorail is decorated for a stretch with imaginative abstract graffiti of coloured neon, as if to say: 'We don't care that nobody much uses the damned trains that run on these tracks – or that they don't lead any-where you might want to go, like the airport or the Beach. At least we can make them *look* good!'

We head towards Kendall on a road slick from a brief but heavy shower. A trance tape plays on our car's mighty sound system and Argentinian-born Veronica, sixteen, entertains us with a story worthy if not of Marquez, then at least of Isabel Allende, of the neighbourhood woman from her Buenos Aires childhood who was known by everyone to be sleeping with her dog.

'It was a big dog,' Veronica laughs, 'and one day somebody went to the house and there was no answer, just the dog barking. So the police came and they find the woman dead in her bed! She had been fucked by the dog, they did forensic tests and everything, but something must have happened, something must have disturbed the dog, because it had killed her – savaged her to death!'

In Kendall, a quiet, comfortable suburb of strip malls and leafy housing developments, some of which edge perilously close to the far-eastern stretches of the Everglades, we wait outside the house where Jennifer is staying, while she goes in to get her stash of grass. Like most of the kids I am with, Jennifer has a parental home to go to, but at the moment refuses to live there. In the other car, Bobby, who is eighteen, from Jacksonville in north Florida, and who is driving, says that he hasn't been home in months. Mostly he has been sleeping in his car, though for the past week he claims to have had no sleep at all. During that time, he says, he has taken thirty-six hits of acid. Danny, who is with him, seventeen and puppy-faced, doesn't know where he will be sleeping tonight. He also has run away from home – not for the first time – and may wind up sharing the car as a bed with Bobby.

We make an unscheduled stop at another house, Raoul's, because his parents are away and he has some Mad Dog, a particularly cheap and lethal brew, in his fridge. While we are there – eight or nine of us, slumped on the sofa and chairs and on the wood floor of Raoul's parents' clean, department store-elegant living room – he grins and asks if we'd like to do some freon.

'Cool,' someone says.

'What's it like?' Diana asks.

'It's like . . .' Raoul ponders a moment. He's a large, dark boy of seventeen, heavy-set but carrying extra weight in any case. His parents are Colombian, but he looks more like a white boy trying to look black in his loose T-shirt and baggy shorts. 'It's like whippits,' he says. 'Only bigger!'

(Whippits – or 'hippie crack' – are glass capsules of nitrous oxide, a CFC, sold to make whipped cream, but also inhaled for a sudden, brief high.)

Everyone laughs as Raoul and Danny go outside, to raid the neighbour's air-conditioning unit. When they return, Raoul is clutching a thin white plastic shopping bag, inflated like a balloon and gripped at the neck. He hands it to Bobby.

Bobby looks at him and laughs. 'Freon, huh?'

Raoul nods. 'Just take a hit . . .'

So Bobby does, sucking in a couple of times from the mouth of the bag, then holding his breath – and the bag – while a monster grin broadens across his face. His eyes light up and blank out in the same instant, and he passes the bag to me.

'Isn't freon what's destroying the ozone layer?' I point out, wondering at this moment, unfamiliar as

I am with air-conditioning units, just how the gas was drained. But curious as ever, and in the strict interests of science and accurate reportage, I raise the bag to my mouth, loosen my grip on its neck and take a couple of very small breaths before passing it on.

The taste is unpleasant – a mix of plastic and something stale and chemical – but suddenly there is an almighty rush through my body and to my brain, and I feel as if I am in a cathedral or some large, echoey space: bells are ringing, and I imagine myself standing at a railway crossing as lights flash and a huge express train thunders past – all while still stuck inside this vast, dark, church-like chasm which turns out, after a minute or so, to be Raoul's living room.

The bag makes its way round the assembled group and reaches Raoul last. It is sagging a little now, so when Raoul brings it to his mouth, he sucks deep...deeper...and again. There is a big, '*Aaaaauuuuhh!*' sound as he takes his last breath then holds it, keeping his lips shut in a happy grin.

But next, as I watch him, sitting there on the floor in the centre of the room, his eyes roll up, so that his brown irises are barely visible, his lips turn an ugly blue colour and a dark stain appears on his shorts where he has pissed himself.

He remains sitting in this position for a moment, then simply collapses sideways onto the floor, drooling at the mouth, the dark stain on his shorts growing larger. Everyone laughs, but it occurs to me that this boy whom I've only just met may be about to die in front of me, and I get up and go over to him to try to sit him back up.

'Will someone help me move him?' I ask. 'I think we should get him standing.'

Amidst much continued amusement, Bobby is the first to help, but by this time the colour is returning to Raoul's lips and his eyes are focusing again. We help him to stand and he looks down at his shorts and smiles, embarrassed. As he goes to change, Bobby shakes his head and turns to me.

'It freezes your lungs and your brain, that stuff,' he says. 'That's why it gives you such a rush. It's fucking up the environment – you can be sure as hell it's fucking up our bodies!'

Plans change. Diana and Paulina decide they're not going to the after-hours party after all. Their parents are at home, and they want to try to get in while they're still sleeping. As we sit in the car outside their Spanish-style apartment building, a looming mass in a quiet, tree-lined courtyard, Diana admits that she went to rehab, two months ago. I ask if her parents sent her there.

She stares at me in the early light. 'Actually, yes, I guess my parents. I kind of wanted to go. I thought I needed help.'

'Why?'

'I guess I needed help with my drug problem and because of depression. I was really depressed. I was doing Ecstasy and a lot of acid, almost every day. And pot – but that's like a cigarette, a baby drug!' She laughs. 'Straight from Mother Earth!'

'How long have you been doing drugs?'

'Since birth.' She touches my hand and laughs again. 'Since the summer, the beginning of the summer, last year. It's been a year now. My parents found out because they saw wraps – from the mari-juana – and a pipe and stuff. Then I was tripping at school and I freaked out. They called me down to the office, and they're like, "*You're tripping.*" I was like, "Uh-uh-uh." "*Yes, you are!*" Whatever. So they found out. They called my parents.'

I turn to speak to Paulina, but she is dozing on the back seat. As I glance again at Diana, I have to remind myself that Paulina is the sixteen-year-old and Diana fourteen, because it always seems the reverse.

'Has Paulina had any problems?'

'Yeah, but not as bad. The first time our parents talked to her, she quit. But I was still in it. I ran away from home, I started getting really messed up. I didn't care about anything except my drugs.'

She seems suddenly the little girl she is, not the sexily dressed club kid she aspires to be. I think about a time when we were all at another club on the Beach, and they were showing hard-core porn videos on TV screens suspended from the ceiling. As we danced, Diana and her friends watched close-ups of women giving men head, of actual inter-course, even gay sex. I was pleased when they told me they didn't enjoy the videos, that they didn't want to think about sex that way, they'd rather dis-cover it for themselves.

Diana lights another in a constant stream of cigar-ettes and continues: 'Actually, my parents went to school and the school told them about rehab, and they said, "Yeah, we suggest it." They took me to a lot of psychiatrists and one of them said that I was really fucked up in the head.'

'Why?'

'I don't know. You know how psychiatrists know right away – the things I would say, the way I would look at them, that sort of thing. I hate that.'

I watch the tip of her cigarette brighten then diminish, like a tiny star. Her eyes are wet.

'Did he say why you were fucked up?'

She smiles. 'I never asked him. I didn't really believe him.'

'Where is rehab?'

'It's here, downtown, around Bayside. I stayed there, slept there, for two weeks.' She opens the car window a little. 'When I first went in there, it was very scary. I felt alone. Like I didn't know what was going to happen.'

'Did it feel like going to hospital or going to prison?'

'Like going to prison, because they have bars all over the windows. The first question they ask is, "*Do you do drugs because you're depressed, or did you get depressed because of drugs?*" Me, I was depressed already, because my mom was really sick, she got – what do all women get? Cancer, she got cancer. I thought she was going to die, you know, but they stopped it in time. But I'd already tried drugs, and it got me away for a while from everything, so I liked it. And I started doing more and then I started fucking up in school, I wouldn't come home sometimes, my parents were like—'

'You know, I wish my mom could hear this,' Jennifer interrupts from the back seat. 'Because my mom thinks I'm a devil-woman! She thinks I'm psychotic. I've kept a straight-A average in school, straight As, but she tells me every day, "*You're fucking crazy!*" She should hear this . . .'

Squashed next to Jennifer and the sleeping Paulina, Lucy leans forward into the gap between the front seats, between Diana and me. Eighteen and a surgeon's daughter, also from Chile, Lucy is pretty, with a taste for tiny-print floral dresses. Like several of her schoolfriends, she sometimes sells acid to supplement her allowance.

'I did rehab when I was Diana's age,' she says. 'In Chile. I was there for three months. I was going through a severe depression, I was pulling my hair out, I didn't eat anything. I thought I was insane until I went to rehab.'

'Exactly,' Diana nods emphatically. 'I thought, *"God, I'm such a fuck-up."* But if you go to rehab, you look at everybody else, they've been sexually abused, they don't have parents, and you're like, "*I never had a problem. Compared to these people, I never, ever had a problem."* '

Paulina stirs, then she and Diana get out of the car and say goodnight. We watch as they climb the stairs to their apartment, then Jennifer, Lucy and I drive back to the Beach. The downtown skyline appears again before us, set against the blaze of the rising sun. On the front seat, Jennifer squeezes my hand and smiles.

'You're too old for this,' she says, 'and I'm too young!'

I think about tonight and other nights I have had like it. These kids are not losers. They're articulate, self-aware and see a future for themselves, shaped by what they know and have learned and have seen on TV and imagined. While they're not total street kids or runaways with nowhere left to turn, they have all run away from home at some point, and some will spend time living hand to mouth, staying wherever they can, probably selling more drugs to survive.

One or two may burn out, may even suffer tragedies from overdoses or accidents, but the others will eventually find jobs and go back to school – even if it means working in a restaurant or the Gap to put themselves through college. If you look at them and see only the problems, or see the problems as the cause rather than the effect, you merely adopt the traditional blindness of one generation for another.

For most of these kids are struggling to cope with family situations which are at best strained, at worst chaotic. I think of Luke, a young black friend who jokes that the only drug problem he has is that his parents are always asking him for some – they're both addicts. Or Todd, the most gentle and unlikely graduate ever to come out of the Marine Corps, nineteen years old, gay and still fighting to win approval from his father but never finding it. Or Amy, physically abused throughout childhood by her father, whom she last saw from behind the barrel of the gun she was holding, as she told him, 'Stay the fuck away from me!'

It's too easy simply to blame the parents – and certainly there are other factors – but sometimes it seems as if a whole generation of adults has fallen apart and its children are trying to pick up the pieces. Mostly they do pretty well: they show more courtesy and respect than many of the adults around them; they have values of their own which they cling to. But they still have the relative freedom and idealism of youth. The test will come when they move into the adult world.

7

I TOLD YOU NEVER TO CALL ME
FROM JAIL!

Sometimes, perhaps much of the time, Miami seems
like a movie – and not just any movie, but the self-
reflective, lived on the surface, trash-literate films of
Quentin Tarantino. Miami is full of stories and
shootings and dumb but fancy dialogue. *Reservoir
Dogs* could happen in Miami; *Pulp Fiction* could
define Miami.

Perhaps because it has no real history (Miami
was only incorporated as a city in 1896), people
need to invent or reinvent themselves here, need to
create their own epic poems and mythologies. And
the culture, the wider American culture of glamour
and celebrity, music, movies, gas stations and
malls, is exaggerated in Miami because there is
nothing to detract from it – no real industrial or
high-tech manufacturing base, no gut-grinding,
ball-breaking, life-shortening work to spread
gloom and despondency; only service industries
such as banking, real estate and, especially,
tourism, to stoke the slow-burning furnace of the
Sunshine State.

Background texture – atmospheric colour – has
never been in short supply in Miami, a city founded
on dodgy land deals, selling parcels of mangrove
swamp to the gullible. It has enjoyed a fruitful

relationship with crime and violence ever since — from Al Capone and Meyer Lansky in the 1930s, through the drug barons of the 1980s, to exiled Latin American dictators and their thugs now — with an abundance of corrupt lawyers, judges and politicians fleshing out the cast.

Against this background, it is not hard to imagine a character like my friend, John Hood — a studiously cool, Miami-born, Yale-educated (until he dropped out), New York-honed amalgam of Humphrey Bogart and Dick Tracey. A man of many parts but perhaps no particular focus: nightclub promoter, nightclub doorman, book reviewer, music critic, DJ, former low-budget film actor, recording artist, performance artist, sometime pimp (read on) and fugitive from the law.

If John Hood did not exist, it might be necessary to invent him, but exist he does, even if the name is not real (though it is certainly the one he goes by on the Beach). The fact is, John Hood has invented *himself*, and if South Florida generally is a place of transformation, then he is a walking advertisement of the possibility here to be however and whomever you wish to be — and to be accepted, for the large part, at face value.

Like Bogart, John was born with something of a silver spoon in his mouth. He can trace his family on his father's side back to 1638 in Connecticut. His mother is a staunchly Republican public figure, another reason for his fictional name, given the trouble he gets into. John was probably not the toughest boy at school, nor at Yale — a university not noted for producing gangsters. But like Bogart (whose mother used to dress him effeminately, in

68

the style of the day), John has assumed the mantle of tough guy.

When I first met John, he was the bouncer at Mayday, one of the clubs on the Beach more popular with my teenage friends than with Miami's glitterati. You couldn't miss Hood: he was the guy on the door who looked like a 1950s B-movie gangster, always sartorially elegant in suit and hat, and never less than courteous when offering firm denials to underage girls trying to talk their way in. Even the uniformed cops keeping watch seemed to like him.

But if Hood was a figure out of DC comics – a malleable, youthful face buried, like his motives, beneath the *noir*-ish brim of his fedora – then he was a character who had travelled a circuitous route, through some pathologically cool, American gangster-inspired Parisian semiological text, back to the pages of the good ol' USA.

Fast approaching thirty, Hood was a one-man combination of trash culture and intellect, a self-described 'literary thug', as likely to give you the Latin root of a verb as the toe of his boot. It was as if the spiffy John Travolta hit man from *Pulp Fiction* had fused with Anthony Burgess – and somewhere in the process incorporated just a hint of Dick Dastardly and Muttley.

We talked briefly on those first doorstep encounters about writing, music and movies. Even in passing, Hood's conversation was laced with literary allusions and wit – rare enough commodities in Miami. We agreed to meet one coming Monday at six p.m. for a drink, but at five p.m. on the allotted day, the phone rang and I heard John's voice on the line.

'It's Hood. Hey, I'm not going to be able to make our drink. I'm downtown. I got busted.'

'You *what*?'

'I'm in the slammer. I was arrested for beating up two Canadians.'

'Shit. *Did* you beat them up?'

'Yeah – I found them at my girlfriend's apartment at four in the morning. You know, these guys are in town for three hours on a stopover. They come to South Beach, to the Spot, meet her and get beat up. They said they were just doing coke, but it didn't look that way to me. And then they *ratted* on me.'

Clearly, jail had done nothing to dull the thrust of Hood's dialogue, or its quaint, gangster movie bite.

'If I'm in Chicago, and I'm at some dame's house at four in the morning, and her boyfriend comes in and clocks me, I've two choices: clock him back or leave. Or both. *Never* rat, *never* fucking rat! They ran out and called the police, said I had a gun and was going to kill them. In New York, you know what they would have said? "*You let this guy beat up both of you? Get the fuck outta here!*"'

We talked some more about the severity of the charge and the likelihood of making bail. Our six p.m. drink was obviously out of the question, but I was impressed by John's courtesy at remembering the arrangement and, with all the restrictions prison places on telephone use, making the considerable effort to call. As we ended our conversation, Hood gave me advice, should I ever be arrested:

'Don't wear plaid pants [tartan trousers] in jail. They think you're from some fucking country club – and the other inmates aren't members!'

Now, a couple of years and many meetings later, I call Hood to see how he's doing. His Monday night club, the Fat Black Pussycat (the name borrowed from Woolworth heiress Louisa Carpenter's infamous Tangiers nightclub of the 1950s, haunt of William Burroughs and Allen Ginsberg) is booming, and John is very much the man about town.

We arrange to meet for dinner, but first Hood invites me over to the lowish-rent Ocean Drive hotel where he lives, to check out his library. His room is at the end of a shadowy corridor which smells, like many of even the more expensive Deco hotels on Miami Beach, of recycled air and old carpet. But when he opens the door, the clutter inside is a tiny oasis of knowledge in a town dedicated almost singly to the sensual pleasures.

Admittedly, some of the knowledge is a little arcane, not to say threatening. Like a man on a major caffeine jag, constantly speeding ahead of himself, Hood whisks me through his crime section, many of them 'how to' handbooks of a variety not usually found at Waterstones or Dillons.

'OK,' he says, running a trigger finger along the titles. 'Here's the crime: *Techniques of Revenge* . . . *Counterfeit Currency: How To Really Make Money* – it gives you the blueprints of how to make money, it's by an ex-Treasury agent. *How To Kill, Volume One* – this is not playing, it's really how to kill people! See how they all use pseudonyms, like "Uncle Fester" – from *The Addams Family*? There's a company I get these from . . . This guy's a very unique individual. His first book was *Making Crime Pay*. *Successful Armed Robbery* was his second. It tells you how to rob a bank!'

'Are these books legal to publish?'

'Yeah.' Hood pauses barely a second to smile. 'America, the Land of the Free!' He sweeps me past more of the same: *How To Survive in Prison, Professional Killers: An Inside Look.* 'I wrote about these guys in New York, for *Details* magazine, *Spin, Egg.* They have some of this faux-anarchist stuff: *Reborn in Canada, Reborn in the USA*; those are about changing your identity. *Physical Interrogation Techniques: Mouth – Intrusion Into Body Orifices.* They're serious, these guys. When I interviewed them, I called the publisher, then they would call me. I couldn't call them direct.'

We check out the more traditional occupants of John's bookshelves, members of what he calls his 'Heroes of the Month' collection: Dickens, Shakespeare, Ataturk, Ivan the Terrible, D. H. Lawrence, Joan of Arc. Hood remembers a favourite quote from Eugene Ionesco ('"*Is there life without geography?*" It makes sense, huh, because life is about where you're sitting') and then, like a jazz musician who's found a theme and wants to run with it, we're off on an Ionesco riff:

'There's a couple of these nonsense, back and forth things in one of his plays, and I discovered that it was written while he was trying to learn English from a textbook! He had to relearn the most fundamental things. So in the play, he gives instructions on how to make a vicious circle. Do you know how to make a vicious circle?'

He frowns at me, waiting a moment for a reply that is not forthcoming. He smiles again – more of an amused grimace – then answers for me.

'*You take any old circle, a plain circle, and caress*

72

it until it shows its vices. That's great. I live for this shit, you know!'

My eyes glance over the shelves at Graham Greene and Alberto Moravia ('He's like Calvino with tits'), then back to the crime – the cultish Black Lizard paperbacks and their Vintage Crime offspring.

I look at this man, with his speed and his intelligence and his insistent elegance (it is not common in Miami to wear a suit during daylight hours unless you absolutely have to), and wonder: 'Who is he?' If people come to South Florida to reinvent themselves, it is usually with coconut-palm-infested ease in mind. Not this. John seems like a man trapped in his dream of a world which never quite existed, except on the page or on celluloid. He is the essence of Philip Marlowe, whom Chandler always intended as a knight out of his time.

Hood has the same mix of street toughs and chivalry, the same battered innocence. And if he falls farther than Marlowe sometimes, with his illusions and his excesses, legal, financial and drug related, I feel compelled to forgive him.

Even Hood's club is an extension of his desire to reimagine the world in black and white. ('What I'd like really is Technicolor *film noir*. Like *Rumblefish*, where only what's important is picked out in colour. See, not everything deserves colour. Colour's wasted.') It's not the decor of the Fat Black Pussycat that's monochrome so much as the thinking behind it. The club itself is in a dark, intimate-seeming space featuring private booths provided with soft velvet cushions, but what gives the Pussycat its underworld, speakeasy edge is the fact that each week John devises a different password, without which you cannot enter. To learn the word, you must first get hold of the club's phone number, then call for a voicemail message in Hood's own clipped yet jazzy tones:

'Some people say the world is a ghetto, others say all the world's a stage, but the Fat Black Pussycat says the world's one big playground of possibilities, and we've got the biggest swing set around. This Monday, let's get lost to a time when Nick and Nora were tops on the silver screen, Walter Winchell and Hedda Hopper spilled ink on the scene, and Chandler and Hammett were must-must reads. When Fifty-second Street was Swing Street, and the hep cats at the clip joints invented terminal cool with nothing but a wink and a nod and a snap. And in honour of the man who led his band to stomp at the Savoy a full two years before old Benny Goodman, this week's Fat Black password is Chick Webb. One more time: Chick Webb. A name without doubt you should know.'

We dine in the subdued glamour of the Strand on Washington Avenue – opened in 1986 and thereby part of the first wave of the South Beach revival (as opposed to a truly historic restaurant such as Joe's Stone Crab, at the bottom of Washington, which has served justifiably famous seafood since 1913). As we start working our way through a bottle of Merlot, John launches into his own highly sin-dividual assessment of Miami Beach's position in a Galilean cosmology:

'South Beach, I think, would be Dante meets Milton. To me, Milton is Heaven, and Dante, obviously, is synonymous with Hell. I think it's a hellish version of Heaven.'

(To give Miami Beach its due, despite the cultural wasteland it often seems, I was once able to purchase a collection of Milton's works at the News Cafe, a twenty-four-hour restaurant which doubles as a bookstore and magazine stand, at three a.m.)

John takes a sip of wine, glances round at the Strand's *de rigueur* beautiful people, then makes the vaguely rat-like tightening of his mouth which seems almost a studied Bogartian gesture. He adjusts his hat, which even here he wears as a testament to his chosen role, and tells me about his metamorphosis from plain John — [real name omitted], to the quasi-mythical John Hood.

'I was at Yale, being groomed to inherit the WASP tradition. I was taking the standard BA thing, I had dual majors in art and literature. And I decided I'm either going to *do* this and go into politics – Yale is recruiting territory for the CIA, of course – or go into business or law. I'm not saying that it's a bad thing, but it's a mapped out thing.

'I had this whole thing with college, that it was prolonging my dependence. So I went to the Chelsea Hotel in New York. I gave them nine grand and said, "I'll move out when this runs out." In fact, I had ten grand. I kept one. Then I got a job in a bookstore, and everybody's, "Read this, read this!" And I just did. The books cost me absolutely nothing. I read everything in sight. I joined the Marxist School, I went for a couple of sessions, and I'm like, "This thing was created to combat something that doesn't even *exist* anymore." I said, "Fuck these people!" You know: everybody's got to share in the wealth. No, I believe in the exercise of individual

75

will. Sovereignty. I wasn't a Republican then, but I'm sure that was a strong reason why I became one.'

Hood started writing for hip New York publications like the *East Village Eye* and *Paper* magazine (an author friend told me that John's book reviews were among the best he had ever read), and graduated into other activities such as performance art, songwriting and recording.

'Then I was in a movie called *Alphabet City*. This was mid-1980s. I was supposed to be this gangster, Cochran, wearing a hood, and this dame I was hanging with, Donna Domino, started calling me "Hood". She says, "*Hood, you look like a hood.*" So I decided to use two four-letter words, each of one syllable, instead of my real name. It simplified things greatly. I would be John —, and people would say, "Who? What?" So I just said, "John Hood". The movie was a big flop, but when I signed with Warners to make dance music, I kept the name, "Hood". I was twenty-three.'

I glance at him now and can't decide whether he looks younger than his thirty years or older. Somehow he manages to seem both. I find it hard, too, to credit him with being quite as tough as he claims, though he has the arrest record to prove it. But where, I wonder, was this love of the gangster milieu born? On the streets of New York? Inside the bookstore?

'No, in Miami. I grew up in Miami – yes, people do grow up in Miami!' The Bogart rat-grin again. 'And Miami is a place with really no history. Miami's history is purely that of the carpetbagger or the criminal. Selling swampland. It's the grifter. I think it's the first city to be founded upon the merits and the true definition of grifting. And it was the first city where the class of a grifter was less important than his talent. A good grifter, be he blue-blooded or barbaric, can make it.

'You know, most of this island came from Biscayne Bay. They just dredged up whatever was at the bottom of the bay, put it here and this is Miami Beach. I call this the Sixth Borough of New York, with so many New Yorkers here. But here's the difference between Manhattan and Miami Beach. Here, we have causeways between us and the mainland. In Manhattan, you have bridges and tunnels. Same thing. The difference is that Manhattan is a rock and being a rock, Manhattan pulsates. And this is sand. Sand, due to its chemical make up, isn't capable of making a pulse. And the worst part: this isn't quicksand. This is slow sand. It's a grimy little Venus fly-trap.'

Aloft in near poetic form, Hood's subtle but unceasing gestures become ever more agitated – not so much anxious as impatient, as if words are merely a brake on the speed of his thoughts.

'I think making money down here and having great ideas are sure to succeed,' he says, 'but they rank in a dubious realm compared to surviving with your spine intact. Down here, I find it's real easy to trance yourself out and wake up in the morning and dump yourself in the cleansing waters of South Beach. I think it's the last best place for decadence. You could swallow a jellyfish, step on a bottle, have unsafe sex and, after an eight-ball evening, still feel like, "*Well, I'm OK. I've got a sun tan!*" Because it's true. When you look in the mirror and you have a sun tan, it's a great deceiver, it's so alluring.'

77

Our food arrives, and I touch on Hood's recent elevation to the pantheon of American religion: prime-time TV. He tells me how, almost by chance, he scammed the *Geraldo* talk show, posing as an unlikely, MBA-educated, new wave pimp known as 'The Mack', taking along his current girlfriend, Lorena, and another woman friend, to pose as his hookers.

A friend of a friend had been approached by Rivera's research team in their quest, presumably, to find personable pimps willing to tell all on TV. That they were prepared to believe Hood was a pimp may say something about the rest of America's image of Miami. From the perspective of New York, South Florida seems like a place where anything goes, where the climate is too balmy for anyone to work at a real job, and where crime, drugs and wild nightlife are so rife that prostitution is probably listed in the Yellow Pages. Of course, John's arrest record may have helped convince them.

On TV, Hood, in his customary suit, low-brimmed hat and breast-pocket handkerchief, was accused by Geraldo of being 'cartoonish'. An ex-New York City cop, shipped in for the occasion, attacked Hood and the other, apparently genuine (and considerably less endearing) pimp for the benefit of the cameras: ' "*Parasites*" is not the word that would actually describe them. "*Sleazebags*" is certainly very, very mild.' Rapturous, Roman amphitheatre applause from the studio audience. 'These people are the scum of the earth.'

John smiles at the memory. Aside from the entertainment of being part of the grand circus of American TV, he got a trip to New York out of the deal, was put up at a swank hotel, and was paid 'one grand for my troubles, while the girls each got five hundred bucks'. The fiction goes on.

And so we come to the full story of John's arrest. This he tells with an element of bravado, a little at odds with reports I have heard from mutual friends, not so much of his behaviour on this initial incarceration, but of a subsequent rearrest for breaking his parole (actually, I believe, for failing to turn up for 'Anger Control Classes'). I have been told tales of John crying down the telephone from jail, of begging for money to bail him out, but I can only say that when he called me, that first time from jail, to cancel our drinks appointment, he sounded as he always does: cheerful, almost playful, as if his Chandleresque lifestyle had in fact been validated by a spell in the slammer.

The night Hood was hauled downtown to the holding tank, he was, he says, relatively sanguine: 'I'm like, "No big deal, friend. You know, I'll be in for a few hours, then I'll be out." Then I get the news: "No bond." [No bail.]

'I'm like, *"No bond? I beat up a couple of Canadians, you know?"*' John says this in an affronted tone, as if assaulting Canadians (a race not held in the highest esteem in America) should rank perhaps with a minor parking offence. 'But because I had a weapon and was in somebody else's home, they charged me with armed occupied burglary, which is the third most severe felony they can charge you with in the state of Florida. It's a home invasion offence, and it carries with it a maximum sentence of life in prison!'

We're still staked out at the Strand, enjoying the dog-end of our meal. I glance around at tables filled with richly attired young men and women all trying to impress each other – a strange environment in which to contemplate the possibility of a life sentence.

'What weapon did you have?' I ask.

'A blackjack. I had a pistol in the car, but I didn't bring it in. I mean, I've carried it around for years.

'So I'm like, "Oh, shit. This is serious. No bond." I'm flipping! So I get the phone call. And they don't tell you how to make the phone call, either. So I'm not getting through, I'm not getting through, and they're saying, "You've got one minute." And then one guy goes, "Dial nine", or something. It wasn't even a nine, it was a seven, I think. And I was thinking, "What the fuck is going on?" I mean, you get so flustered, the most simple things become tremendous, torturous tasks. I was thinking: "Life in prison." I didn't know at the time it was life, but I knew it was serious. No bond for Mr Clean.'

John sips from his wine and lights another in a steady flow of cigarettes. Even these he smokes like some B-movie hood, pinching the filter between forefinger and thumb, and exhaling the smoke in a punchy, no-nonsense stream.

'When you're charged,' he goes on, 'these people don't care what colour you are. They don't care where you went to school, they don't care if you can spell Baudelaire, or you know the history of Franz Anton Mesmer, or even some butthead thing like when *Banana Splits* went off the air. They don't give a shit. None of that matters. They don't care if you're the most popular guy in the world, all they

80

know is you have these charges, and these charges demand this redress.

'So I call my mother. I'm like, "Look, Mom—"

'And she says, "*If I ever told you one thing, I told you never to call me from jail.*"

' "When did you tell me that?" I ask. "When I was four or five years old? This is serious!"

'But you know, I can see her point of view. Say, for instance, that one of her political opponents finds out that her son is an ex-con or a convicted felon or in jail or whatever. It's dirt. And she's worked long and hard to achieve her position. So then she's like, "*My friends make the laws, they don't break the laws.*" And it's true.

'She could easily have called a judge, or called this or called that, and fixed it. But that's the kind of favour that is real hard to repay. It's different for you or I – you know, I wouldn't hesitate to call in a favour big or small from someone, because I'm always ready to do that kind of favour in return. But for her, it's different.'

(Just to give a little balance to Hood's tale, he has since been seen quite happily in his mother's company at a party for Miami's Summit of the Americas, an event presided over by President Clinton. John may play the rebel and ne'er-do-well, but he is not one to cut all filial ties.)

'Then they put me up somewhere else, where I had more access to a phone – that's when I called you, remember?' A grimace, a smile. John pauses not so much for reflection as breath. 'So I get an attorney and the first thing he says is, "You've got to get rid of this armed occupied burglary charge." So my girlfriend comes down and says, "No, he lives

81

there. It's his place. He has a key." So they dropped that right away. But it still took five days.

'And what happened is this thing went here and then went there. They shipped me to an ICDC from a DCJ. A DCJ, a Dade County Jail, you still feel like you're close to the mechanism. A DCJ, that's where the courts are and that's where the processing is, and you're still only an elevator ride away from freedom.

'But an ICDC is something like an inter-correctional facility for Dade County, and this is where you're going to stay. Everybody's like, "You're going to be here thirty to thirty-four days, easy." And I'm like, "Wow, this is serious." I'm like, "Look, can I have someone bring some books for me?" But they tell me, "No, you can only get books from a store. Someone can *buy* you books and have them sent to you, wrapped and sealed."

'And I'm like, "Well, I have my own library." ' John allows a wry grin to cross his lips. ' "I'd prefer hardcover!"

'It was really heavy. I saw some heavy shit in there. I saw a guy get raped. I didn't see the actual act, but I saw his feet. I was sleeping on the floor. They said, "There's no beds," so I slept in a corner on the floor. The beginning of the assault, I turned over and shut my eyes. Apparently they'd had some kind of relationship before. Maybe they were play-acting.

'Other times, I saw guys get crocked. One guy reached across another guy's plate, and *boom!* One guy changed the TV channel. Never do anything without asking the house man! The house man runs things. The house man is like the veteran, the

82

toughest. I have no idea how they appoint them, all I know is that you don't push their authority. You *ask* them if you can take a shower!'

Another toke of the cigarette. John looks at me with his sharp, dark eyes, an assumed weariness masking the boyish sense of fun.

'You know, two things I could recommend in jail,' he says. 'One, I told you: don't wear plaid pants. The other is, don't ask to watch *Northern Exposure* when it's Monday night football!' He laughs and affects a slightly squeaky, affronted black accent. 'They were like, "*What?* What the *fuck* you talkin' about?"'

I smile and try to picture John Hood in jail, the ex-Ivy League college kid talking smart and doubtless trying to dodge the fate that befell the guy he heard being raped.

'They'd be looking at me weird,' he says, 'so I'd pull out my arrest record – and mine was two pages, most people's were only one! And they're like, "Oh, shit, white boy!" Or "GQ", they'd call me. "Oh, shit, GQ, you got a fucking temper, huh? What you do?" I'd go, "I beat up a couple of fucking squares." And they'd go, "Over a girl?" "Over a dame," I'd say. "Right."

'One time, I was handcuffed to this one guy, a big fucking guy . . .' Again, John assumes a black voice, now dropping an octave to a *basso profundo* growl. 'He's like, "What are you in for?"

' "A couple of assaults," I go. "What about you?" '

If anything, John's voice drops still further, mimicking a slow, almost childlike rhythm.

'He goes, "*Well, they say I killed him . . . but he wasn't dead when I left him!*" And this guy's biceps were bigger than my imagination!'

All this chat about guns, dames and killing is fun because it's designer violence, one step removed from reality. I have never seen John Hood commit a violent act. On club doors, he certainly looks able to take care of himself, but I have never seen him so much as lose his temper.

So when I ask how he would feel if he shot someone, and he laughs and replies, 'If I shot someone? It depends . . .', I can't take him seriously. Hood has a clear (well, clearish) moral core, and while he's no candidate for canonization, I have never sensed that he might actually enjoy hurting another human being. As he says, 'The worst part about violence is that your shoes get ripped.'

Even on the issue of Miami's reputation for violence, John has his doubts. 'You know what's weird? Miami is still a cowboy town, and yet I'm rarely in fights here. Rarely. I carry a pistol, and I had a guy who wanted to shoot me once, but I talked my way out of it. It's different from New York. New York is a tough town. New York is attitude and swagger. Here, they can't *spell* "attitude"!'

John is not quite so self-delusional as he might on occasion appear. Once, when I asked him what he wanted from his life, he replied, 'I expect nothing, but I'm going to have the world. But that doesn't mean that I want to be Trump or Huizenga. It means that I want life on my terms.

'But I'm sick of the whole feast or famine thing,' he went on. 'With the club, I made thirty thousand dollars in forty-six Mondays, yet I had my landlord lock me out of my apartment yesterday. I'm sick of that. I'm not twenty-three any more. But at the same time, the one saving grace is, it's on my terms. It's my choice to be here. I live the life.'

And so, in this town of invertebrates, as he calls it, Hood walks the mean streets. And with his mix of pragmatism and fatalism, his charm and his wit, his movie-screen tough talk and his impeccably good manners – John Hood walks alone.

8

I'M NOT A HOOKER

At the corner of Calle Ocho (Southwest Eighth
Street) and Southwest Eleventh Avenue, Cuban-born
Isaura has lived a life that makes years in-
determinable. She might be twenty-five, she might
be forty. Her dress hugs her figure and reveals much,
both of her legs and bust, but the slightly split and
frayed seam at the back lends a quality of pathos
which somehow confirms her account of why she's
waiting by a pay phone now.

'I'm not a hooker, though I dress like one,' she
says, almost by way of introduction, and it is difficult to doubt her or not to like her.

'My boyfriend started coming on to my little
sister.' She pauses, to greet a friend who walks by.
'I caught him watching her, getting a hard-on, playing with himself, so I told him, "*Stop the car! I'm
getting out now!*" That's why all my shit is out here
on the street.'

She points to the doorway of a bar, where a dozen
or more plastic carrier bags of clothes rest against
the glass. 'I'm trying to call my mother to ask if I can
stay with her. I have nowhere to go. Maybe next
you'll see me dancing in that bar to survive!'

The whole story is delivered with great spirit and
no hint of a hustle, or even a desire for sympathy, as
if her telling it to me gives it more sense or shape –

or perhaps simply passes the time until, as I move on, another friend arrives to help her move her stuff.

Isaura might seem like just another extra in John Hood's mean-streets vision of Miami, but in fact her neighbourhood, Little Havana, is a world apart from the neon madness of South Beach. Calle Ocho is the heart, both figuratively and geographically, of Miami's Cuban population, and while it lies only a few blocks away from the southwestern fringes of downtown Miami, it might almost be an island like Cuba itself, so intense is its identity, its self-absorption and its residents' commitment to a cause – the 'liberation' of Mother Cuba, the downfall of Castro.

In a Calle Ocho bar which, even at three in the afternoon, is as dark as it is musty, I mention to one old man, Charlie, that I am writing about Florida, about Cubans in Miami. Immediately his wizened face lights up and he becomes strangely excited and affectionate, hugging me repeatedly and announcing, from beneath his faded white baseball cap and behind his large-rimmed spectacles, his crazy verdict on the situation that has kept a whole generation of Cuban exiles in Miami, waiting for Fidel to tumble.

'Castro, he make a mistake! England, she make a mistake! God and your momma make a mistake!' Charlie's eyes shine in the darkness. He seems almost tearful as he hugs me, shaking my hand at the same time, as if his sole appointed task on earth is to make me see what he sees, feel what he feels. 'I love you!' he says. 'Don't make a mistake!'

Back outside on the street, I gulp for air and

glance around at buildings which would make even Barnsley look beautiful. I walk a couple of blocks past seemingly endless furniture stores – *muebles* – selling mostly overly ornate tables, lights and bed-room suites, their electric candelabra alone worthy of a miniature Versailles palace. Then, eager to get out of the sun again for a few minutes, I duck inside a smaller, more promising establishment, the Botánica el Indio Amazónico, its window filled with kitsch religious statuary, ceramic Native American figurines, heavily decorated with painted feather head-dresses and beads, and a whole range of other weird shit demanding immediate investigation.

The interior is gloomy and cluttered with an amazing array of beads, charms, bottles of healing oils, saint statues, plaster Madonnas, bleeding heart icons, a figure of Christ with a golden halo and a lurid purple and gold robe draped around his body, more painted ceramic Native Americans – plus an almost life-size, free-standing wooden Indian by the door, perhaps a blood relative of one of those traditional American cigar-store Indians, but somehow much more intimidating.

I smile idiotically at the tiny old Cuban woman behind the counter, half expecting her to produce some cute, squealing, ultimately deadly *Gremlins*-like creature for me to take home. But instead she smiles back and answers my unasked question with the words: 'Is *santería* . . .'

'*Santería?*' I mumble, in a daze.

'Is Cuban,' she says, in her heavy, at times almost impenetrable accent. 'Saint worship – like voodoo. From Africa, *los esclavos*, the slaves . . .' She reaches behind her to a wall stocked with hanging beads of every description, but mostly large, darkly coloured and irregularly shaped. 'For luck,' she tells me, letting me hold a couple of the strands. 'Different beads for worship each god. Is for Chango,' she says, showing me a string of white and red beads. 'Chango is god of thunder and fire. Has three wives, many lovers . . .' She grins, then hands me another strand. 'For Orula. Like St Francis . . . You are *católico*?'

'No.' I shake my head. I remember now hearing about *santería* on TV, when there was a controversy on Miami Beach over the ritual sacrifice in an apartment building of goats and chickens. WSVN7, the local English-language station most sympathetic to exiled Cuban causes (and part of Rupert Murdoch's predictably sensational Fox TV network), had visited the apartment and filmed a *santería* priest preparing to slaughter a chicken. Outside the apartment, animal rights activists protested against the killing. The local city council was concerned about public health aspects. But it had also become an issue of freedom of religion, protected under the Constitution. In the end, the sacrifices were stopped by the priest's landlord, who argued that they constituted a breach of the lease and threw him out.

When later I read about *santería* (what little I can find in English, which is not much), I learn that it was originally a four-thousand-year-old Nigerian religion, brought to Cuba by Yoruba slaves, who were forced to convert to Catholicism but who fooled their Spanish masters by substituting images of Catholic saints for African deities and continuing their own forms of worship, including animal sacrifices. *Santería* worshippers in the United States, among Cuban, Caribbean and Latin American immigrants in Miami, New York, Los Angeles and other major cities, now number around half a million, up almost 400 per cent in the past decade.

All of the Catholic icons have their *santería* equivalents. Jesus Christ is identified with Obatala, the god of energy, wisdom, purity and peace – yet somehow Obatala also represents Our Lady of Mercy. Saint Lazarus is associated with the musically named deity, Babalu Aye, the tobacco or cigar saint, traditionally depicted on crutches (not perhaps the best advertisement for the tobacco industry) with two dogs.

Here in the *botánico,* the old lady, whose name is Marisol, explains with some difficulty the mysteries of *Yoruba* – or the *Orishas* or *Lukumi* or *Regla de Ocha*, as *santería* is also known. The seventeenth of December, she says, is *San Lazaro*'s saint's day, and is marked by blowing cigar smoke onto an image of the saint. This she proceeds to demonstrate, showing me how you must first light the cigar, then insert the lighted tip into your mouth and, with puffed cheeks (to prevent burning the inside of your mouth), blow smoke back through the cigar onto the deity. Just why you would want to do this, she doesn't say.

We are not alone in the store. Under a sign which reads, '*Consultas*', three or four people sit waiting on sofas and thick, padded armchairs for a reading of some kind or another. As they wait, they watch on a colour TV a particularly tacky Cuban talkshow presenter called Christina, who's described to me as

90

'the Cuban Oprah Winfrey'. She and her live audience here in the store seem somewhat at odds with the large poster above their heads of another Indian, *El Indio Amazónico*', from whom presumably the *botánico* gets its name. He's a moody-looking bugger, with a feather through his nose, surrounded by various astrological symbols – *Acuario, Escorpion, Libra, Geminies* – whose powers are revealed in an explanatory leaflet in Spanish, which Marisol falteringly helps me to translate:

'*Consulte ya al más grande y mejor vidente* ... consult now the greatest and best soothsayer, astrologer, *parasicólogo*, healer, botanist and spiritual counsellor, that with only a reading of the eyes, the tongue, the hands, the aura, the Tarot, the crystal ball, the Spaniard playing cards, the tobacco or the seashells, will tell you *toda su vida* ... your entire life ... does all sorts of cleansings, treatments and works to solve *todos sus problemas* ... all your problems, even ... *los que otros no han podido arreglar* ... the ones no-one has been able to fix.'

'*Spaniard* playing cards?' I ask.

'Is cards from Spain,' replies Marisol. 'Special cards ...'

'A reading of the seashells?'

'*Los caracoles, sí.*' She looks at me, searching for an explanation. 'He throw him on ground and read future from how he falls. You want he read for you now?'

As she says this, a large, somewhat retarded-looking man in a feather head-dress and Native American garb appears from behind a curtain. He seems neither Indian nor Cuban (perhaps Colombian, since somewhere in the store I have seen another leaflet for '*El Indio Amazónico de Colombia*'), but the grim expression on his lips and the vacant stare in his eyes promises, as far as I can see, only the most troubling of futures, and I have enough problems coping with the present. So instead I make my apologies, ponder a moment over whether to buy a plastic Jesus night-light, but opt for a couple of glass-jarred votive candles guaranteeing good luck, love, power and money – ingredients I have always sought in my life – and make my way back out onto the street, reflecting once more on how in Miami magical realism is not just some high-flown literary term, it's the very essence of life for many of its citizens. This place is *weird*: voodoo, doll worship, hexes and curses, are in the air.

(A sense confirmed a little later when I read in the *Miami Herald* that one of the tasks required of janitors working at Miami's criminal courthouse is to 'report any voo doo objects which need to be removed'. Apparently relatives of defendants frequently dump dead chickens on the courthouse steps overnight in order to cast a spell and help win acquittal. Hexes even make their way into the courtrooms: at one time, during a break in a cocaine trial, a bailiff found two dead lizards, their mouths wrapped shut with twine, inside a court. A government informant who was supposed to testify later refused.)

Further along Calle Ocho, attracted by a vision through the window of middle-aged Cubans sitting at tables handrolling big fat stogies, I step inside Ernest Perez-Carrillo's small cigar factory. The smell is the first thing that hits me as I walk through the door: that beautiful, rich aroma of cigar leaf, earthy and funky and already burnt by the sun – a smell like the best, dirtiest sex you've ever had, sex rolling around in a mud wallow, covering yourself in filth (while guzzling vast quantities of brandy) and then baking like a pig.

I used, briefly, at a very pretentious stage in my youth, between the ages of about eighteen and twenty-two, to smoke Havana cigars, *Monte Cristos* especially, though a box of twenty-five (then about twenty-five pounds; today practically the price of a single smoke) represented a ridiculously high proportion of my meagre film journalist's income. Now, a few puffs on one is enough to make me gag – and the thought of mouth cancer doesn't help. But I know enough to understand that these Calle Ocho coronas aren't quite the real thing, no matter that their labels carry names such as '*La Gloria Cubana*' or '*El Rico Habano*'. Because of the United States's crippling thirty-year trade embargo against Castro's Cuba, no Cuban products, including cigars or even raw tobacco, are allowed into the US, so *Señor* Perez-Carrillo must import his tobacco leaves from elsewhere. At least the staff are the genuine article, though exiled from their homeland, and their work environment seems far more the sort of humble, dark-wood interior that you would expect in some steamy Latin American capital, rather than a modern American city. (Hopefully their pay and employment contracts are a little better than those of their Third World compatriots, though the statutory minimum wage in the US is hardly generous.)

In any case, it is fascinating to watch as they roll the inner and outer leaves skilfully in their hands,

93

using sharp blades to cut the cigars and ancient hand-operated presses to shape them. And perhaps best of all is the sight of an old black Cuban in a hat, with a face full of character and seeming generosity of spirit, who smokes his own stogie, chewing a little on its damp tip and moving it from side to side of his mouth to relish its flavour as he works.

In Little Havana's chess park, a few more blocks up Southwest Eighth Street from the cigar factory, if you ignore the offensively ugly McDonald's next door, you could almost forget you're in the United States altogether. This is a meeting point for old Cuban exiles. (You must be fifty-five or older to join and, as far as I can tell, women are excluded – Cuban culture is still actively *machismo*.) They come to sit at shaded tables and play chess, dominoes and other games outside in the humid Miami heat, while endlessly discussing *la lucha* – the struggle against the arch-demon Fidel.

In an atmosphere condemned by a recent United Nations Human Rights Commission report on Miami for its almost total lack of freedom of speech (although at least there are no more terrorist bombings, as there were in the 1980s, against Miami Cubans who failed to voice the proper condemnation of Castro), there are still those who will go against the grain and express a more balanced, perhaps more objective opinion.

As he ends a fast-paced game of dominoes with a smile of quiet triumph, I start talking to Orlando Menes, a gentle-voiced Cuban of sixty-seven, simply because he speaks English when virtually everyone else in the park doesn't. Orlando is no fan of Castro.

The mere mention of his name makes him glance cautiously around before saying anything. But his words lack the savagery that colours so much dialogue in Little Havana.

'Everybody here,' he tells me, 'everybody here, at the beginning of the revolution, they open their *heart* to the revolution! Now, all of them, they *hate* the revolution! What they want is to bring the revolution – not only Fidel – the whole thing down.

'But before Castro, it was not good. It was better than now, but Batista, he was a dictator, he steal the power – it's not because he win some election or something. It was not good. He kill people, like this guy. He torture people, like this guy. You live in Cuba and you have no political opinion under Batista, you can live. But you say something against Batista, you go to jail. So he is a dictator like this one. Batista was not good either!'

Three dates more than any others mark Miami's recent history with Cuba. The first is New Year's Day, 1959, when Fulgencio Batista finally left Havana for the Dominican Republic, his departure marking the success of Fidel Castro's revolution and beginning a flow (at times a trickle, at times a flood) of Cubans leaving their country and coming to Miami, to escape communism, economic hardship or their own sometimes shadowy pasts.

The second is the seventeenth of April, 1961, the date of the aborted Bay of Pigs invasion of Cuba, by a force of Cuban exiles trained in and supposedly supported by the United States. An invasion whose failure – largely as a result of President Kennedy's not unwise refusal to commit the US military to the

95

assault – is still regarded by many among Miami's *exilio* community as an unforgivable betrayal of the anti-Castro cause.

To imagine Florida during this time, and particularly during the following year, 1962, during what became known as the Cuban Missile Crisis, is to picture a war zone. Miami was awash with soldiers and tanks, preparing to invade or be invaded by Russian troops reportedly massing in Cuba – or worse, preparing for the consequences for either side of a nuclear strike. From the exiles' point of view, the Kennedy–Khrushchev accord which brought an end to the crisis was only further evidence of betrayal, despite Kennedy's assertion in Miami in December 1962 that the flag of the 2506 Brigade, the exile invasion force which had suffered such heavy losses at the Bay of Pigs, would *'be returned to this brigade in a free Havana.'*

The third significant marker in this increasingly hostile tale of two cities, Miami and Havana, which stand a little over two hundred miles apart, came in the spring of 1980 with the *Mariel* boatlift. Following a crisis at the Peruvian Embassy in Havana, when thousands of would-be Cuban refugees claimed sanctuary in the embassy grounds, Castro designated the Cuban port of Mariel a temporary collection point at which Miami Cubans with boats could come and pick up their relatives, *'Ésta escoria,'* as Cuba's *Radio Rebelde* put it: 'This scum'.

Seizing both a tactical and a propaganda opportunity, Castro opened his prisons and his insane asylums, dumping on the shores of Florida, among the 125,000 new Cuban refugees, a vast number of the sick and the criminal – 26,000 of them with prison records – as well as a high proportion of homosexuals, homosexuality being a crime in Cuba.

The impact of this massive influx, in a matter of months, on the already volatile racial mix of Miami was unsettling. The *Marielitos*, as they were known, were quickly credited with turning Miami Beach – where many of them landed and took up residence in the early 1980s in the then declining and often derelict Art Deco hotels – into a rabid, crime-ridden, crack-driven combat zone.

Back in the Little Havana chess park, I ask Orlando Menes what he thinks will happen when Castro dies.

Orlando shakes his head sadly. 'Oh my God,' he says, 'that's something which nobody can imagine: what will happen. But I think it will be something very dangerous, will be blood. Bloodshed.'

'What would you and the people here most want to happen?'

'No, no, no, not me – because I have nothing against anybody in Cuba. But you see, a lot of the people here, you have to consider this question: here, maybe ninety per cent of these people are illiterate. Ignorant. What they have in mind is revenge – revenge and revenge. You can't get that thing from their mind . . .'

'Even thirty years later?'

He smiles grimly. 'It doesn't matter – a hundred years. They have a dream. What is their dream? As soon as Castro falls down, they go to Cuba, soon as possible, with whatever they have in their hand. They want to kill their neighbour, or something like that. Because right here—' He looks around at the other old Cuban men settled over their chess boards, their chequers games. Orlando lowers his voice a little and confides: '*I can say this to you, because everybody here don't speak English.*' He continues: 'Right here – one guy there, I know him, his brother was a military under Batista, and Castro – no, not Castro, Che Guevara – Che Guevara took the power and they put him against the wall, and *bang*!

'And this guy,' Orlando says, 'he know who shoot his brother. Ah, yes! He has the name, the four soldiers and the lieutenant. He wrote the name on a piece of paper. He said, "*The only thing I want to do before I die, it doesn't matter what it cost me, even I give my life, I go back to Cuba, I look for those people and I kill them one by one!*" This is something I think the United States don't want – to make some move, to release Cuba from Castro. I think they think is better Castro is there, because everything is tight, everything will squeeze, nobody move. As soon as they remove Castro and open up, *ai* my goodness!'

In spite of the passion and hatred Castro inspires in Miami, there is also humour. On the Internet, the Fidel For President page set up by an alternative cigar smokers' newsgroup, offers suggestions drawn from the 'Top Ten Reasons To Help Elect Fidel Castro The Next US President':

> 8. *43 per cent of Perot voters think Fidel looks like Santa Claus.*
> 7. *After the release of* Look Who's Talking Too, *he offered political asylum to John Travolta.*
> 6. *Drab green fatigues guarantee the vital Generation X vote . . .*

2. Willing to arm-wrestle Colin Powell: winner-take-all for the free world.
1. Cigars for everyone!

The aforementioned Channel 7 runs nightly propaganda television reports on the latest bizarre attempts inside Cuba to poison or overthrow Castro, whom it rarely fails to refer to as 'the Teflon dictator'. These reports are frequently presented by a local Cuban-American newscaster, Rick Sanchez, whose air of self-importance and unblanching righteousness prompts jokes such as this: 'You walk into an elevator and standing inside are Rick Sanchez, Castro and Hitler. You have two bullets in your gun. Who do you shoot?' The answer: 'Rick Sanchez – twice, just to be sure!'

Orlando Menes, meanwhile, is becoming quite wistful as he talks of his homeland. We are still surrounded by Spanish chatter and the click of dominoes and chess pieces. For a moment I lose myself in a reverie, gazing at a wall mural of Hispanic and black leaders, listening to the bustle and laughter around me, drinking in the pungent cigar smoke, the particular scent of old men gathered together, then noticing that the hands of Orlando's wristwatch are stopped at five past twelve, although it is now late afternoon. It seems symptomatic of Little Havana and Miami's Cuban population, this freezing of time.

'Right now,' he says, raising his voice a little against the increasing rush-hour traffic, 'every week, about two thousand people travel to Cuba from here – from United States, mostly from Miami. Two thousand! Visit friends and relatives. Everyone go to

99

Cuba with big luggage. They put inside the luggage, goods, coffee, sugar. *Sugar!* Cuba is the mother of sugar, but if they want the sugar there, they have to bring it from the United States! They have a shortage of everything. So people go to Cuba with everything the family need there. Medicine – any kind of medicine. Razor to shave. *Razor!* You can't believe that? Soap – they have no soap to wash themselves. It's really the most poor country, the poverty there is more than Haiti, it's incredible. A rich country before Castro! Maybe was the number one in Latin America.'

I choose not to argue that perhaps much of the poverty is the result of the United States's thirty-year embargo – aggravated by the collapse of the Soviet Union, formerly Cuba's main trading partner – and instead ask if Orlando would like to go back one day.

'Back to Havana?' he replies. 'No, no, not now. Not with Castro there. If something happen in Cuba, if Cuba become some kind of free country, a democracy or something, maybe then I would go back. Oh yes, it's my country! I love my country! I want to sit there and read, something like that . . .' His eyes light with an emotion somewhere between yearning and quiet acceptance. 'I can live in Cuba, free. *Free* – that's very important, to be free. I burn to be free! Then I would go back to Cuba, like everybody here.'

9

AN ENGLISHMAN IN HAVANA

But of course I have already been to Cuba, in my first month in Miami – a trip organized by *GQ*, which seemed a gift from the gods. ('While you're in Miami,' they said, 'would you write a piece on Havana as well?' I jumped at the chance: Cuba had long fascinated me; I had even outlined a novel set partly there.)

That early trip to Havana lives in my memory as a jolt from the underworld, or another world, at any rate: a country steaming with a sticky, sweaty mix of exuberance and enforced restraint, of tropical colour and a kind of communism that I doubt was ever grey and austere; a land where politics could never drown out the more vital forces of sensuality, *salsa* and an all-embracing lust for life . . .

Six o'clock in the morning, and I'm in a taxi bound for Miami International Airport. It's a Monday in late October, 1990, I've been up half the night writing, and only now do I discover that I have absolutely no idea which airline I'm flying to Havana.

'When I flew there in 1960,' says Maurice, my French-Canadian taxi driver, 'it was American Airlines. Of course, that was 1960 . . .'

Maurice had once gone to Havana and had met Castro. 'My cousin owned a hotel there and phoned to say that things were getting bad, the government was going to take it away from him. He said I should come over, so I went, and while I was there, Castro came to the hotel. He came with his men, drinking whisky and smoking big cigars. He was hung like a bull! He was standing in his army fatigues with a girlfriend – a secretary or something, a scrawny woman – and my friend said, "Do you see that? He has a penis like a missile!" '

The size of Castro's dick is not uppermost in my mind as I rifle through my papers in search of some clue as to which terminal we should try. All I have is a name, Suzy, and a number at Airline Brokers, useless at this hour, plus a note instructing me to pay two hundred and forty-eight dollars cash over the counter for my return ticket.

'Don't worry, we'll find it,' says Maurice. 'Maybe someone at American can help you?'

But the American Airlines staff seem affronted that I want to go to Havana. Finally, someone at Air Venezuela points me in the direction of Terminal B, and I find an Eastern Airlines clerk who reluctantly admits this is where I check in for Cuba.

'Are you an American citizen?'

'No.'

'Why are you going there?'

I remember my Cuban tourist card, hastily arranged in London; there wasn't time to organize a journalistic visa.

'Tourism,' I say. 'I'm British.'

'You're not allowed to go there as a tourist from here.'

'Well, actually I'm a writer, working on a magazine article.'

'Fill out this form.'

The form reveals just how restricted travel is between the US and Cuba, only ninety miles distant from Florida's southernmost tip, but light years apart ideologically. Unless you have close Cuban relatives, the US Government restricts travel to journalists or professional researchers. A fact which becomes abundantly clear as I prepare to board the plane: everyone else on the flight is Cuban, they're all in their sixties, and they're all wearing the same hat.

Touching down in Havana less than an hour later, America quickly fades to dust. The flight from Miami is hardly enough to drain me, but the culture shock is immediate. The heat seems somehow more tropical; the people noticeably less affluent. The first thing I notice are the cars. The cars are incredible: a reminder of America, but not the America I've just left.

I stand staring at beautifully maintained Dodges, Plymouths and Chevrolets from the 1940s and 1950s, feeling as if I've stepped through a time warp. Thanks to the US embargo, no new American cars have been imported into Cuba since the revolution in 1959. Cuba's trading problems have limited the import of new cars from other sources mostly to Soviet-built Ladas and a few highly prized Japanese models, so the Cubans have been forced to keep their pre-revolutionary American classics in tiptop condition.

The sight of a gleaming white 1941 Plymouth makes me happy in a way I don't think any new car could. Its owner approaches and laughs, saying, 'The whole of Havana, the whole of Cuba, is a museum!' He asks where I'm from and immediately wants to discuss music: 'You like rock music? Rush, I love Rush!' I tell him I prefer soul and jazz, but he knows what he likes. 'Z Z Top. Jimi Hendrix. The Doors.' He starts singing 'Light My Fire'. I can't help but join in. I haven't left the airport yet, and already I'm singing along to Jim Morrison's greatest hits. I think I'm going to like Cuba.

In truth, I want to like it. I've always had a sympathy for socialist causes. I believe in public health care and public education, two areas in which Castro's Cuba has, for the most part, earned international respect. I find romantic the image of Fidel Castro and Che Guevara setting sail from Mexico in 1956 with a force of eighty-two men on board a tiny American yacht called the *Granma*, their intention being to overthrow the corrupt and repressive dictatorship of Fulgencio Batista. And I find Castro's success in holding out for thirty years against a neighbour as powerful, as hostile and as close as the US impressive to say the least.

So it is with some excitement that I look out of my taxi as we drive into Havana, past murals of Che and Fidel and posters asserting, '*Socialismo o muerte*' ('Socialism or death'). I am aware that I have come at a difficult time. The collapse of communism in Eastern Europe has led to massive cuts in Cuba's foreign aid. Castro is under pressure from just about everywhere to reform his hardline stance. A whole generation of Cubans has grown up to whom the revolution is history, making it difficult to blame the sacrifices expected of them on US interference.

Add to this the ever explosive political manoeuvrings of the Cuban exiles in Miami, and the fact that, by opening itself up further to tourism as it hopes to do, Cuba is exposing itself to the values and temptations of a more affluent and materialistic lifestyle, and it is hardly surprising that the country is widely reported to be straining at the seams.

This would not, however, be your first impression at the quietly elegant Hotel Inglaterra. Situated in the old part of Havana, the Inglaterra's nineteenth-century exterior is no match for the impressive Gran Teatro de Habana next door, but inside it is a different matter. One glance at the high-ceilinged, Moorish-styled bar and I envisage an endlessly rolling tab of *mojitos*, daiquiris and *Cuba libres*, followed by a dawn disappearing act leaving the bill in the hands of the Cuban government. If challenged, I will simply claim to have been disorientated by the bar's Moroccan tiling: 'I thought I was in Marrakech. My credit's good there.'

I take the lift to the third floor, discovering that the control panel has a logic of its own: the indicator shows '3' when in fact you are on '2', so to get to '3', you press '4'. My room is fine by any standards, with a large bathroom, marble floor and a balcony overlooking the palm trees and Spanish-colonial splendour of the Paseo de Martí (the old *Prado*) and the Parque Central. Havana was once considered the jewel of the Caribbean. Despite a good deal of climactic wear and tear – and, if you listen to the exiles in Miami, a criminal lack of maintenance under Castro – it still rates as one of the world's most beautiful cities.

I turn on the TV, keen to get my cultural bearings. Seven hours ago, I was watching MTV while I packed. Now I'm confronted by a fast-cut sequence which, given my atrocious Spanish, I can only guess is a trailer of some sort, since it combines fragments from a Goofy cartoon with footage of family life in an impoverished village and a clip from an Hispanic soap opera. The pace isn't quite as frenetic as a music video, but not far off. It's followed by another montage, this time of black-and-white images of Che and Fidel in army fatigues, followed by children cheering, then a young Castro in action with a gun.

I spend the rest of my first day in the city wandering around Habana Vieja, observing just how close some of the buildings are to crumbling into dust and watching out for falling masonry from cracked balconies.

I also get my first real sense of Cuba's most serious problem: a shortage of food. Having failed to find a café, restaurant or pizzeria with anything to offer, I return to the hotel in the hope of eating there. I realize I have missed both breakfast and lunch and feel extremely hungry, but the Inglaterra's restaurant is not open for another two hours, and when I ask at the bar for a snack, I am shown the one remaining sandwich: an unappetizing affair which consists of two slices of dry bread, a chunk of ham worthy of a funeral parlour and some gelatinous cheese.

Grateful even for this, I offer to buy the bartender a drink once he has toasted the sandwich. This has a magical effect in terms of my popularity – though it produces no hidden cache of more edible snacks – and from now on my arrival in the hotel bar is treated as an excuse for a party. The bartender, Raul, introduces himself and shakes my hand, while his colleagues joke about his family ties with Fidel,

Raul being the name of Castro's brother, the Minister of Defence.

Over the next few days, I check out the old town, the decrepit glories of the Plaza de la Catedral, the Hemingway haunts – his favourite watering hole, La Bodeguita del Medio, is one of the few restaurants where you can still regularly find food in Havana, if you're prepared to wait. (His opinion regarding this and another favourite spot a few blocks away is immortalized on a plaque inside the restaurant: '*Mi daiquirí en el Floridita, mi mojito en la Bodeguita*' – 'My daiquiri in the *Floridita*, my *mojito* in the *Bodeguita*'. A *mojito* is a rather splendid concoction consisting of white rum, sugar and fresh mint.)

The feel of the streets is very much that of any Spanish-colonial city. The architecture is beautiful, the colours suitably dusty and Caribbean, the street-life busy, with children everywhere in their government-subsidized mustard-and-white uniforms.

The strange thing is, just as in Miami Beach, I experience a kind of geographical dislocation. Here, I'm reminded more of Morocco than of Spain. And this isn't simply the influence of the *Inglaterra*'s bar. The poverty here, the bustle, the ethnic mix of Hispanic and African, all make Cuba seem far more a part of the Third World than its often unwilling role in US and European history might suggest.

It could also be the constant assault of the street hustlers that brings to mind Marrakech. Here, as there, it is impossible to walk through the city without at least half a dozen people trying to change money, sell you marijuana or show you around for a profit. The approaches are mostly friendly and diminish once you're recognized, but the pressure is greater than in most capital cities.

Trying to unnerve them, I ask several of the dealers what it's like to live in Cuba, how happy they are with Castro, and discover a distinct lack of paranoia about speaking out.

'I like Havana,' one of them tells me, 'but I don't like the system. Too much *burocracia!* Still *ricos y pobres* – rich and poor. This is not *socialismo*, everybody equal! No perestroika for Cuba. Castro would not like! Many people come to Havana just to survive. There are many problems in the country-side, much poverty.'

The young man smiles at me over his wispy goatee. I ask if he has travelled outside Cuba at all, and he says, 'Not possible for Cubans.' He laughs. 'Maybe Angola. Many Cubans in Angola – in the army!'

I talk to another money-changer, Eduardo, about music and tell him I'm interested in what's going on in the clubs here – not the overpriced tourist shit at the Tropicana, but the sort of place he might go to. A couple of his friends join us and we start talking about reggae. One of them is a musician, and we make a date to meet the next night and check out a little entertainment.

I walk along the Malecón, Havana's magnificent seafront promenade and watch fishermen in 'boats' made from the huge inner tubes of trucks with canvas tied across the bottom – the same crafts the rafters use to try and cross the shark-infested waters to Florida.

Behind me stand truly handsome colonial buildings, ravaged by time and the Atlantic spray but with a sense of history and an emotional impact far removed from even the prettiest 'island-style' wooden houses in Key West, just ninety miles across the water.

I think about conversations I have had in Miami with young Cuban-Americans such as Dulce, whose family left Cuba in the 1960s, but who has never seen it herself.

'Havana was once the jewel of the Caribbean,' she told me. 'Now everything is crumbling, the stores are empty, the people are hungry. My uncle went back to visit and cried to see what it had become.'

But I have been reading Graham Greene's *Our Man in Havana*, published in 1958, a year before the revolution, and from that it's clear that Havana has long been in disrepair:

> The pink, grey, yellow pillars of what had once been the aristocratic quarter were eroded like rocks; an ancient coat of arms, smudged and featureless, was set over the doorway of a shabby hotel, and the shutters of a nightclub were varnished in bright crude colours to protect them from the wet and salt of the sea.

At least the Malecón's facades seem vaguely suited to decay. Exploring Vedado, the more modern and residential quarter of Havana, it is impossible to avoid the Habana Libre — the Hilton in pre-revolutionary days. Its run-down tower-block exterior looks as ugly as hell, but it can't have looked much better when it opened in the 1950s. Although still in theory a luxury hotel, it has the cosmetic charm of an aeroplane toilet, only with rather more dubious water in its pool.

I sit beside this grey-green murk and try to imagine what Havana was like when it was a playground for rich American tourists. Gambling and prostitution were rife under Batista (the latter is now making a sweeping comeback under Castro), and where official American investment left off the Mafia took up. No doubt to the tourist it all seemed like innocent, heady fun, but at the same time a vast proportion of the population lived in the direst poverty and ignorance, while Batista was imprisoning and torturing his opposition.

Of course, Castro's own human rights record is far from immaculate, and he is under constant fire from Miami's largely ultra-right-wing *exilio* community. In the international arena, one of Castro's most vocal critics has been Armando Valladares, a former US envoy to the United Nations Human Rights Commission in Geneva. Imprisoned by the *Fidelistas* for twenty-two years, and only released after pressure from President Mitterand of France, Valladares's book of prison memoirs, *Against All Hope*, was a first-hand account of the violent and inhumane treatment of political prisoners in Castro's Cuba. But other leading Cuban human rights activists and former political prisoners outside Cuba cast doubt on Valladares's own behaviour in prison. And even within the US, he has come under fire for his increasingly vocal attacks on Castro's opposition and the Cuban human rights group which made his work possible.

I ask Arturo, the young Cubatur guide sitting beside me at the poolside bar, what the feeling is within Cuba towards Valladares.

'The man is a delinquent!' Arturo complains. 'You cannot trust anything he says. While he was in prison, he claimed to have been paralysed by a hunger strike. He was in a wheelchair. So the prison authorities set up a concealed video camera in his cell. When he thought he was alone, Valladares got up out of the wheelchair and walked fine!'

Arturo might, of course, be a victim of his own government's propaganda, but he is nonetheless a fairly open critic of Castro himself:

'We must wait till Castro dies for there to be change in Cuba. Or we must have another revolution. The principles of the revolution were good, but it's not socialism when you have party leaders with a Mercedes and maybe two or three other cars, sending their family on holiday to Europe. There will have to be change. A few months ago, food was rationed perhaps sixty per cent. Now there is one hundred per cent rationing. You can take many things away from people – petrol, other goods, maybe even their home – but you cannot take away food.'

The following night, I meet my dealer friends outside my hotel and go off with them in search of good music. I am more than a little wary of what to expect – not so much musically, as from my companions. They are essentially small-time crooks and anything could happen. As a result, I have left my wallet behind and carry only a small stash of dollars, divided between different pockets of my jeans.

To show some degree of trust, however, I have brought them packs of Marlboro from the hotel shop. There is a different economy for tourists in Cuba than for the Cubans. Tourists are expected to spend US dollars, and in hotel shops can buy products such as European chocolates and Marlboro cigarettes at less than the prices Cubans would have to pay on the black market. Of course, the biggest irony of all is that Cuba is rapidly becoming a dollar economy. There are rumours that Castro even prints counterfeit US dollars himself, although no-one I spoke to would confirm this.

The Marlboros go down well with Eduardo, Carlos and Miguel, despite the fact that they have to bum lights off passers-by, since one of the shortages Cuba is suffering from is an almost total absence of matches. They lead me through the hot, shadowy streets of central Havana, lit in many cases only by the headlights of parked cars.

I ask Eduardo why it is so dark.

'The oil shortage,' he explains. 'We get less oil from Moscow, so there are many economies. Even the streetlighting is cut.'

He asks if I will pay for some beers. I give Miguel five pesos – less than a pound – and wait while he disappears to get four unlabelled brown bottles.

We drink these standing waiting for a bus. One arrives within minutes, its front emblazoned with multicoloured lights, like a police car gone crazy. The buses in Havana – known locally as *gua-guas* (pronounced, 'whah-whahs') – consist of two carriages, linked by an articulated section. During the day, they are packed to capacity. Now, at ten-thirty p.m., there are only three other passengers, and we make our way to the back.

The *gua-gua* rattles across Havana at quite

112

startling speed for about fifteen minutes, heading into the modern blandness of Vedado. The houses here are one- or two-storey and set back from the road by small gardens. They were once the homes of rich men; now they house Cuba's equivalent of a middle class.

Eduardo ushers us out onto a gloomy residential street, opposite a building site. There is not a night-club in sight, and I begin to wonder what the hell is happening.

'Where are we?' I ask. 'Where's the club?'

The three of them sense my anxiety and laugh, slapping me on the back.

'We have to walk,' says Carlos. 'Five minutes!'

We follow the road up a hill, ducking under palm fronds. 'What kind of music will it be?' I enquire. '*Son*, *salsa*, reggae?' We have been talking about Bob Marley.

'A mixture,' Miguel, the musician, replies. 'Maybe some jazz. It's a local band.'

When we get to the club, it's not what I expected. The atelier is situated in the basement of a modern high-rise and seems disturbingly respectable inside.

Things look up when Carlos has an argument with the manager, who informs us that we can't order a bottle of rum unless we are accompanied by women. At first, I assume this to be a prelude to the arrival of management-supplied, high-cost host-esses, but instead it seems a policy designed to limit the excesses of groups of men drinking alone. Two of the band's girlfriends who are sitting at the next table start up a conversation with us, and a bottle is brought.

What kind of joint is this, I wonder, where not

even a gringo tourist is hustled?

The kind of joint where, for reasons left un-explained even to their girlfriends, the band has decided not to play tonight. I look at Eduardo, Carlos and Miguel, who seem faintly embarrassed by this development.

'Would you like to go to another club?' Eduardo asks.

'A better club,' Miguel adds.

'Or perhaps you would like to get high?' Carlos enquires. 'Ganja!'

And so we hightail it back across town in a *gua-gua*, then thread through the maze-like streets of Old Havana on foot. Fourteen pesos change hands and a paper tube filled with grass is bought. A few more pesos and a bottle of rum is obtained, then we head off again, stopping now while Miguel dis-appears inside an ancient apartment building.

Eduardo, Carlos and I sit waiting on a step oppo-site. People are still wandering the darkened streets. Two soldiers drive up on a motorcycle, slowing to take a look at us. The bag containing the marijuana is on the pavement between us. I find myself wondering what a night in a Cuban jail – or perhaps many nights – would be like, but the soldiers drive on.

Miguel is gone a long time. Finally, he emerges with some music cassettes and we walk a little further, down more shadowy streets. We turn into an open doorway and climb a stairway in a partly gutted building, the stairs lacking a banister on one side and offering a twenty-foot drop onto rubble below.

Carlos leads us along a corridor to a large room

114

where we're greeted by four other young men and two very attractive women. I seem to be something of a novelty, but any doubts as to my soundness are quickly dispelled by the rum and grass.

I am invited, amidst much giggling, to sit on a sofa between Maria and Giselle, who are clearly prostitutes, but who seem relaxed and off-duty. While Carlos rolls a joint, using a torn brown paper bag in place of cigarette papers, I take in my surroundings.

The room is tidy and clean, with a balcony opening onto the warm night. The men – apart from Eduardo, Carlos and Miguel – are all stripped to the waist, and the women are wearing short, flimsy dresses. One of the men, sitting opposite me, has a thin, rat-like face and a hyped-up intensity that makes me nervous. When he laughs, revealing stained teeth which seem to have been filed to points, I feel still less easy, but I have no option but to try to relax.

There's little furniture: the sofa, two chairs, a stereo, and a mirror with a shelf almost at floor level, decorated with a few ornaments. There are also two photographs, of a baby and a little girl. Giselle sees me looking at them and smiles.

'Where are you from?' she asks.

'England.'

'England!' one of the men, Jorge, proclaims happily. 'Do you know Sting?'

'Not personally.'

More laughter. 'No, I mean his music.'

'Yes.'

'Do you know he sings in Spanish? And Portuguese. Listen!'

He puts on a bootleg tape of Sting singing 'Fragile' from *Nothing Like The Sun*, in Spanish. It sounds great – a good deal better than it does in English.

We start dancing, seven or eight of us weaving about the room to the echoing music, smoking spliff and drinking rum. One of the men keeps watch out on the balcony for passing police or complaints from the neighbours, while Giselle reminds us occasionally not to dance too heavily on the floor because the baby is asleep below.

As Sting's voice continues to bellow out in Spanish, Jorge translates the lyrics for me. At one point, he makes a joke about Sting's song, 'An Englishman in New York', pointing at me excitedly and shouting, *'An Englishman in Havana! An Englishman in Havana!'*

We smoke all the grass and drink all the rum. Waves of paranoia strike me from time to time, that this is a set-up and I am about to get ripped-off or busted or worse, then I realize how ridiculous my fears are – if anything were going to happen, it would have happened by now. I have not even been pressured for money: so far this evening I have spent less than twenty dollars. I have perhaps another sixty on me, so there's not much to steal.

The question I feel most uncertain about is Giselle and Maria. No outright advances have been made to me, and I don't want to sleep with them, but I waver between thinking that I might be committing some breach of etiquette by *not* asking to stay with one of them, or feeling that I would be stepping over a line tonight if I made such a suggestion – this is Giselle's home and I get no sense that it is used for business.

There is also the small matter of Aids, especially

here in the Caribbean. Cuba has a strict but inhumane policy towards Cubans who are HIV-posi-
tive, forcibly isolating them for the remainder of
their lives in a sanatorium, but that hardly guaran-
tees safe sex among the rest of the population.

So, hoping that it won't precipitate an ugly
change of mood, I announce that I am feeling tired.
'I can find my own way back,' I lie, wanting to
appear cool. But Eduardo, Carlos and Miguel insist
on accompanying me. We stroll through the quiet
streets, blitzed out of our minds, and say goodnight
a block from my hotel, after I have given Eduardo
twenty dollars to change at slightly below the going
rate.

10

THE OLD MAN AND THE SEA

Next morning, after a breakfast of cold scrambled eggs and fresh fruit (early morning being, for some perverse reason, the only time fruit can be found in this naturally abundant land), I realize my time in Havana is running out and decide to explore a little outside the city.

Catching *gua-gua* number seven, I ride about eight miles southeast to a town called San Francisco de Paula, where Ernest Hemingway bought a house in 1940. As we pass through the town, everywhere there are faded reds, greens and blues, small wooden houses, washing on lines, a woman sweeping her floor, astonishing light, glimpses of people's lives – but there's a temptation to romanticize the poverty.

Hemingway's house is set back from the main road in lush grounds lined with palms. Now a government-run museum, it has been kept exactly as he left it when he was encouraged – by America, not by Cuba – to leave the island in 1960, a year before he shot himself in a cabin in Idaho.

As soon as I see the house I want to move in, but the museum attendants quickly inform me that visitors are not allowed to enter or even photograph through the windows and open doorway the scattered magazines, shoes and ugly stuffed animal

118

heads inside. Presumably the intention is to preserve Hemingway's effects, but the result is also to make a visit here less than fulfilling. You can wander the grounds, admire the striking view over Havana towards the sea, buy Hemingway memorabilia – T-shirts, a video, a framed photograph of Hemingway and Castro, their beards and cigars practically intertwined – but you come away with little insight into the love the writer developed for Cuba over twenty years.

For this you have only to open the book which did more than anything to win Hemingway his Nobel prize (it received special recognition in the citation accompanying the award): *The Old Man And The Sea*. Written here, eight miles from Cojimar, the fishing village where it's set and from where Hemingway, then fifty-two, spent a great deal of time game-fishing at sea, its story of an epic struggle between an old man and a giant marlin – or perhaps his own faith – reflects more than any other of his books Hemingway's strengths, weaknesses and grace, as a man and a writer:

> He was an old man who fished alone in a skiff in the Gulf Stream and he had gone eighty-four days now without taking a fish. In the first forty days a boy had been with him. But after forty days without a fish the boy's parents had told him that the old man was now definitely and finally *salao*, which is the worst form of unlucky, and the boy had gone at their orders in another boat which caught three good fish the first week. It made the boy sad to see the old man come in each day with his skiff empty and

he always went down to help him carry either
the coiled lines or the gaff and harpoon and the
sail that was furled around the mast. The sail
was patched with flour sacks and, furled, it
looked like the flag of permanent defeat.

To understand Papa – and Cuba – a little better, I
make the journey north to Cojimar. While not
quite as tightly nailed down as the Hemingway
Museum, it still requires a leap of the imagination
to connect this built-up suburb with the simple
fishing village of the book. I have made two new
friends, Gloria and José, while changing buses to
get here, and they make much of the bronze bust
of Hemingway and the old fortification next to the
dock.

'This fort was built by the Spanish to keep out the
English. Why are you here?' José demands, grinning.
In his early twenties, he is a good deal taller than
Gloria and six or seven years younger.

'Did you know the British once control Havana?'
Gloria asks, as we pose for a photo in front of Papa's
statue. 'In 1762, they capture it for a year, then trade
it with Spain for Florida. Imagine, we might have
been British!'

'Or American,' adds José. 'After the Americans
fight the Spanish in 1898, there was a time when
Cuba consider joining the United States.'

I sense a certain wistfulness and ask whether
José and Gloria would like to be American. Both
were born into Castro's revolution and have an
ambivalent attitude towards their country's most
troublesome neighbour.

'Not everything is good about America,' says

Gloria, 'but not everything is good about Cuba. There is no opportunity here. We have thirty years since the revolution, but still we have rationing, still we must make sacrifice. There is a slogan: "*Cuba will always be in a state of revolution.*" Why must that be?'

'There are two things Cuba can be proud of,' José asserts. 'Hospitals and schools. We should keep those and get rid of the rest. The system here is shit. This isn't *socialismo*, this is *fascismo!* No liberty! Discrimination because of my hair and the way I dress.'

He is dressed not so differently from me, in jeans and a T-shirt, but his hair is long.

'You must be careful,' he says. 'G2, the security police, are everywhere. Be careful what you say, who you see.'

This is the first time anyone has mentioned possible surveillance to me, though I've thought about it. I have been careful with the notes I have taken and have changed names so that no-one can be identified, but it is clear that G2 represents more of a threat to José and Gloria than to me. The worst I could face is deportation; they would face imprisonment.

Their home in Guanabacoa is modest in the extreme – a shack the size of a one-car garage, with an outside toilet which is precisely that: a porcelain bowl set into the earth and surrounded by bushes.

Showing enormous generosity, they cook me a meal which consists mostly of a thin broth with slivers of fried plantain. Gloria shows me their ration books. Until recently, everyone was

121

guaranteed one piece of meat every nine days and fish was free. Now, meat is almost impossible to find and fish is rationed. They get one bag of flour a month, one bag of detergent. Food, soap, matches, shoes, underwear – all of these are difficult to obtain. The food shortage is such that there is a policy of moving people voluntarily (or such is the official line) from Havana into the countryside, to help with food production.

'Cuba needs change,' says José, 'but Castro will not permit it. Gloria has an uncle in Florida. One day, she will join him there. For me? My only chance is a boat!' He mimes paddling in a tiny craft.

We take a bus back into Havana, and José shows me round the hospital where he works. Despite his criticism of Castro, he is proud of Cuba's healthcare system. He shows me a refrigerator where drugs are kept.

'Medicines are free to everyone,' he tells me, although recently they have been in perilously short supply. 'If a Cuban needs medicine or treatment, they will get it. People come from all over the world for surgery. Less babies die in Havana than in many cities in the United States.'

On the street, we run into Carlos, my dealer friend. Gloria and José laugh.

'He is *aseré*!' they tell me. 'A hoodlum, a punk. *Aserés* have a particular dialect, *un dialecto africano*. *Aserés* have a particular walk. They strut, with a comb or a knife in their back pocket. There is a Ted Nugent song about *aserés*.' They squint at me, as if seeing me for the first time. 'You – you would make a good *aseré*!'

122

For my last two days in Cuba, I fly to a tiny island fifty miles south of the mainland, called Cayo Largo. This is absolutely a tourist trap; so much so that a kind of apartheid exists, whereby Cubans cannot go there unless they work there.

A sand-strip measuring roughly fifteen miles in length, Cayo Largo has all the expected trappings of a tropical island, including vicious mosquitoes, white sand beaches and three clutches of hotels each dedicated to maximizing Cuba's dollar income. It also has food – fresh lobster cooked on the beach at fifteen dollars a throw – but I find it hard to swallow when the rest of the country has so little.

I fly back to Havana in an aged, high-winged Russian cargo plane, an AN24, a fact which greatly excites my fellow passenger, Tomas, a Czech diplomat treating his family to a weekend break from Havana.

'We are flying in history!' he announces. 'Did you see the Douglas DC3 we came out on? A beautiful plane, a flying museum, but very reliable.' He raps on one of the AN24's few windows, shouting, 'Look!'

Below us are the swamps of Playa Girón, the Bay of Pigs, wild and inhospitable, thick with mangroves.

'Can you imagine trying to land an invasion force there?' he asks in disbelief. Ignoring the fact that it was an operation led principally by Cuban exiles, he continues: 'Only the Americans would choose such terrain!'

For my last afternoon in Cuba, I visit Havana's main cemetery, for an hour of quiet reflection in the sun.

Even here I find that the literacy and culture of Cuba contrast strongly with those of America or Britain: the attendant at the gate is reading a book on the German philosopher Leibniz, instead of a tabloid newspaper.

As I walk among the graves, I am struck by the fact that they seem better tended than anything else in Havana. Clearly, the dead command respect – even if some of the stones have the additional decoration of plastic dolls and other *santería* charms. I think about my son, who has been much on my mind in Cuba: it seems inconceivable that he died, that I will never hold him again. I remember that today is my father's birthday and make a mental note to try and call him, regardless of Cuba's sometimes less than spectacular telephone system. I wish I could see them both, hug them.

I realize that I have felt lonelier here than in Miami – at times quite tearful and nostalgic. Maybe this is partly the result of my inability to speak Spanish but it seems also a reflection of the atmosphere here in Cuba. Despite the ebullience of the people, despite even my grudging respect for Castro, Cuba does not seem an entirely happy land.

A flash of Miami comes to mind, and it is the advertising sections of the *Miami Herald*, with their cut-price material abundance on display. Cars, refrigerators, washing machines, video recorders, personal computers – all the things which seem perhaps excessively available in America, but which are impossible dreams for most Cubans.

Then I consider the almost tangible soul of Cuba, the sense of a society that is not motivated solely by principles of gain and greed. Of the apparent innocence of the schoolchildren in their uniforms. Of the cemetery attendant reading Leibniz.

And suddenly Havana and Miami seem like the light and dark sides of the moon – only I'm not sure which is which.

As the sun sets, I take a final walk through the streets of Old Havana. I drink a final *mojito* or two at La Bodeguita del Medio, but decide against waiting three hours for a table. I try to get my mind off food, but have to admit that I'm looking forward to getting back to Miami and going to a restaurant that can actually serve what's on the menu.

I walk up Calle Empedrado, leaving behind the throng outside La Bodeguita, nursing their drinks happily enough as they wait to eat. The street is dark; voices from the same TV channel echo from different windows. People sit on their steps, trying to stay cool in the heat. The air smells acrid and fruity, a heady mix of flowers, piss and petrol. A group of young boys play baseball in a side street; a little girl runs about dressed only in a swimsuit. It is nearly midnight.

I find Giselle sitting on a bench, outside a hotel. She asks if I have any presents for her, and we sit and talk. Beautiful American cars drive by from a different era. I feel as if I am in the 1940s or a Fellini movie or a Graham Greene novel. Havana *is* a Graham Greene novel, but the ending hasn't been written yet.

125

11

THE ARGENTINIAN FIELD
HOCKEY TEAM

Four years later, by way of comparison, I return to
Cuba on a flying three-day visit, to spend time with
British friends at the Havana Film Festival.

It is December, 1994, and my routing is different:
the only direct flight now between Miami and
Havana is on an Haitian air freighter, which I unsur-
prisingly decline. Instead I do what an increasing
number of Americans are doing (travel restrictions
to Cuba still being in place) and fly via Nassau,
switching there from an American Eagle craft to
a Russian-built Cubana YAK-42, whose air-
conditioning system produces a dense and
somewhat disturbing emanation which rises from
the floor like dry ice mist in a 1980s nightclub.

When I land, the changes in Cuba are immediately apparent. Despite constant propaganda in
Miami that Fidel's regime remains unaltered, the
airport officials now seem remarkably less ideological and bureaucratic. Whereas in 1990 it took
me three hours even to penetrate beyond passport
control, this time I'm out so fast that I miss Danny
Boyle, the thirty-something British director of the
cunningly horrifying *Shallow Grave*, who's here to
meet me – and instead find my own way to the vast
Hotel Nacional in a taxi, its radio's *salsa* and *soca*

rhythms filling night streets otherwise strangely devoid of traffic and light. Attitudes may have changed, but clearly the shortages haven't.

Manchester-born and looking like a wilder, more tropical Morrissey in his lethal haircut, Gap shorts and floral shirt, Danny is here with a contingent of other Brits for the festival. I'm here to discuss with him a movie we might be making, but this being the British film industry, we're both on tight budgets and when we do finally meet up, I'm smuggled into the hotel to share his room free of charge.

'Hide your toothbrush and make your bed,' he advises, in a no doubt futile attempt to fool our maid.

The next morning, at breakfast, I feel as if I'm back in Britain – I see more Cubans every day in Miami than are visible in the hotel's dining room. I find myself chatting with Stephen Frears, the British director of *My Beautiful Laundrette*, *Dangerous Liaisons* and *The Snapper*, who once directed Norman Wisdom in a BBC TV drama. Wisdom told him that when the Rank Organization originally saw his first film, *Trouble In Store*, they thought they had an unmitigated dog on their hands.

'Then,' says Stephen, 'once an audience had seen it, their attitude changed completely.' He scowls gloomily over his *café Cubano*, takes a sip and grimaces. This, I interpret as approval. 'You know, in Russia, he was a big star . . .'

'Norman Wisdom? In *Russia*?'

'Yes. When he went to Moscow, they would line the streets to cheer him!'

Reflecting on this unlikely revelation, we board a

bus for a trip to Havana's International Film and Television School, which in fact is an hour's drive, out past the town of San Antonio de los Baños (the *baths* need a saint?), to the middle of what used to be an orange grove. The journey is not so different from my trip four years before to Hemingway's house at the similarly sainted San Francisco de Paula, except that the festival bus is marginally more robust than the public *gua-gua* I travelled on then.

Not much has changed outside Havana. While a sense of bustle and some renewed investment animates the capital, the surrounding countryside looks as poor as ever. But still the roads are awash with colour and life – and little or no traffic. Everywhere, brightly dressed, seemingly enthusiastic Cubans go about their business on bikes (Cuba having recently imported two million Chinese bicycles in an attempt to deal with its worsening petrol crisis), on foot or by trying to hail our bus. As our driver presses on unheedingly, Danny stares out of the window and remarks: 'We've forgotten how to do that in Britain – how to walk.'

Back at the Nacional, after a spirited discussion about whether the revolution was Soviet-inspired or merely turned to the USSR in response to America's hostility, we are distracted by our fine view of the waves breaking on the Malecón below – and by the sight of seven or eight young women in bikinis, sunning themselves by the hotel pool, who volunteer, somewhat bizarrely, that they are the Argentinian Field Hockey Team. Suspicions run deep that Fidel has shipped them in to bring a touch of much-needed glamour to the festival; certainly our attempts to discover just where the hockey is being played prove fruitless.

More glamour is on display later in the evening, when finally I make it to that rat trap of *turista* dollars and indulgence, the Tropicana. This is a festival-organized excursion, and while the more drunken and thuggish among our party chant cries of '*Viva Batista!*' – and after a delay as rain stops play for thirty minutes or so – we finally bear witness to a show billed as 'Paradise Under The Stars' ('Celebrating 1939–1994'). The exuberance, sensuality and marked physical charms of the dancers are undeniable, but it is the *smell* above all which strikes me: the circus scent of make-up and perfume, mixed with perhaps a fragrant misting of sweat, as the showgirls sweep by, the feathers of their regulation-exotic costumes brushing our faces and inducing clandestine urges of lust.

As I sit back, drinking it in, sipping my rum and briefly reminding myself of the flavour of a fine Havana cigar, I reflect on the possibility that Cuba may be headed, with or without Castro, back towards the 'pleasure-ground for the rich' role it had in the 1950s. Right from my arrival this trip, I have been aware far more so than before of startlingly attractive, well-dressed, well-educated and frequently quite relentless *putas* – whores – outside the hotel, inside the hotel and lurking around every corner. On my first night, while waiting with Danny in the hotel bar for some friends to join us, two women sat at our table and practically grew roots there, despite polite entreaties to move when our guests showed up. While it's difficult to begrudge

129

anyone the opportunity to make some money in this hard-pressed economy, I think back wistfully to the relative innocence of Giselle and her friends, my first time here.

The last day of this dizzyingly brief trip provides two quite distinct glimpses of the old and the new Cuba.

In the afternoon we are whisked (by bus again) to a party at the British Embassy – real Graham Greene territory, with a neatly marshalled tropical garden and a dazzling old interior swimming pool. The ambassador and his wife seem predictably charming, and I come away with a sense of Havana as a lush fairy tale kingdom, from which the evil giant (in this case, America) has been absent for many years, leaving everything cracked, faded and overgrown with vine.

In the evening, the reborn Havana makes itself felt in the shape of a hip new restaurant in the old town, whose opening night is accompanied by a band of musicians playing in the courtyard outside, and whose internal decor is worthy of South Beach – the 'distressed' paint job so fresh that if you touch it it might smudge. Unlike my last trip to Cuba, food now seems freely available – to tourists, if not to the local population – and we harbour a sneaking suspicion that the restaurant has some sort of 'Cuban Mafia' backing.

We're in the company of a group of students from the film school, who have made a big effort – a tortuous bus journey – to get here, and who reflect the school's under-resourced but truly international approach to cinema. As we sit eating with two

130

Japanese women (one of whom, Mari, admits that her decision to spend two years here, rather than at an American or Japanese film school, was prompted in part by a desire to shock her father, a wealthy Tokyo businessman), a Bajian and a Belizian, someone jokes, 'Hey, we're the united colours of Benetton!'

The mix of races, the abandoned beauty of Havana, plus the fact that Cubans and foreign investors alike are starting to open businesses all over the city – from tiny shoe repair shops to clubs, restaurants, a Benetton store and the new Fiat showroom on the Malecón – remind me more of Miami Beach when I first arrived, when it was still very cool and not quite rediscovered, than my first visit to Cuba. Havana, I sense, will be the next trendy place to be (I know Americans and Europeans who are already investigating buying clubs here), and while there are dangers inherent in that – a return to the corruption and inequality of Batista's 1950s not least among them – there is also some hope of a brighter future.

'This is a city on the edge,' Danny says, as we walk back to the hotel. 'One minute, it's like it's on its last legs – the next, there's a real buzz . . .'

And as we fight our way through the crowd of hookers waiting outside the Nacional's entrance, I wonder if, politics and more legitimate commerce aside, sex is the true currency of Cuba. At sunset this evening, as we all stood on the hotel roof gazing out over the pink-hued city, Rosa – here for the festival from Barcelona – had perhaps captured the island's essence with a throwaway remark about the booming sex trade with Spain:

'They come here, the Spanish, because they know Cubans are very good at it. So they marry their mulatta or mulatto and take them home. Because it's a fact: *Cubans are very good at sex!*'

12

DON'T FUCK WITH THE MOUSE

Back in Miami, I feel displaced. The first time I returned from Cuba, in 1990, I was so hungry I seriously considered stopping to eat a hamburger at Miami International Airport. This time, better fed and more relaxed, I pass the time talking to an old Cuban-American man, an employee of American Airlines, who notices that I have a poster from Havana with me and strikes up a conversation. Initially wary because in Miami Cubans rapidly become quite hostile if you admit to having visited the island and spent money there (thus supporting Castro), I discover that this man's personal history is in fact pre-Batista. He left the island in 1952, forced to make a swift exit when Batista deposed the previous leader, Carlos Prío, to whose niece my new friend here at the airport was married.

'How is Havana?' he asks, a sad expression lighting his face. 'Is it still beautiful?'

'It's beautiful,' I tell him. 'It's crumbling, there are many problems, but it's beautiful. I love your country and your countrymen . . .'

Other friends in Miami are less sympathetic to my observations. I find myself arguing about what I have seen on both trips. They tell me my eyes were closed to the real Cuba – the true suffering, the arrests, the political prisoners, the torture, Castro's cruelty. I tell them that many Cubans now blame the Cuban community in Miami, which lobbies aggressively to maintain the United States embargo, for aggravating the problems in Cuba. And they are worried that when the situation changes, Miami Cubans will flood back in with their wealth and take over.

'It's going to happen anyway,' one more cynical, non-Cuban offers. 'It's the American Way.'

'What? For Cuba to get fucked again by America?' I ask.

'Well,' he retorts, 'how many countries has Britain fucked in the past?'

So to get to grips with Florida again – and to face the American Way head on – I take off with some of my younger friends for a weekend at Walt Disney World.

The only way to do this *right*, it seems to me, is to do what local high school seniors of seventeen or eighteen do on Grad Night, when they load up on illegal chemicals – despite the presence of high school faculty supervisors – and celebrate their graduation at one of several officially organized nights in the Magic Kingdom, which closes its gates to other visitors and stays open until five a.m. for such occasions.

Because you have to understand: Walt Disney World is a very ugly proposition, stone cold sober. It is Middle America gone rampant, with all that that entails, topped off by the overweeningly cute spin on life that Disney and his workforce have made their own.

Even now, writing this, with the reality months,

134

perhaps years behind me, my spine shivers and my mind freefalls at the memory of all those singing animals, those freaks in furry costumes, those plastic masks and head-suits – like some terrifying Greek ritual, only here in modern-day Florida.

'*Get me out of here! This is hell on earth!*' I screamed, as I was led to the ambulance. But I am ahead of myself . . .

Our troubles begin at the gate, after the numbing, four-hour journey by road from Miami north to Orlando, an odyssey past endless farmland, fast food restaurants, budget motels and gas stations. As you near Orlando and Disney's fiefdom, the ugliness conjoins and multiplies, so that the International House of Pancakes becomes the HoJo Inn, which seems suddenly to be offering its guests Exxon and Texaco for breakfast, while Denny's and McDonald's and Burger King are pumping oil.

We urge our rented minivan forward towards the vast Magic Kingdom parking-lot and realize, somewhat belatedly, that we have not a dime between us (not that a dime would even begin to take you through the parking-lot gates) – only a galaxy of credit cards, none of which, for one reason or another, the Disney staff are prepared to accept.

'You came to Disney without any money?' The until-this-moment perky woman at the portal gazes at us in wonderment. '*Are you out of your minds?*'

She calls over a co-worker, a young man with acne on his face but a crisp press to his shirt and trousers. 'What's going on?' he asks.

'These guys have no money!'

He looks at us, a cloud of suspicion now

darkening his features. 'Well, you're at the toll point,' he tells us. 'You can't go past the barrier – but you can't go back!'

Cars full of eager American families are lining up behind us. No-one has honked his horn yet, but I can feel the tension building. I glance behind us, scanning the vehicles for a glimpse of a shotgun, an easily deranged face: this could quickly develop into one of those Michael Douglas *Falling Down* situations.

'Well,' I say, 'I guess we're really trapped.'

Our crisply creased gate-guardian eyes us warily. 'Well,' he says, no hint of mockery brightening his face, 'I guess you'll have to go through the barrier.' Now his voice becomes deadly serious and he warns: 'But you know, if you go through this barrier, you'd *better* turn around!'

So we drive through the barrier and it all seems ridiculous, so we think maybe we'll just park the van and take things from there – but suddenly there are uniformed Disney police everywhere, waving us back, escorting us out of the parking-lot, and we realize we have broken the first cardinal rule of Walt's kingdom: '*Don't fuck with The Mouse!*'

A little later, having hunted down various bank machines on the fringes of Orlando and raised some hard currency, we mount a second assault on the parking-lot entrance and this time emerge unscathed. We are directed to park our vehicle in a zone marked 'Donald 63' – the name more like some ominous suburb of *Alphaville* than a reference to a Disney cartoon – and then we listen and obey as faceless electronic announcements herd us onto

136

trailer-trains to transport us, like the doomed of
Schindler's List to the smokestacks and Nazi death
camps, beyond the Magic Kingdom's gates.

'*Mousechwitz!*' my mind keeps prompting,
'*Mousechwitz . . .*' Of course: the movie industry
nickname for the Disney Studios in California,
noted for their generous working hours and
hospitable terms of employment.

Because something's wrong here. Maybe it was
the coffee I had, or the copious jugs of freshly
squeezed Florida orange juice at every rest stop
along the road, but I'm starting to hallucinate.
Jeremy, my good friend Jeremy, twenty, a film
student and a handsome boy under normal circum-
stances – *Jeremy is morphing into Mickey Mouse!*
First the ears, then the button-black nose, then the
wide, annoying grin . . . it's like that scene in
Pinocchio where he smokes a cigar at Pleasure
Island and starts to turn into a donkey. And Yojin,
nineteen-year-old Yojin, a Korean student, *suddenly
Yojin looks like E.T.!*

Beside me, my girlfriend, Charong, usually coolly
beautiful in a classically Chinese-American way,
seems caught in some transformation between Snow
White and Daisy Duck. I touch my face and feel fur
where there was none before. My nose suddenly has
a life of its own, I hear myself slobber and growl, and
when I glance nervously at my reflection in a window, I see an ugly, flesh-distorting struggle taking
place within my body, as skin and bone erupt and
contract to form the gangly lineaments of Goofy one
minute and the surging power of the Beast, the next.

We are waiting in line to buy our tickets. All
around us, kids pester their parents for candy,

drinks, attention. Jeremy is first at the window. His big black mouse-ears bobbing, he laughs in that halting falsetto of Mickey's and asks for admission for one. Yojin is next. Reaching an elongated, frog-like arm up to the booth, I hear her voice and she seems to be pleading, '*Phone home!*' But the even-faced Disney goon behind the glass does not blink. She hands E.T. a ticket and some Disney dollars (the bills graced by guess which rodent's face) in return for some regular US notes.

And I realize: '*We're safe!* We don't have a problem, we absolutely don't have a problem . . .' Because they're used to it here – they're used to people looking like seven-foot cross-species mutations! They're used to great bags of fur with ping-pong-ball eyes and flipper feet dancing around all day like those balletic ostriches in *Fantasia*. They're used to the bizarre and the gaudy – and to Normal American Families, laden down with soft toys and mouse hats and stepping out in battery-operated flashing sneakers. We fit right in, Mickey, E.T., Snow White and I. What they couldn't handle here would be something *real*, something natural . . . say, a young gang member who wanted to spray-paint Space Mountain . . . a woman who wanted to sunbathe topless on the grass . . . or anyone who wanted to walk on the grass at all.

Inside the gates, the volume increases and we know we are in our element. Little children come up to Jeremy and want to shake him by his large white three-fingered hand. Others gaze with joy at E.T.'s frail form and nervously press their ears to Yojin's alien breast, to hear whether her heart beats like theirs.

138

We stand surrounded by comic-book architecture, looking cruelly plastic in the harsh Florida sunlight – a fairy tale castle that doesn't quite promise dragons or princesses; a candy-coloured American Main Street that makes me long for the urban squalor of Miami's Overtown; a vast, quaintly nostalgic New Tomorrowland (whatever happened to the Old Tomorrowland?). And then we stand some more, waiting in the first of many purgatorial lines to ride the Big Thunder Mountain Railroad, the mere mention of mountains being a plus in a state which rarely rises more than three inches above sea level.

And suddenly I understand whence the magic in Magic Kingdom comes: a spell is woven as you enter the gates so that queues which in a post office or supermarket would spark a riot, here are accepted by an obedient multitude as the (added) price of the fun.

The volume grows ever greater as we move from ride to ride, attraction to attraction. We plunge heedlessly down a roller-coaster rail into water, only to be assaulted by Br'er Rabbit singing mercilessly in our ears. In a darkened auditorium, strange contraptions descend around our seats, seemingly locking us in place, and we actually feel an alien's breath tickling the backs of our necks (it is not our friend, Yojin) and are splattered by some kind of extraterrestrial gunge as a poor creature explodes in the central dematerializing chamber. We fly with Peter Pan over London, my Beast-nostrils flaring at scents which are intriguingly chemical and electric – but definitely not those of Pall Mall – then emerge once more into daylight and those vicious happy

Mouse songs coming from each concealed speaker, calling forth the demons of Goodness and Light, the way the vast bat-like creature at the end of *Fantasia* raised the darker spirits to swirl about him in a tempestuous cloud.

We glide upwards towards a rocket ride in an elevator car shared with weird life-forms from Ohio or Nebraska – two mid-western tourists, each with Walt-clone moustaches and a child's shoulder lodged beneath their hands, who lovingly compare the performance and gas consumption of their respective minivans, then face each other across the elevator and chuckle in ape-like tones:

'This here's my Sam . . .' Walt Clone No. 1 pats the five- or six-year-old girl beneath him. 'As in Samantha . . .'

Walt No. 2 gently urges forward the innocent-faced five- or six-year-old boy in his grasp and responds: 'This is my Sam, too. He would have been called Samantha if he'd been a girl!'

'Well,' says the first, the daughter-father, 'my Sam's a boy – a real tomboy!'

Thus ensuring either a healthy degree of gender flexibility or a lifelong search for true sexual identity on both children's parts – and driving Goofy perilously close to a criminal act.

We spend hours in the bathrooms, simply listening to the recurrent flush of the automatic toilets, and it is while I am here, studying my Beast reflection and wondering at the great palace and chandeliers which stretch boundlessly behind me, that I ponder a moment over the begetter of all this, Our Lord and Father, Walt Disney: a man of much inspiration and many contradictions, whose impact on this century's ways of seeing was remarkably large – comparable in some respects to Picasso's – and yet who could not even draw especially well himself.

What seems enlightening, and not particularly surprising, is that the man who created a world – and a worldwide industry – of brightly coloured, excessively curved, usually quite sexless yet nurturing anthropomorphic cartoon creatures, instilled with an unerringly positive outlook on life (Thumper: 'If you can't say somethin' nice, don't say nothin' at all'), was himself driven by demons, no matter that he cultivated a warm and homespun 'Uncle Walt' public image.

Clearly possessed of a powerful will to achieve and control – witness the way he almost single-handedly took credit for his films, or transformed this flat Florida farmland into a hugely lucrative international tourist lure – Disney was rumoured to have suffered a nervous breakdown in 1941 as a result of a strike by his studio workforce for better working conditions and greater recognition. Virulently anti-communist, 'Uncle Walt' was also alleged to have had a twenty-year working relationship as an FBI informer, as evidenced by his six-hundred-page FBI file, eighty per cent of which is still blacked out, 'for reasons of national security'.

And yet he also took animated films to where they'd never been before, transforming them from shorts into features and filling them with flights of the imagination that, especially in the early days, were not afraid to touch on dark and truly dreamlike moments – Pinocchio in the belly of the whale; Snow White fleeing through the forest, as

141

nightmarish tree-fingers reach out from the id to grab her.

And he created Disneyland, which in turn spawned Disney World and their mutant siblings in France and Japan, putting the old-style carnivals, with their tacky sideshows, rickety ferris wheels and run-down ghost trains, onto the production line and creating a McDonald's or Ford of theme parks.

Here in Florida he added an extra touch, siting right next to the Magic Kingdom the strangely self-contained realm of Epcot (the 'Experimental Prototype Community of Tomorrow' – well, let's hope not), with its World's Fair approach to geography and its lakeside pavilions representing a slightly skewed cross-section of the planet: Disney-China, Disney-Italy, Disney-Norway, Disney-Morocco – but, curiously enough, no Disney-Cuba!

Despite the presence of specially imported, genuine-article native labourers from the countries in question (those who come from afar to work for Disney have little chance to see much beyond the Epcot Stalag's gates), the accent, as it is throughout The Mouse's fiefdom, is on not merely a sanitized, but a soundly capitalist, vision of the world. *Everything* is for sale, from food and trinkets to bags, shoes and high-tech novelty items, though while the imported workforce smiles predictably and politely, they are not permitted to exhibit any true local colour: no haggling over prices in this Moroccan souk.

Ultimately, both in Epcot and the Magic Kingdom, the relentless selling of the world, together with the parades and music and fireworks, starts to feel perversely Maoist in its propaganda intent. Just as Chinese schoolchildren used to drill daily in the name of their leader, so we seem to be being brain-washed with a small-town/Main Street/Disney language of childhood and world citizenship – a sugar-coated, carefully calibrated medication closer to Valium than to Ecstasy, designed to pre-empt individual thought and produce reliable, controllable drones.

And it's all too much. The endlessly flushing toilets, the ceaselessly joyful singing animals, the Disney storm troopers with their crisp uniforms and milk-fed Disney faces . . . My mind starts to rebel and I can't take it any more. I race outside, but everywhere I look, tiny furry animals – racoons and rabbits, baby deer, cats, mice, dogs, even pink trumpeting elephants with wings – are screaming at me, raining down upon my head a hailstorm of sharp-edged or smotheringly soft Disney merchandise.

I hear voices – more voices – ritualistically squeaking broken phrases from ancient hymns: 'THE SEC-OND STAR TO THE/WHEN YOU WISH UP-ON A/JUST THE BARE NE-CESS-IT-IES OF/ WHIST-LE WHILE YOU . . .'

And then the scene turns truly ugly, as the cartoon characters get vicious, ripping at me with their teeth, desirous of blood – *my* blood!

'*Heellppp meeee!*' I cry, mindlessly lashing out, but seeing nothing now, only an endless sea of Technicolor munchkins, white goggle-eyes staring, slash-like cartoon mouths snapping open and grinning. 'Get me out of here! *This is HELL ON EARTH . . .*'

And suddenly I am in the quiet of a vehicle, and

143

Cinderella's castle or Snow White's – or whosever it is – is melting into the soft Florida night until only the distant prick of coloured fairy lights remains, then vanishes beneath the stately silhouettes of palm trees. I bathe myself in the cool wash of the air-conditioning and feel calm and reason returning to my body, as I glance around and realize this is not an ambulance but our minivan. I am safe, and I will not have to venture back beyond the beanstalk to Walt's enchanted land until perhaps I am a parent again and have good reason to brave the snarling, singing furballs.

I reflect aimlessly on a statistic I once read but cannot now quite bring into focus – that by the end of this century, a number equal to the world's population will have passed through the gates of the various Disney parks – and wonder what, if anything, this means. Maybe that number has already been surpassed – maybe the statistic was that *four* times the earth's population will have entered a Disney park, or that each of us will have visited four times? Whatever, clearly someone somewhere is doing something right: even the French have not been successful in bringing Disney to its knees (though perhaps EuroDisney would be a popular spot for French nuclear testing).

As neon-lit malls and dark empty stretches of wilderness flash by, we turn on the radio and hear a local news story about an Orlando couple who kidnapped a young woman at a nightclub and held her hostage as their sex slave – forcing her to perform sexual acts blindfolded. After what seems like a lifetime of enforced wholesomeness, I feel almost reassured by this and lose myself in the memory of a visit to a Miami Beach strip club with my friend, Jennifer Rubell, who had thoughts of becoming a stripper herself.

We spent many nights at the club, but none was quite so satisfying as our first. As the only female patron, Jennifer — who is the beneficiary of a very sizable trust fund and for whom therefore the question of stripping was not one of economic survival — excited a good deal of attention among the dancers, many of whom came to sit in her lap.

We talked to Gabi, twenty or twenty-two, Venezuelan and darkly beautiful with long, lustrous black hair, who told us she had been working in the club for only four days.

'I'm *sueño* — sleepy,' she said, rocking a little on Jennifer's knees in her bra and panties, and staring straight into Jennifer's wide green eyes. 'This morning I go to school at seven to learn English.' She rocked a little more. 'In Venezuela, I am actress. Here, exotic dancer.' She smiled, content for the moment to nestle in Jennifer's warmth and let the other dancers work the more lucrative tables. 'I try to move with sensuality — not just sexy.'

But it is Debra I remember now, on the road in Florida's flatlands, the endless night slipping by outside. The incredible Debra, who knew better than any how to work the pole — which is just what it sounds like: a vertical metal support the dancers wrap themselves around and hang from, sometimes with extraordinary agility.

Debra, who's Swedish or German or Dutch, but who clearly has absorbed enough of American culture — and specifically American TV culture — to

145

turn it to her advantage.

'She's good,' says Jennifer. 'So funny – laughing, mocking us, totally in control.'

And as we watch, suddenly Debra removes her black bra and positions it across the slightly balding head of a peculiarly embarrassed man in the front row, so that it resembles large mouse ears.

Then, loudly and accurately, and smiling dazzlingly all the while, Debra belts out each letter of the *Mickey Mouse Club* TV show theme song:

'*Em-I-see, kay-ee-why, em-oh-you-ess-ee!*'

She laughs. The man blushes and fumbles for a dollar. We drive on.

13

LIFESTYLES OF THE RICH AND FAMOUS

You could die in Palm Beach and not know it. This is a place where age and wealth go hand in hand, and even those not advanced in years play at being dull – or perhaps commit weird and dangerous acts behind the manicured façades of their million-dollar mansions but still put on a zombie face to fool the disadvantaged into thinking that money can't buy you love . . . or life . . . or action.

I'm on the road again, on another quest – to get to the heart of Florida – in another minivan, this one shared with a different group of friends: Dara Friedman, twenty-seven and an independent German-American filmmaker; Mark Handforth, Dara's English sculptor husband; Adam Kuczynski, an artist friend visiting from England; and Brian Antoni, a thirty-six-year-old, Miami-based Bahamian novelist and millionaire.

Dara grew up in West Palm Beach, which is mainland Florida and less affluent than its glitzy neighbour, but tonight, Saturday night, Night of Wildness and Abandon, we are approaching the gilded isle of Palm Beach itself via the Southern Boulevard Bridge, ready for – indeed, *willing* – anything to happen.

And it doesn't. Nothing much happens in Palm

Beach on a Saturday night or anytime else, so far as I can tell. Maybe on Sundays the dead rise from their graves and tool into town for brunch, but on a Saturday night, Worth Avenue, the island's commercial artery – an obese Bond Street of flashy jewellery stores and art galleries – runs dry. This is the closest Palm Beach gets to Miami Beach's Ocean Drive or Lincoln Road – both abuzz on the weekend with cafes, bars, restaurants, galleries, the thump of bass-heavy music and the press of massed humanity – but Worth Avenue is like the rest of Palm Beach: silent and sedated.

Perhaps in the good old days, before the William Kennedy Smith rape trial, when the Kennedys still had their 'compound' here, drunken madmen would charge up and down Worth Avenue screaming obscenities in pursuit of pleasure, but I doubt it. ('The Kennedys are fine,' I remember a prospective woman juror saying on TV, 'until it comes to women. Then, their brains stop working and they think with their penises!' For some mysterious reason she didn't make the final twelve.)

Tonight the only citizens on the street, aside from us, are two or three microprocessed Stepford couples, their dress so studiously and expensively casual as to put Gucci to shame, their skin stretched so taut by face-lifts and tummy-tucks that you could bind a book with it.

Spurred by that thought, and to escape the breakneck pace on the sidewalks, we step inside one of the few establishments open on Worth Avenue – a bookstore – and browse. While Brian, a large, powerful man with shoulder-length hair, a Jack Nicholson scowl and much the same manic charm,

148

chats with the manager, shamelessly plugging his latest book, Dara and Mark scoff at the local histories on sale which extol the life of Henry Flagler, the oil and railroad tycoon almost solely responsible for opening up Florida's east coast and, in particular, developing Palm Beach.

'He was a real scumbag!' says Mark, pointing out a photograph of Flagler, an imperious-looking individual with white hair and a white moustache, amid a sea of people alongside one of his East Coast Railroad trains. 'He wanted Palm Beach to be a posh island for his rich northern friends, so to get rid of the Blacks and the Indians, he organized a circus on the mainland, then took the bridge up and burned all their houses while they were at the circus, and kept the bridge raised until the island was established.'

Tall, sideburned, faultlessly English yet strangely hip in a style that somehow only works in a place like Florida, Mark grins and directs my attention to a photograph of the vast Royal Poinciana Hotel which Flagler built in 1894 on the shore of Palm Beach's Lake Worth – a building so large that it was said you could see the curvature of the earth along its palatial waterfront façade. Boasting 1200 windows, 1300 doors and a main dining room that could seat 1600, the hotel made Palm Beach *the* place to be in the winter, and was the site of the season's end Washington's Birthday Ball each twenty-second of February, which regularly drew more than two thousand of America's social élite. At its peak, the hotel's guest list included such hallowed names as Harold S. Vanderbilt, John Jacob Astor, Admiral Dewey and Countess Boni de

149

Castellane; you would think that such a building might have been preserved as a museum or college, but this being Florida, hurricanes took their toll, and after severe structural damage it was decided in 1934 to tear the Poinciana down.

Dara, meanwhile, has found a slim volume – little more than a glorified pamphlet – written by one Theodore Pratt, author of a favourite book from her childhood, *The Barefoot Mailman* (a fictional account of the pioneer mail carriers of Florida who, from the 1880s onwards, literally walked barefoot the sixty-six miles along the beaches and through the surf from Palm Beach to Miami, to deliver the mail).

That Was Palm Beach seems curiously out of touch even for its publication date of 1968. We read a passage with open mouths:

> An Afrimobile is a special vehicle in Palm Beach. It consists of the rear half of a bicycle, to which is attached, in front, with wheels at each side, a white-painted wicker padded chair for two. A Negro pedals the delightful contraption for $2 per hour, and gives it its name. If you are really somebody and want to do the smart thing, you hire your own chair at a $10 daily rate all during your stay . . . There are a few Afrimobiles still in operation in Palm Beach today . . .

'Afrimobiles?' I mutter, staring at a photograph of one and wondering aloud: 'Do they still have slaves here?'

'Practically . . .' Dara laughs dangerously, like a David Lynch heroine under threat. 'They were

150

talking recently about forcing the blacks and immigrants who work here to carry identity cards – they'd only be allowed on the island to work!' She shakes her head. 'This place is so weird. Even in the 1960s, there were signs: *"No Blacks and No Jews!"* '

This prompts a recent memory of Dara's and Mark's, of driving one night, somewhere around West Palm Beach, and seeing a whole group of cops bunched at the side of the road, strip-searching a black man – the victim standing there in the darkness with his pants down around his ankles. Mark further embroiders this scene by imagining the cops later holding the unfortunate man by his feet, upside down and naked over a bridge, until he told them what they wanted to hear. 'And then, of course, they'd drop him . . .'

We climb back in the minivan and take a drive around the island's slumbering mansions. At Whitehall, the dread Flagler's white marble palace – now the Henry Morrison Flagler Museum – we try to sneak a peak at the railway carriage sitting outside, but it's eleven p.m. on a Saturday night, the museum is closed, and a uniformed security guard escorts us off the property.

We wander through the vast, vaulted lobby (like a slightly smaller Sistine Chapel) and elegant garden walkways of the Breakers, Palm Beach's most striking remaining hotel, built – predictably enough by Flagler – on the ocean front in the Italian Renaissance style, on a scale which would dwarf anything but the Poinciana itself. Like the Poinciana, the Breakers had its problems: originally constructed in 1896, it twice burned down, but has survived in its present form since 1926.

Here, particularly after a drink or two, I finally start to feel the somnolent allure of Palm Beach working its magic. I have been resistant, because this just isn't my kind of place. I understand better the negative reactions of one or two friends who visited Miami Beach and felt, as I do here, that sun, surf and comfort alone do not necessarily make for a fulfilling experience. 'It's like Leicester in the rain,' one especially suicidal houseguest once remarked of South Beach, eager to board the first available plane and fly home to England.

But now, as I watch a charming, wizened man of about ninety chatting happily while his girlfriend, a modest young student of the Anna Nicole Smith school, hangs on his arm and every word, I see that my standards have simply been too high. What else can a concentration of wealth and an easy climate produce but expensive homes and bored rich people?

It's definitely time to get back on the road, zip past a couple of Palm Beach's more famous monuments and imagine our whirlwind tour narrated in the strange Antipodean-Atlantic vowels of Robin Leach, for his *Lifestyles of the Rich and Famous* TV show.

'Welcome to Mar-a-Lago!' I hear him articulate in his ebullient style. 'Built for the cereal heiress to the Post Toasties fortune, this Moorish manor is not only the largest mansion on an island of large mansions, but the jewel in the crown of its present owner, that Monarch of Monopoly Money, The Donald himself . . .'

I recall a tale of a party here, thrown by Donald

Trump shortly after he had bought the house, at which the champagne was served in paper cups and the bus transporting a phalanx of models from Miami Beach broke down on the highway. Luck was not with The Donald that night: prompted largely by the matter of the cups, rumours were that he was on the skids once again. He has since turned Mar-a-Lago into a private club.

But it's Dara's voice I hear, not Robin's, as we trace a route along Lake Worth – the intracoastal waterway separating Palm Beach from the mainland – to Estée Lauder's house. We can see little in the darkness, but for Dara it's a window onto her childhood:

'I remember the first time I went in there as a girl, another girl served me a glass of water on a silver platter, and we were just kids and I thought, "Shit, that's so chic!" And I always felt that it was so blatant that the lake was called Lake Worth, because it's worth a lot! Actually it's named for Colonel William Worth, another scumbag . . .'

We stand listening in the dark for a moment to the crickets and trying to make out the five Greek columns at the front of the house, then Dara says, 'I've a feeling that this is a decoy house now – that Estée bought the house behind it, and that's where she lives.'

Brian mischievously suggests paying a call on Estée tonight, but Dara doesn't think so: 'You know, the ultimate irony is that Estée was refused membership of the Everglades Club – because no Jews were allowed. That's the real Palm Beach: the kind of place where everybody talks about being rich rather than being wealthy. It's a distinction somehow . . .'

Back in the van, as we cross the bridge, leaving

the island and perhaps some of its more striking inequities behind us, the conversation veers, as it always does with Dara, towards sex:

'But you know, we had some great parties on Palm Beach! Once, when I was thirteen, I went to a party with all these Vassar women dressed up in tartan skirts. We played Van Halen songs on the piano, and it was just all these women – they couldn't get dates – but it was such fun. That's what made me want to go to Vassar.' (She subsequently did.)

'This girl at the party, Nancy, told a story of how she'd been abducted at the Poughkeepsie train station, near Vassar, and driven out to the woods by some men who tried to rape her – but she ran out of the car and walked all the way back to campus. And she was really gorgeous and chubby, and I remember thinking the walk must have been good for her.

'And that was when I had my first lesbian experience. We were obsessed with the Rolling Stones. This was when I was thirteen. I would have these intense dreams of Mick Jagger. We wanted to be rock'n'roll chicks. We were hanging out in Palm Beach, looking really good in bikinis, meeting Kennedys on the beach, and then zipping through these vacant posh houses – because everybody had left for the summer. This was Elizabeth, Nancy's younger sister, and me. She was the chubby one and I was the babe, so I could really turn her on and she knew that. It was like I was Mick and she was Keith – we would just have adventures.

'It was a summer of cruising through all these Palm Beach houses, and every house was ours, because if you could walk through the house naked, it belonged to you – if you could skinny-dip in the

154

pool, it was yours . . . And we were reading Xaviera Hollander, this really tacky porn, and we learned all about amphetamines from her before we ever did them. She wrote about being a prostitute and having a really good time, and she would fuck anything. *The Happy Hooker* was her big novel, and we were embodying the spirit of Xaviera Hollander as thirteen-year-olds on Palm Beach while everyone was gone for the summer.'

As we turn into the driveway of Dara's parents' almost rurally situated West Palm Beach home, she seems quite wistful. 'Palm Beach is very mixed,' she says finally. 'It's deeply sexual and deeply repressed at the same time. It's like nowhere do I feel so sexually charged in a way, and yet nowhere is less sexual. Yet it all seems set up for sex – everyone has these big houses with private rooms, and what else is there to do but fuck?'

And then we're inside the house, and Gundula, Dara's mother – everyone's mother, a wild German artist with more than a hint of pagan forces beneath the surface – is making us drinks and showing us her work: huge, striking canvases filled with earthy colours, great swathes of ochre, green and gold. Abstracts which, after the buttoned down anality of Worth Avenue, revive the senses and somehow consolidate in my mind an image of the Palm Beach we've left behind as a mythical isle, a place so perfect and so strange that the swimming pools are filled only with vintage champagne, where residents enact troubling sexual tableaux behind closed doors but refuse to venture outside without a shirt – and where even the lawns are sprinkled by giant dogs whose urine turns to the purest water.

155

14

YOUR SPICS, YOUR NIGRAS AND
YOUR POOR WHITE TRASH

The next morning we're up with the dawn and on the road again, this time with Gundula cramming into the minivan beside Dara, Mark, Adam, Brian and me. It's a Sunday, and as we drive down Route 710, past orange grove after orange grove, all ripe with fruit, we know we're on a mission – a mission from God! Dara is partway through a script set in the sugarcane fields and trailer homes of 'white-trash Florida' and wants to remind herself of the real thing. And I . . . I have this sense that what I need most is a break from Miami and a journey to the heart – if not geographical, then metaphorical – of the state. If we rid maps from our minds and just focus on the long, dusty road and the mournful, gospel-style Elvis song on the minivan's stereo (a tape Gundula picked up at a gas station), then we could be anywhere in the depths of Nowheresville, USA.

We turn the tape off and listen instead to a preacher on the radio, barely noticing the difference. Route 710 cuts straight through a landscape that's so flat the power lines and occasional water tower are a welcome relief from the horizontal. Florida pines, palms and oaks line the roadside, battling for space with the exotics – the melaleuca tree, with its peeling, papery bark, and the Australian pine, both of which spread so aggressively they're in danger of crowding out the indigenous species.

'That's a Brazilian pepper,' Gundula points out as more green flashes by, though with my usual acuity I'm not entirely certain which tree she's talking about. 'It gives you a horrible rash if you touch the leaves.' She smiles charmingly. 'That tree knows what it's about!'

We pass through a tiny, no-horse town of precisely three buildings – a 'packing house' next to a dirt-poor general store and a derelict-looking barn – then back to another ocean of oranges, which remind Brian of a time he did some research for a writer friend. Jay McInerney (*Bright Lights, Big City*) had called him up and said, 'Brian, I need to know who picks the oranges in Florida for this book I'm writing.'

'Which book was it?' I ask.

'A novella and part of it takes place in Florida.' Brian snarls, in a basically good-natured way. 'It's about a guy befriending a guy that picks, a black person. And Jay wants to know if there are any black people who pick, basically that was the question.'

We bounce around for a moment in the back of the van as the wheels hit some Florida potholes.

'So I called up all the state agencies and nobody would talk to me, the minute they heard I wanted to know about migrant workers. I called the Florida Department of Citrus – citrus is the state's second biggest industry – and the Department of Agriculture, the Department of Labor. So finally I just called the library and asked for the names of

157

some groves in central Florida. I called a grove, I don't remember which one, Indian River maybe, one of them, and I got a woman on the phone and I said, "I'm calling to find out who picks the oranges . . ." '

He laughs and lets his voice slacken into a rural Florida accent – closer to a southern accent than Miami Floridians, who tend to sound more urban, more northeastern, more New York or New England (which are where many of them are from).

'The woman says, "Who picks the oranges? *Well, you got yourself your spics, your nigras and your poor white trash. And them's what's ruining the country!*"

'So I said, "Well . . . um . . . I agree with you . . . but what I need to know is exactly what type of nigra you have out there picking, because it's a black person in the book and I have to figure out where to make him come from."

'And this is the best bit . . .' Brian grins and makes his southern/central Florida drawl even thicker. 'She says, "*Son, a nigra is a nigra!*" And she's mad at me because, "*You're writing about those ingrate migrants that's ruining the country!*"

'And I'm thinking, "How does she know I'm not a nigra at the other end of the phone – or a spic or a poor white trash?" But I said, "I agree with you – ruining it. So go outside and ask those black people where they're from."

'So finally she goes outside and she comes back five minutes later and she says, "*We got nigras from all over – and them don't talk good English!*" '

We crack up laughing at this, but it's a reminder too that those placid Florida fields out there aren't quite as docile as they seem. This state is effectively part of the South, and still harbours racism. Even if the darkest days of the Ku Klux Klan are largely gone ('Those sheeted jerks,' Florida governor Fuller Warren once called them as, in the early 1950s, he enacted a law forbidding Klan members to wear masks), ingrained attitudes remain and hate crimes still occur: a young Vietnamese student beaten to death at a party in Coral Springs, north of Miami, in 1992; a Chinese restaurateur who died from a beating at a Jacksonville gas station a year later; a black man set on fire on New Year's Day 1993, in Tampa.

We turn north on Route 98, skirting Lake Okeechobee, the huge body of water at the centre of the state from which the wetlands of the Everglades drain. The name is Hitchiti Indian: *oki* is water, *chubi* is big and the lake certainly is big, so much so that you can't see one side from the other. What we can see, when we stop for a rest by the J&S Trailer Park at the edge of the water, is a true central Floridian: a good ol' boy in a baseball cap with a Tasmanian Devil on it (from the Warner Bros. cartoons, not the other side of the world), aged about forty, wearing sunglasses, a beard, a plaid shirt and jeans with a buffalo belt buckle.

Elvis is warbling again on our stereo – a country-sounding tune now. Faced with tightly clustered rows of mobile homes, each with washing or engine parts or children scattered about outside, Brian confides his dream of living in a trailer park:

'It's perfect! There's one for sale right there. You make a lot of friends, you barbecue. You'll never be

159

lonely again! You read a lot of catalogues, you play shuffleboard . . .'

Our surveillance subject, TasDev 1, is getting into his pickup, so we have no option but to follow. As he pulls out and we stay close behind, Dara – who's driving – draws our attention to a bumper sticker on his tailgate.

'He's a hippie!' she cries. 'He's got a peace sticker on his truck. *We've found the only liberal here!'*

We follow where he takes us and arrive at a perfect spot, by a bridge and a canal inlet, where the water practically laps at the edge of the road. Here truly there is peace: only the rustle of the reeds in the gentle wash from a couple of boats taking Sunday morning fishermen out onto the lake. An osprey flies overhead with a huge fish in its bill. A lizard suns itself on a rock. The air smells like . . . air.

Dara is determined to persuade someone to swim in the lake – not that she wants to go herself, she just wants to watch.

'Mark will go!' she decides for him. 'Mark will go swimming.'

'There are snapping turtles in that water,' warns Brian, fishily reared in the Bahamas and able to spot a predator – a shark, a rival novelist – at a thousand metres.

Dara turns and smiles. 'Mark's a wildlife innocent. He can deal with them!'

I wander off to the edge of the canal, where I stand chatting with a local, Bob Mack, eighty-two years old and here to fish. Somehow we touch on the subject of hurricanes and he tells me about the big wind of 1928 which killed two thousand people hereabouts.

'Two thousand?' I ask.

'Well, yeah, the hurricane actually pushed the lake out onto the land.' His voice is soft and has a slight country twang, but it doesn't sound like down-home Florida. 'This land is all pretty flat,' he goes on, 'and a lot of Indians lived back here at that time, too, around Okeechobee town. Two hundred eighty-five lost their lives at Moore Haven, across the lake on the other side. And Herbert Hoover was president at that time, and after that disaster happened, he saw to it that it wouldn't happen again, and that's why he started building the dam around the lake.'

Listening to him, I do some quick mental arithmetic to work out if he could have been around then, he sounds so immured in all this, so authoritative – but when I ask if he grew up here, he says, 'Nope, been here fifteen years. I come from Minnesota originally, I'm a Minnesota man. Might as well spend my time where it's nice, instead of where it's—' He laughs and looks at me. 'You'll understand what I mean, if you know anything about Minnesota weather! Gets *cold* up there. In 1936, we had below zero for thirty days. Thirty days . . .'

Back in the Florida sun, or rather the cool of the minivan's air-conditioning, we drive a few miles on and bypass Okeechobee town, but hit a smaller burgh, whose name, so far as I can tell (it's not on my map), is Cypress Hut. We're about to roll straight through when Brian spots a Sunday market set up in a field under a series of tents and announced by a sign slung from a traffic signal, which reads:

161

'CYPRESS HUT FLEA MARKET (OKEECHOBEE'S OLDEST).'

Nearby, beneath oak trees hung with Spanish moss, is another wooden notice decorated with a hand-painted icon of a pit-bull terrier and the words, 'WARNING: PIT-BULL WITH AIDS!'

'Don't these people go to *church*?' demands an affronted Mark (the son of a singularly congenial and laid-back Anglican minister).

'Obviously not,' replies Brian, who's out of the van so fast at the sight of old junk that you could light a match with his shadow.

We wander around the tents, examining broken toasters and abused toys, and realizing that the gulf between this impoverished, almost unsalvageable material and the Deco furniture and trendy 1970s clothes of Miami thrift stores says much about the gap between their respective owners' lives. Even Brian is hard-pressed to find much of interest here, beyond some truly ugly plaster Negro figurines – including one of a naked woman whose buttocks provide the slot of a money bank!

Then, as I'm making a few brief notes on a spiral-bound legal pad, a large redneck in, appropriately enough, a red T-shirt sidles up to me and says, 'Excuse me, what are you writing about?'

Surprised, I turn to him and say, 'Pardon?'

His eyes roam threateningly over my notebook, then he repeats the question. I glance at Brian, picturing the two of us, beaten and bound, tarred and feathered and both made to squeal, *Deliverance*-fashion, in a field not far from here – victims of some righteous, local gang of foreigner-hating/ Miami-cityboy-hating, inbred, twisted, Nazi/White-Aryan-Race sugarcane farmers out for a bit of

Sunday fun.

'I'm doing a book on Florida,' I respond edgily, mentally calculating just how much damage I can inflict with a spiral-bound notebook if I have to. 'My friend loves flea markets. We were just looking around . . .'

'I'm security around here.' He sounds almost apologetic. 'I have to ask . . .'

(Though what kind of tented flea market needs security? And what type of threat could a stranger with a notebook possibly provide? Did he think I was casing the joint, drawing plans in preparation for a lightning midnight raid?)

So we drive on, past the Brahma Bull restaurant, offering 'The Rib Special For Rodeo Weekend' ('It's Rodeo Weekend!' exclaims Gundula excitedly), past Fat Boy Burgers and a huge fibreglass ice-cream cone advertising 'Six Flavours' ('Whatever happened to "Thirty-two"?' inquires Dara). Past the Brahman Movie Theatre ('They must raise Brahma cattle,' explains Brian), past the lake ('That god-damn lake!') and out of the town, such as it is, past a massive sign announcing, 'The Churches of Okeechobee Welcome You,' and listing about forty of them.

Then we're back out in the flatlands, the farm-land, on Route 70, following a line which cuts directly across Florida, according to my map – and I wonder: 'Was that it? Have we just experienced the pulsing beat at the heart of Florida?'

15

TWIN PEAKS

The road to Arcadia, across the Okeechobee Highlands, is Florida – and America – at its purest. Aside from the herds of Brahma bulls ('The highest breed of all,' Brian informs us with remarkable authority), the prime feature along an otherwise almost featureless roadside is a series of signs which, at intervals of an hypnotic regularity, read:

> 3 Things
> Every Man
> Should Do In His Lifetime
> Trust God Love A Woman Plant A Tree
> We Have The Trees

The sight of all this farmland prompts Mark to remark that the dream of every English public schoolboy is to become a farmer: 'You own a county or two, and between the computer and the Range Rover, you need never get mud on your boots!'

An old boy of Dulwich College himself Mark sadly missed this vocation and instead established himself as a sculptor on Miami Beach – after a brief period as an illegal alien, making ten-foot chicken-wire flamingoes to promote the Florida Lottery.

We drive through Brighton, a nothing town in the middle of nowhere – impossible to relate to my old home town in Sussex, and nowhere near the sea. Then, as the Florida flatlands envelop us once again, the conversation, the mood and the music start to turn seriously *weird*, despite the pleasantly distracting perfume of gardenia sneaking in through the minivan's partially open windows.

At the side of the highway, a buzzard is eating a roadkill, while on the radio sepulchral organ music accompanies a plaintive female voice singing:

> '*Why should He love me,*
> *A sinner undone?*
> *I do not merit*
> *The love He has shown . . .*'

The tone is so morbid and yet the voice so camp (it could almost be the Beverly Sisters) that we begin to feel as if we're trapped in a David Lynch movie. Just to heighten the tension, Brian is reminded, by God knows what, of something he saw on Miami Beach before we left: a decidedly un-p.c. tale that my sister – in a wheelchair from multiple sclerosis and blessed with the darkest sense of humour this side of Dali – would love.

'I was having a coffee on Eleventh Street,' Brian says, 'and I saw a cripple on one of those little electric machines that they drive, leading a blind man. And the blind man was holding onto his machine and he walked into something, and the cripple turned and said, "*What's wrong with you – are you blind?*" And the blind man goes, "*Shut up, you cripple!*" This actually happened, I swear to God, I couldn't make it up.'

Stunned into something between silence and

wild, cackling laughter, we listen as the radio continues to provide the perfect soundtrack for our 'descent' into Arcadia. A sombre-voiced preacher announces: 'I'm going to be singing just as I am, without one plea. That's the way God wants you. Don't try to fix yourself up, you come as you are. Let Him do the cleaning, let Him do the forgiving.'

It could almost be a commercial for the Church of the Holy Bathroom, were it not for the earnestness in the man's voice. An announcer interrupts:

'You are tuned to special Sunday morning programming on WOJC, FM 103.1 in Okeechobee, Florida, KC 103 . . . You've been listening to the Sunday morning worship and praise service from the First Baptist Church of Okeechobee, with Pastor Richard E. Wipple . . .'

'What?' exclaims Mark.

'Did he just say, "*Wipple*"?' demands Dara.

'Can they say that on the air?' inquires Adam innocently.

'These messages are available on cassette tapes,' the announcer goes on.

Then there's a blast of country music and a happy-voiced band enthusiastically chirping, '*Coun-tree gos-pel!*' and a different announcer, sounding even more down-home than the first, saying, 'It's time once again for Country Crossroads. Hello, everybody, I'm Bill Mack [a relative, I wonder, of my fisherman friend, Bob Mack, out by Lake Okeechobee?], and today Columbia Records recording artist Joy White is bringing her music to the Crossroads. Stick around, there's a lot of good music coming up . . .'

And as someone changes the channel and finds

another preacher, counselling about sex ('Dick, you are a man. Judy, you are a woman . . .'), we know we're in the heartland – this is it, there is no other. Adam mercifully slams in a cassette of the theme music to *Twin Peaks*, and as that oddly mournful, twanging guitar begins and the strings kick in, it's left to Gundula to observe, 'Now we fit right into the landscape!'

In Arcadia, just after the one-storey Burger King and Radio Shack (which seem to come from a different universe), a sign proclaims: 'Welcome To Arcadia – The Best Small Town in Florida.'

As it floats by my window, I realize that this is a *country* of signs – that despite European prejudices about America's overall literacy rate, in fact everyone here can read, one way or another, just enough to get by. And if they can't read, they can look at the pictograph – the Smiley face, the Mickey Mouse grin, the pyramid and the eagle on the dollar bill – and intuit a meaning. This is a country dedicated to communicating, maybe not always well, but people here *want* to connect . . . at least for as long as it takes for those pyramids-and-eagles to change hands. (In Britain, I sometimes feel the reverse is true: our famed irony is a way of shutting people out, putting them down without them even realizing you're taking the piss. We can be warm and wonderful, but sometimes it's like cracking a walnut before you get that far.)

With the sign behind us, Route 70 becomes Magnolia Street – Arcadia's main haul – and we are in a town not only as American as apple pie, but as 1950s as a Norman Rockwell painting . . . or maybe a little emptier and darker, an Edward Hopper painting . . . or maybe, a lot darker still, *Blue Velvet*.

We pass one of Arcadia's larger buildings, a classically Hopper hotel, with a big, vertical sign outside announcing, 'MOTOR LODGE', and beneath that an old-style wooden board hanging down, graced by a hand-painted Pepsi-Cola logo and the words, 'DESOTO *Restaurant* – AIR-CONDITIONED RESTAURANT'. We pass The Depot, Arcadia's old railway station, which looks as if it hasn't seen a train in fifty years, then roll on, past furniture stores with dusty windows – past an entire townscape which appears to have been sprinkled with a layer of magical, brownish-grey dust that has somehow frozen everything in time.

'Oh, my God,' Brian cries, joy in his voice, 'look at the bed with the mirrored circular frame there. There's some black people in town! I love that, that mirror. Alexander, you'd like that, the mirrored headboard . . .' Our van glides on and Brian passes sentence: 'The town's dying, though. Look how many empty shops on Main Street. Look at the barbershop, everything's closed. The town's over.'

'It's Sunday,' I point out.

'It's Sunday,' agrees Gundula. 'That's why.'

Having already reached what seem to be Arcadia's city limits, we decide to turn back and explore some more. We pass a little, neo-colonial town hall, of the kind you might find in New England – a reassuring façade of local power (behind which who knows what goes on: intrigue, scandal, subterfuge, death?), a reminder of order in the wilderness.

We turn down residential streets and find tiny, pretty, Colonial-style wood-frame houses, set back from the road by small gardens, some well tended, others completely overgrown.

'I think we should move here,' I suggest, as we spot one particular clapboard structure – little more than four walls precariously balanced against one another.

'It's for rent!' notices Brian.

'That's a great house,' says Mark.

Gundula laughs. 'They'd give it to you to take it away.'

'It's a fixer-upper,' says Dara.

'It's beyond a fixer-upper,' I say.

'It's a cross-your-fingers-and-pray-upper!' says Brian.

'It's sort of lilting to one side,' I observe.

'All good places lilt,' replies Brian, ever the property expert.

We pause a moment outside a nondescript office building, staring in disbelief at the quite Dickensian name painted on the brick wall:

Parking For
BEESTING & BEESTING
Law Offices
Only

Then we roll past a small church – one of probably twenty-five in town – and back on to Magnolia. Even before we stop the minivan and get out to investigate the Motor Lodge Hotel, it seems apparent that Arcadia is well on its way to becoming a ghost town.

While the others go on ahead to take a look around

the hotel, Dara and I wander down Main Street, drawn by the distant allure of gospel music. And indeed, inside a hall, across the sidewalk from a vast Oldsmobile Tornado with a crown air-freshener on the dashboard and a satellite-dish antenna on the boot – a throng is gathered, rejoicing to the accompaniment of a stirring drum beat and an almost James-Brown-funky organ.

> *Got to send a message to Jesus!*
> *Got to send a message to the Lord!*

The two-line chorus repeats and repeats, as the almost entirely black congregation (we can see one white woman) keeps up a joyous rhythm while a black preacher sings and shouts his faith in time with or in counterpoint to the chant.

In the window of the hall is a sign which reads:

Assembly of Praise
C.O.L.J.C.
Overseer: Lorenzo Dixon, Sr.
The Church Where Everybody
Is Somebody

And behind the altar and the preacher – who doesn't look so very senior, more like a stylish thirty-year-old – is still another offering in this land of signs: '*One Lord, One Faith, One Baptism.*'

We stand in the doorway enjoying the music for a while longer, then a young black man, perhaps in his late twenties, approaches and tells us, 'You're welcome to come and join us any time. We're here every Sunday. Every Sunday, eleven o'clock service.

We have an evening service at six o'clock.'

Somehow as he says this, despite the invitation, we move farther back out onto the sidewalk and he follows us, his suit neatly pressed, his eyes bright and sharply focused, taking the measure of us, it seems. I glance at the sign in the window and ask, 'What do the initials stand for, C.O.I.,J.C.?'

He has to raise his voice a little over the music from inside, which is building in intensity to the accompaniment of several, *'Hallelujahs!'*, but politely he explains: 'The Church of the Lord Jesus Christ.'

'The music's really beautiful,' I say. 'Is this part of a bigger church?'

'Well, he has four churches. He's got one in Mississippi, one in Lake City, one in Atlantic Water, and this one. He's the overseer.'

I glance back inside the hall at the preacher, who seems to be bringing the service to some kind of a near-apocalyptic conclusion. 'And that's Lorenzo Dixon?'

'Lorenzo Dixon, Senior,' the young man confirms. 'We're trying to get a church now in Punta Gorda, Florida.' I look at him blankly and he says, 'You've heard of Port Charlotte, Fort Myers? It's close.'

At the front of the hall now, people are lining up in their Sunday best to be blessed by the Reverend Dixon. The stirring music has not stopped for a moment – hell, I'm seriously considering asking to be saved, too.

'So you'all's welcome to come in any time we have a service,' the young man tells us, glancing back inside the hall himself now. 'Al's my name. Pleased to meet you.' He reaches out a hand to shake ours, then turns and disappears into the enveloping wash of gospel music.

We listen for a moment more, then move a few paces down the street, where Dara laughs and says, 'That was an incredibly courteous way of getting us to leave.'

'I thought he was genuine,' I say. 'I think we were welcome in there.'

But Dara shakes her head. 'I don't think so.'

And we watch as the Reverend Lorenzo Dixon Sr. comes out of the hall, flanked by people on every side – like a rock star or a boxer with his minders and his entourage. While Al holds open the door, the Reverend gets inside the sleek Oldsmobile with the satellite antenna on the boot and the crown air-freshener on the dash, and – like a boxer or a rock star – is whisked away to his next engagement, perhaps with the Lord Jesus Christ himself.

Back at the Motor Lodge, we find the others deep in darkness. It's hard to figure out whether the hotel still functions or not, but certainly there's no-one around and the front desk not only looks old but smells of decay. Displayed around it are still more signs – 'WITNESS FOR CHRIST – Have A Good Day!', 'KEEP SMILING,' 'NO PETS ALLOWED,' 'Rent Must Be Paid On Time' – as well as the room rates, 'Single: $18; Double: $25', which may or may not be current.

Across from the lobby is the ancient Palace Barber Shop, furnished with magnificent old barber chairs, cracked white marble sinks, an antique Coke machine and a seemingly prehistoric Lance snack dispenser stocked with peanut brittle and adorned with the slogan, 'Don't go 'round hungry!' All it

172

would take is a dwarf talking backwards and brandishing a cut-throat razor to make the ghost-hotel effect complete.

I finally make human contact in the men's room, which is shared with the Desoto Restaurant next door. A short, stocky man in his fifties washes his hands beside me, and when I ask if there are many people in Arcadia, he surprises me by saying, 'Oh, I reckon around six thousand.'

'What do they do?' I wonder. 'Is there much work locally?'

'Used to be a bottling plant of the Coca-Cola company,' he tells me, smiling thinly as he dabs his hands dry, 'but it closed many years ago.'

And then he's gone, like the barman in *The Shining* – vanished into the past.

When we walk into the dining room of the Desoto, I know at last I've found what I'm looking for: Florida's true heart, unadulterated by tourism, by The Mouse, by northeasterners or even by the second half of the twentieth century. Here, solid white American families sit leadenly eating their Sunday lunch (tiny, Freudian baby chickens; entire carcasses of beef with the horns still attached) and talking *sotto voce* of murder, crop failure and religion. Until we enter, that is. Then, all heads turn slowly in our direction and we feel the full collective stare of Arcadia directed towards us – an almost tangible wall of energy and light closing around us as the Pod People, the Children of the Corn, the Undead, rise dully from their seats and advance, stumbling and shuffling forward, forks and knives menacingly outstretched . . .

And it's too much for Dara. We're all immensely

173

hungry, but she says, 'Let's leave, let's go now.' She glances at the townsfolk and their wives, good solid burghers all, shotguns doubtless somewhere close to hand, holey sheets perhaps not too far off. 'Let's get out of here,' Dara stresses, more urgently now. 'This is too Ku Klux Klan for me!'

16

TRASH FISH!

Beyond Arcadia, things gradually return to normality: Florida normality.

The next town we hit, after a KKK-free lunch at a roadside diner and a detour or two, is a little spot identified on the map as Gibsonton, but better known as Carnie Town. This is not, it has to be said, a place of great architectural import. Its interest lies in the fact that it is the winter resting home of carnival folk and circus people from all over the country – the only place in America with a residential/show business zoning, so that if you want to keep elephants in your back yard, you can; if you happen to be a fish-tailed bearded lady, happier living outside in a large seawater aquarium than inside watching TV or surfing the Net, then so be it.

At the right time of year, we've heard, all manner of strange stuff can be seen in Carnie Town. But of course this is not the right time of year. It's spring, and the shows are already on the road, so instead of conversing with Strong Men and Human Skeletons and Two-Headed Hermaphrodites, we have to content ourselves with a drink at Showtown USA, Gibsonton's colourfully decorated 'lounge and package store', and a chat with a few Carnie retirees.

Just south of Tampa and a few miles from Florida's Gulf coast, Gibsonton is also only forty miles north of Sarasota, the town circus promoter John Ringling put on the map in 1926 by building, at a cost of one and a half million dollars, a thirty-room replica of Venice's Renaissance Doge's Palace as a gift for his first wife, Mable Burton. We have bypassed this, and the John and Mable Ringling Museum of Art (home reputedly to one of the world's finest Rubens collections), in favour of the living, breathing folk of Carnie Town, and as we emerge, tired, beaten and bruised, from the minivan and stand facing Showtown's simple, one-storey structure, painted *trompe-l'oeil* fashion to appear as if a large yellow car has just smashed straight through the front of it, we're certain we've made the right choice.

'*You got a nice set of gams there, honey!*' one charming, but raucous-voiced old woman remarks of Dara's legs the moment we enter the darkened lounge. And, sure enough, as we find stools at the bar and order Cokes, mostly, from Rocky, our warm and courteous barman, we know we're among friends.

'Who did the paintings?' is the first thing I want to know, as I turn to stare at another *trompe-l'oeil* mural – this one of a woman sitting at a table which seems, especially in the bar's atmospherically low lighting, just another part of the furniture.

Rocky plonks a drink down in front of me, smiles and declares, in a reassuringly homey accent, 'Bill Browning done all the paintings. He did the outside as well – that's about the fourth different painting that we had out there. Bill does fantastic work. He's done a lot for Disney World up there, and he just had an art showing down in Sarasota about six months ago that went over real well.

'But this one over there, one of the band members wanted to build a shelf first, so that when he set his tea up there, it would look like it was sitting on the table.' Rocky glances over at it himself and laughs a generous laugh. 'And there has been a few people in here,' he ambles on, 'that has asked that lady to dance! So you *know* they had a buzz!'

'What about the outside?' I say. 'How did that come about?'

'Well,' Rocky replies, 'this guy – a regular guy, he's in the carnival industry also – well, I guess he'd had too much to drink and my dad had shut him off from drinking. This goes back to 1974 . . . So he's inside the establishment, so what he done, he went down the street and he borrowed a friend's truck and he come down and he went right through the front of the building! That's just what happened. So when we had the front done, we went ahead and put that on there.'

Rocky's own story, I discover, as Dara settles her gams on a stool next to mine and Brian goes off to explore the bar's darker quarters, is pure Carnie Town.

'I ran away from home and joined a carnival,' he confides (how many people can actually say that?), 'and that's how I ended up down here. When I first come here, I was working the joints and stuff like that. I come down from West Virginia, I had what they call a "six-cat" – you throw baseballs and try to knock little cats over. So then after that there, I worked popcorn and cotton candy for a guy named Liam Tally, travelling all over. Then, when I decided I wasn't going out on the road no more, I just stayed here and I got a job in construction – I was probably about sixteen when I started doing construction work!'

The seasonal difference in Gibson, as Rocky calls it, is marked: as many as sixteen thousand people in town in the winter, falling in summer to below five thousand. 'You could roll a bowling ball through the centre of town,' he says, 'and not hit a soul. But in winter, it's really a madhouse down here! It's kind of like Spring Break over on the East Coast, Daytona [annually invaded by thousands of drunken college kids on the rampage for sun, sex and sport] – only with an older crowd.'

Not surprisingly, carnival life can also be tough. 'They pick up a lot of help up north,' says Rocky, 'promise them the sunshine in Florida, but what they don't tell 'em is they're only paying them ten dollars a day and that makes it hard to survive down here. You've got to have more than one trade to survive.' With a smile and a flourish, he pours the shot of mescal I've ordered to counter the sweetness of the Coke.

Buoyed by the tequila, but on a necessary trip to the bathroom, I pass by Showtown's notice board and find small ads differing somewhat from those in your average newsagent or laundromat window. Beside a colour photograph of a man with a moustache sitting in a vast, oversized chair, clutching a huge beer bottle and ice-cream cone, is the handwritten legend:

For Sale
GAINT CHAIR
With 10x10x10 Tent
& photography equipment
with props
$3,800 FIRM

'Three thousand eight hundred dollars,' I think, 'for a giant chair? Surely the price is too high!' But what do I know?

Below a business card belonging to 'BOZO THE CLOWN, INC', and 'For Sale' notices offering a 'Balloon Machine' ($200.00), a 'Side Show Banner' ($50.00), 'Ferris Wheel Seats' ($50.00 each) and a 1987 Chevy one-ton truck for a more reasonable price of $2,500.00, is another idiosyncratically spelled notice:

Help Wanted
To: Travil with med x lg.
show N.J. Area
Starting pay $200 weekly
Some living quarters avilb.
Start in Maimi, Fl.

And next to that, a personal favourite: 'WANTED TO BUY: I-GOT-IT MACHINES, ANY CONDITION.'

But the true flavour of the Showtown Lounge and Package Store (whatever that means) is captured by its more deliberate announcements — 'IF ASSHOLES COULD FLY, THIS PLACE WOULD BE AN AIRPORT'; 'I KNOW JACK SHIT' — and by its men's room graffiti, which reflect an inescapable but somehow here less overbearing grain of racism:

For a good fuck or suck,
give a Mexican a quarter!

Back at the bar, as Dara, Gundula and the others prepare to leave, I grab a few words with a real circus veteran — already retired, though still in his forties and in excellent shape – Pepe Arturo. The son of high-wire artist, The Great Arturo, with a family history stretching back on both sides through four generations of Austrian trapezists and high-wire performers, Pepe sketches a wild, but mostly positive picture of growing up under the Big Top.

'I was three years old when I first performed,' he says, in his smooth, unplaceable accent, 'and I was the latest to start! I had one brother that was twenty-two months, and my other brother was two-and-a-half years old when he began. All we knew was to perform, that's all – we were deprived of our childhood!' But Pepe laughs as he says this and adds, happily enough: 'I guess I'm in my second childhood now. I collect old cars and stuff like that. This is a great place to retire to – it's very laid-back.'

His father, he says, was the first performer to do comedy on the high wire. 'In 1938, my dad went to John Ringling North and said, "I'll do a high-wire act with my wife – I'm going to do a top hat and tails as a drunkard on a high wire." We went all over the place – all over the islands, we played all fifty states! But the last time I performed was 1986. My brother and I were still doing the high-wire act together and unfortunately we had a car accident in 1979. He quit and I went with the ice shows for a few years, then went back to performing for a while, and then I stopped.'

'Do you miss it?'

'Sure, I miss it.' Pepe smiles. 'My dad's eighty-two and he still misses it – he still thinks he's performing!'

'Were any of you ever injured in the ring?'

'Yes, we lost one.' I hear this, but don't fully appreciate its meaning at first. 'And my oldest brother, he fell, but fortunately he's still ticking. But my sister, we lost – we lost her in Fifty-one. We were born the year after: my mom lost one and she had two, I'm a twin.'

'You didn't use nets?'

'No. It just doesn't have the drawing power, you know. People come to a circus, some of them come to see blood!'

From across the dim bar, Brian calls that they're ready to go, but I urge Pepe to tell me a little more.

'We played towns where they shot us with pins and stuff like that,' he says. 'I got hit right here in the eye, holding a pyramid. That was New Haven, Connecticut – you remember when they had the riots years ago, at the college there? That was the same year. They were shooting everything – we could see in the spotlights these rings and paper clips and pins. And I caught one right here on my eye. My dad said, "That's it." We stopped, they put the lights on, the MC said, "If this doesn't cease, we will not continue with the performance." A guy would come out with the balloons, the balloons would go *pop-pop-pop-pop*, and then he'd go back in! It looked like a clown act, you know. How could we do the show?'

'And that was the only place that ever happened?'

'No, St Paul, Minnesota, was bad, too. There was an incident there. Some of the performers got hit, but they weren't critical. But we had these first aid kids, these volunteers, that would go round and help people, it was such a big place, and another kid got one in the eye and he lost his eye. They brought him right out and stopped the show. I caught the guy that did it – I was standing right there and

181

saw him. I messed him up pretty good, too: I knocked him down a flight of stairs. The cops just said they saw him slip! But the other kid lost the sight in his eye. It was terrible. I don't know, it was just one of those years. The same year as Connecticut, 1971, I think.'

As I stand to leave, feeling a refreshingly cool blast of air from the a.c. and smelling the bar's mingled scents of alcohol, tobacco and perfume, Pepe tells me, 'You missed out on some of the animals. We had a couple of female Africans [elephants] on the next block, but she sold them to another fellow. Lady down the road, she sold her elephants, too. Then we have a friend of mine, he's coming in, he's got bears – I don't know how long you're going to be here?'

'I've got to go,' I say reluctantly. 'I'd love to meet the bears.'

Next stop is Ybor City, the historic downtown area south of Tampa that's like a sort of fledgling South Beach – in this case, full of bricked-up Cuban cigar factories and abandoned casinos awaiting renovation. It looks great ('More like SoHo than the Beach,' observes Brian), and clearly Seventh Avenue, the city's old Broadway, has had some money pumped into it – notably in the form of rows of date palms landscaped down the middle of the street – to beautify it, but we can't figure out whether it's happening or just starting to happen or maybe already over.

We stop and walk around, exploring some of the young, hip indie/gothic boutiques, then stepping off the avenue into a more interesting, run-down area of wood-frame shacks and railway tracks, where three police cars have surrounded two young black guys.

'They're busting some homeboys,' Brian remarks, as we turn and talk to Martha and Chuck, whom we saw moments before working in a store selling records and clothes, but who we bump into again as they are walking to their apartment on the wrong side of the tracks.

'To live on Seventh Avenue, the rent is six hundred dollars a month for a one-room apartment,' complains Chuck, twenty-two, a silver ring through his nose and a neat checked cap crowning his short hair. 'Here, it's thirty dollars a week.'

Martha, who's eighteen and says she's been hanging out in Ybor City for eight years, tells us that three years back, Seventh Avenue was dangerous. 'It started out, it was all crackheads and punk rockers. Now it's a lot safer, more police around.'

Pretty, with red hair and an abbreviated purple sweater exposing a bare midriff above a short plaid skirt, she stands in front of a brick wall painted with gang graffiti ('They're mostly suburban kids who wear the same colour') and 'SID LIVES' in large letters, watching as the police bundle the two black kids into a patrol car.

'It's kind of going downhill already,' she says. 'Weekend nights are just insane – people cruise up and down Seventh Avenue. Weekend nights, there's something going on everywhere.'

'It's just a symptom of what's happening all over,' says Chuck, as he glances back between the buildings at the wrought-iron balconies and ornate Spanish tiling of a former casino on Seventh. 'All the cool cities and cool parts of town are getting the soul kicked out of them. This place will end up like South Beach – it's disgusting now!'

Then it's dusk and we're driving across Old Tampa Bay on the Courtney Campbell Bridge, and Tampa looks beautiful in the fluid-hued, Florida-orange sunset, greatly assisted by the awakening city lights of the St Petersburg peninsula ahead and the vast expanses of space and water below us.

It's too late for St Pete's Salvador Dali Museum (which houses the most extensive Dali collection outside Spain), so we press on, past art of a different kind – a huge *Jetsons* neon sign atop a Tex-Mex joint – and up the coast to Tarpon Springs, an almost exclusively Greek community, once the 'sponge capital of America'.

Home to a fine Greek Orthodox church and what seems like a thousand tavernas, we opt for a dinner of moussaka and salad deterred only from sampling the abundant seafood on offer by a drunken red-faced woman, who having been forcibly ejected from our chosen restaurant just as we arrive, clutches at a lamppost on the street for support and screams with a penetrating ferocity, '*Dino serves the worst trash fish in town!*' Then, endlessly, louder still and with an almost mantra-like rhythm: 'TRASH FISH! TRASH FISH! TRASH FISH!'

17

HAPPY TRAILS

The next morning, after a night in a spectacularly
seedy motel somewhere on Route 19, we have
breakfast at a place called The Koffee Kup, in the
strip mall across the highway from the motel, and I
muse on how much you can tell about a community
from the nature of its stores – here, a bridal store,
a coin store, a liquor store, a power-tool store, a
trophy store and a hair salon. (Presumably we're
close to a neatly coiffed, frequently married,
frequently drunk tribe of coin collectors, driller-
killers and athletes.)

We cross the road back to the no doubt ironically
named Star Motel, and while we wait for Dara and
Mark to shower, Brian sits across from me in a chair
on the motel lawn and against a background din of
traffic speeding by along the highway, reads out this
apocalyptic rant, laid out across a whole page of a
local free newspaper and titled, in large handwritten characters,
'JOHN IMBODEN'S DECLARATION OF WAR
AGAINST STRAIGHT WHITE AMERICA':

> I wonder about a country more worried about
> celebrity transgression as if their lives fucking
> depend on million dollar tabloid tattletale bull-
> shit. This is a rant you mindless fuckers, if you

want white bread, go find a hateful christian person and suck their cock, accept their milky white body of Christ into your mealy, perfect teeth mouth, swallow and you can be like me. I have got it. I am them. Them and us, us means you. We are those people, a whole society so marginalized, so denigrated and exploited by the media, the P.C. cult of the red ribbon, high-minded propaganda bullshitters. The red ribbon somehow exonerates the shame monster that builds up and has built up until it nearly eats you alive. Every time you hear the word AIDS you shudder, thinking those people, those poor pitiful people, this red ribbon should help, and besides it's the thing to do, just ask Arsenio Hall. Yes, I've got it and I am dying. And I pray with my so-called bohemian sisters and brothers who drink coffee, look for the truth, vomit and somehow maintain humour. I pray that I will live long enough to see Americans pull their heads out of the dark recesses, whether that is the 18th hole of denial, or a religion that preaches hate, and redemption with strings attached, or their tight little assholes, and either get a clue or suffer and die, join our side, be them. Draw straws, bargain, we are living in hell and there are plenty of seats on the meat wagon. Yes, I am them, but if I must be the devil, the sinner, the dirty queer, the one who deserves to die, I accept, because I will laugh out loud when you and yours get sick and die the undignified deaths you've been foisting on us. We are us, you are them. Happy trails you fuckers.

'Jesus,' I say, stunned by the anger and passion I recognize from my own flailing emotions during my son's, Joe's, struggle with cancer. I look at Brian, sitting there by the highway in front of this nowhere motel. 'Maybe there is life in Tampa, after all?'

Brian, who has read the whole thing with a high degree of passion himself, stares at it again and says, 'It's incredible! *"Those people, those poor people . . . Them and us, us means you."*' He slams the newspaper down in his lap, turns to me and grins with a terrifying, twisted intensity. '*Happy trails, you fuckers!*'

I take the paper from him and read the poem again, the morning sun scorching my neck, a strange buzz of birdsong and rocket-powered traffic assaulting my brain. 'John Imboden', I say, 'can write!'

'And he's right about that red ribbon bullshit,' declares Brian. 'They've tried to make Aids just another fucking charity bonanza.' His eyes burn with the ferocity of John Imboden's words; among his friends on South Beach, Brian has seen plenty of the reality of Aids. He grabs the paper back and reads: ' *"We are living in hell and there are plenty of seats on the meat wagon . . ."*'

I could not speak to John Imboden that day, wherever we were outside Tarpon Springs, but I tracked him down later by phone, and with all the invisibility and anonymity and static and false silence afforded by AT&T's long-distance lines between Miami and Tampa, we talked about his poetry and his life, about Aids and the prospect of death.

I felt guilty, it was his body and soul we were discussing, but I had been there, as much as anyone

187

can who does not have Aids himself. I had lived through two years, with Joe Buffalo and his mother, of spending months in hospital and out: two years of living with the possibility of death every day and every night; of lying next to Joe in bed and smelling the fevered salt sweat in his hair and begging some greater force – whatever was out there – that we might not lose the child we loved above anyone or anything in the world; two years of making the most painful and horrifying choices for his body, not our own.

So when John Imboden apologizes down the phone that he has to pee because he has trouble controlling his bladder – and then stays on the line talking, while I hear the flow of his urine into the toilet bowl – it feels more normal than all the neon Deco, million-dollar homes and giant *Jetsons* signs in Florida could ever do. And when I edge into the question of death and ask how he deals with that, I hear the absolute truth and clarity and hard-earned resignation in his voice, and sense that this is one of those conversations that goes beyond any immediate or casual purpose.

'Lately I've been thinking about dying,' he says, 'and it's been kind of scary, because I don't want to suffer. I've had the same nurse for about four years and we've talked about it and she said, "I'm not going to let you suffer." I have a plan,' he goes on, even-voiced. 'I thought, if it came to it, I'd O.D.'

He pauses and there are some muffled noises while he moves about, then he says, 'I don't have a problem with death. I've had enough friends die from this disease, and you want to let them go, because you're so fucking sick. It's freedom ... I have spiritual beliefs, but I'm not a Christian. My main problem is I've been having a lot of pain lately. I have a port – a tube into my chest – and they've been giving me Demerol, but I got addicted to it. The problem with all these drugs is they're addictive. They were supposed to give me this experimental drug this morning, but I was in so much pain when I woke up that I called and cancelled.'

'How old are you?' I ask.

'Thirty.'

'How long have you had Aids?'

'Four years.'

We talk a little about my son and John promises to send me some more poems.

'I talk to kids at school,' he says, 'and they ask, "Well, how does it feel knowing you're going to die?" And I say, "Well, how does it feel knowing *you're* going to die?" I'll just deal with it – I'm not going to just lie down and take it!'

A MERMAID WITH LEGS

In Weeki Wachee Spring, a few miles up Route 19 from our motel, all the truth, emotion and power of John Imboden's poem evaporate in the shower-stall-humid air. Weeki Wachee is another of those premeditated Florida tourist traps – the City of Mermaids. The site of a two hundred acre, carefully manicured 'nature park' and what is billed as 'the world's only underwater spring theatre', it plays host to a daily underwater musical extravaganza featuring young women dressed in sparkly bikini tops and even sparklier fishtails, who perform for long periods of time in a vast aquarium by period-ically ducking behind strategically placed weeds and other props to inhale oxygen from concealed hoses.

Elvis has been here, James Darren and Don Knotts too – as evidenced by framed black-and-white photographs of these luminary beings, mostly from the early 1960s, posing with mermaids who by now must be more than a little long in the fin. While a regular turnover of mermaids ensures that those in the current show are young and fresh, much of the audience at Weeki Wachee isn't. It attracts young children, but there are more grandparents – suf-ficient, at any rate, to make our presence in the Weeki Wachee cafe worthy of comment.

'Do you guys work here?' asks one of the waitresses, as we scan the menu, hungrily selecting 'dolphin-safe tuna' and salad. 'You don't see too many younger people here!' A friendly faced woman in her forties, she seems keen to strike up a conversation.

'Any gossip on the mermaids?' asks Mark.

'Are there any cat fights?' asks Brian.

'Oh, plenty!' laughs the waitress. 'We've got a former mermaid working in the kitchen now – you should talk to her . . .'

But when we try, the woman in question, perhaps mindful of her job, is reluctant to say anything beyond, 'It was a long time ago.'

I can't resist sneaking a peak at her feet – to check for fishscales – but there's nothing doing, and with a wan smile she disappears back among the hotplates and deep-friers.

Before we submit ourselves to the mermaid show itself, our motley crew wanders about the Weeki Wachee park, listening to the chatter of macaws and parrots and watching an attractive young woman in a sort of *Pocahontas* costume perform a none too astonishing act with a falcon on horseback.

Then, against the distant shriek of monkeys and the closer cries of small children, as we line up to enter the auditorium of the 'underwater spring theatre', Gundula puts what promises to be a gloriously tacky entertainment into a more mythic context.

'Men are afraid of mermaids,' she declares, 'because they symbolize the deep unconscious, the wonderful unconscious . . . Men crave the unconscious and at the same time are afraid to be

191

pulled into it because they're not in control any more. That is the point! That's why they made mermaids into fairy tales. But we women are really mermaids – because our main domain is the unconscious! We know how to work it, we do! And how to make men do what we want them to do . . .'

Her voice seduces with its gentle Germanic rhythms, lulling us into such a charmed state that we barely notice the unlikely presence, amid an audience of pre-schoolers and retirees, of a group of hard-core bikers, seated together to one side of the huge aquarium, adjusting their bandanas, until Brian points them out: 'Look at that! Five hundred old people and a gaggle of Hell's Angels!'

As the show begins inside the illuminated fishtank 'stage', three mermaids with sequined blue bikini tops and long flowing wigs move languorously through the water, lipsyncing to recorded music and offering only the faintest pantomime-hint of sexuality. Suddenly a 'curtain' of bubbles erupts from the floor, the scene changes and we have the Little Mermaid (not noticeably smaller than the others, but blonde and distinguished by a gold sequined top and tail), riding on a large, colourful seahorse, while other fish-suited creatures appear and perform to a suspiciously Disneyesque Caribbean calypso-style tune.

But the overall mood of the show is tackier than Disney, more Disney-meets-John Waters, though with any campy sex seriously muted. A rather effete prince puts in an appearance at some point, to be rescued by the Little Mermaid, but the show doesn't really liven up until a wicked Sea Witch suddenly sticks her head out of a porthole above the stage/ tank, causing all the small children in the audience to scream in unison and creating an abrupt, synchronized surge in five hundred pacemakers.

'Where's Bette Midler when you need her?' I wonder, thinking this is something she might have done, only with a lot more wit, twenty years ago. But she's nowhere to be found, so I content myself by watching a couple of statuesque mermaids bob about to the music, and remembering one of my earliest sexual awakenings – at the age of five or six – when I spotted a fleshy ladder high on the thigh of a Disney ice-show skater's tights (it was *Snow White*, though she was not) and had fantasies about her for months afterward.

As we emerge from the theatre, Dara voices all our feelings when she says, 'That was crying out for a little sexual tension, that show.'

'It's so sad that she had to surface around South Beach and get a gay prince,' opines Brian.

'There should have been some oil deposits being dropped from a ship above,' suggests Mark. 'That would have made it really sound.'

'Yeah,' Brian agrees. 'It should have been more ecologically correct. It should be the mermaid saving the sea. She should meet this really sexy ecologist, not a prince – princes are over!'

But I am lost in a world of my own, thinking: 'A mermaid, that's what my Florida book cries out for – I must interview a mermaid!'

A few telephone calls to the management, and about a half-hour's wait later, I find myself being transported with a thrilling frisson through an employee entrance marked, 'MERMAIDS ONLY — DO NOT ENTER.' Before I can even catch my breath, in walks Deena, one of the mysterious fishy creatures I have just been watching in the show.

The only problem is that as Deena sits opposite me, her long dark hair still drying, her fishtail sadly vanished, her attractive but too worldly legs emerging from beneath a modest dress, I can think of almost nothing to ask her – and she can think of nothing to say.

I manage to ascertain her age – twenty-one – and the fact that she used to work at Winn-Dixie, a convenience store across the road, before donning a fishy tail for the first time three and a half years ago, but beyond that, our conversation does not exactly start any fires.

She is polite and businesslike when fielding my questions about rivalries and cat fights, suggesting that all is permanently hunky-dory in Mermaidland, and I start to feel uneasy about trying to pry from her information which might land her back before the evil Sea Witch.

She is most fun when talking about the problems of swimming in the fishtails (which are zippered down the side) – 'You tend to want to what we call butt-kick and bend your knees a lot, but mermaids are meant to be real graceful and smooth, and you're not supposed to bend your knees *because mermaids don't have knees!*' – and about the occasional drawback of this particular line of work: 'Sometimes if you have to fill out paperwork and they want your job description, whether it's for a loan or something, and you put, "Mermaid", they're like, *"Mermaid?"* So you have to specify: "Weeki Wachee Mermaid" or "Professional Underwater Performer . . ." '

But overall I regret meeting a mermaid in the flesh and destroying what few illusions I have left. Tacky or not, Weeki Wachee's sirens are definitely best enjoyed underwater, besequined and immersed in a cloud of mystic bubbles. And so I leave my mermaid, whose dream of 'financial security and a house' seems so much more realizable than that of Hans Christian Andersen's tragic heroine – especially as Deena already has legs.

19

THE FINAL FRONTIER

Next we put all the bullshit behind us and head for Florida's final frontier – the Everglades. The journey down the Gulf coast (Mexico lies just across the water) is certainly picturesque, taking us past some of Florida's prettiest resort spots – Sanibel Island and Captiva Island (part wildlife reserves, part hotels, houses and shopping malls) – as well as past sights the travel guides don't tend to dwell on: a gang of largely black prisoners doing hard labour at the side of the road, not quite chained together with leg irons, but heavily guarded.

A little further on, we pass a sign which reads: 'EVERY THIRD CHILD DIES FROM ABORTION.'

'What? Two out of three survive?' jokes Mark, but the placard is an ugly reminder that in this predominantly Republican state, Christian fundamentalist ideas often rule. Abortion is a complex and emotional issue, but in Florida those who argue loudest about the 'right to life' are frequently also those staunchest in their support of the death penalty (Florida still uses the electric chair), gun ownership and cuts in child and family welfare. The anti-abortion movement is dominated by activists who protest outside clinics, intimidating women who try to enter, and by the true extremists, such as Paul Hill, who in 1994 outside an abortion clinic in Pensacola, Florida, shot and killed a sixty-nine-year-old doctor and his seventy-four-year-old 'bodyguard', echoing a similar murder, also in Pensacola, a year before.

The relatively unspoiled wilderness of the Everglades National Park – one and a half million acres, first given federal protection in 1934 – is a welcome relief from Florida's human excesses. As we turn east on US 41, the original Tampa to Miami highway, known more popularly as the Tamiami Trail, we enter an area of wetlands unlike any other in the world.

Situated between the state's slightly elevated east and west coasts, tremendous amounts of water once drained from the Lake Okeechobee area, into this vast, mosquito-infested region of sawgrass, cypress and mangrove swamps and isolated 'hammocks' – islands of hardwood trees. The mosquitoes are still here, and so are the grass and many of the hammocks, but despite efforts to protect this unique habitat, large numbers of trees have been cleared and pollution from farming (especially sugar cane cultivation) and from surrounding cities – as well as the diversion of water for both agricultural and municipal use – provide an ongoing threat to the survival of the Everglades as a whole, and to certain species of animals and plants in particular. Speeding vehicles on the roads are a problem, too. Some drivers seem to feel they notch up extra points for hitting endangered species such as the Florida panther (highway signs read: 'Panther Habitat – Only 30 Left') or, in the Keys, parts of which are included in the Everglades Park, the tiny Key deer.

At a roadside rest stop – a beat-up little shack offering cold drinks and, like practically everywhere else along the Tamiami Trail, airboat rides – we cross a wooden footbridge and sit for a while, surrounded by tall grasses and swamp.

Here, we start to feel the pull of the past, an almost tangible and not so distant past when Europeans had not penetrated this fevered yet beautiful Eden. We hear only the buzz of insects and the occasional cry of a bird or the splash of a fish jumping in the water. Some distance away, an alligator, perhaps six feet in length, lies at the edge of some weeds, sunning its gnarly dark brownish-green body – so still that at first it really does resemble a floating log. An anhinga, a strange, blue-black bird with a long, snake-like neck, sits on a branch of a half-submerged tree. An egret flies overhead.

Curiously, sitting in the afternoon stillness, with the unmerciful sun beating down on my head and mosquitoes feeding on my flesh, I find myself thinking of what the Spanish found when they tried to penetrate beyond the coast of Florida in the early sixteenth century.

Ponce de Leon, a companion of Columbus on his second voyage to the New World, was the first recorded European to set foot in Florida, a little north of St Augustine on the east coast, in April 1513. 'Believing that land to be an island,' wrote Antonio de Herrera, historiographer to His Catholic Majesty the King of Spain, 'they nam'd it Florida because it appear'd very delightful, having many pleasant groves, and it was all level; as also because they discovered it at Easter, which as has been said, the Spaniards called Pasqua de Flores, or Florida.'

That was the good news. Ponce, who was searching for gold and for a magic fountain of youth, of which the Puerto Rican Indians told tales, claimed Florida for Spain, stayed six days in the vicinity, then took off, sailing southward along the Keys. Eight years later, in 1521, when Ponce de Leon had finally won the exclusive right to settle the land he had discovered, he established a colony on Florida's west coast, around what is now Port Charlotte, but lasted only five months against disease and constant clashes with the Calusa Indians, who in one attack sent eighty canoes against him. Seriously wounded, he sailed to seek treatment in Cuba, and the whole colony left with him. He died soon after reaching Havana – sadly never having located the youth-giving fountain – and his heirs lost all claim to Florida through their failure to settle.

Back in the twentieth century, we return to the minivan and set off in search of a tiny Everglades museum Mark and Dara recall having visited in the past. Farther along US 41 towards Miami, this turns out also to offer airboat rides, as well as an alligator show, at which we happily stroke the cool, softly corrugated back of a live baby gator.

'This one's at pre-handbag stage,' notes Mark unkindly.

The museum is funny and depressing at the same time – a sorry collection of stuffed dead animals, gloomily lit in glass cases, with the barest effort made to create some sort of 'natural environment' around them.

'Look at this, it's just a head mounted on a plaque!' cries Dara, and it becomes apparent that, while pretending to celebrate the diversity and beauty of Everglades wildlife, the museum is in part a collection of old – very old, in some cases – hunting trophies.

Outside, as storm clouds gather ominously before our planned airboat ride, we inspect a Seminole Indian hut, or *chickee*, its roof distinctively thatched with palmetto leaves, which somehow has the same air of tattered dereliction as the moth-eaten exhibits in the museum. Though the museum and lone *chickee* hut are privately owned, there are Indian reservations on either side of the highway – Seminoles to the north, Miccosukees to the south. Until recently, both groups were considered to be Seminole, but they spoke different languages, and were finally allowed by the federal government to partition into separate camps.

The history of relations with the indigenous tribes in Florida is shameful. Osceola, the greatest war chief of the Seminole nation – despite having an English father and an Upper Creek Indian mother – was treacherously captured by US forces under a white flag of truce in 1837, and died in captivity the following year, only to have his head cut off and displayed as a souvenir. But perhaps the Miccosukees exact a tiny revenge today through their lucrative casino and bingo hall – the only gambling sanctioned in Florida other than the state lottery.

Slightly chill rain pours from the sky, as our flat-bottomed airboat sets off on its brief and well-travelled excursion through the Everglades swamps. Having just been instructed to stuff paper towels into our ears as protection against the monstrous noise of the propeller's large engine, we now struggle as a group to hold a tarpaulin over our heads. There are four rows of hardy travellers sitting in the boat, and the tarp is not quite big enough for us all. Seated at the front, Brian, Mark, Dara and I pull the canvas forward to keep the rain off our brows, only to have a group of German tourists at the back of the craft tug it the other way. As our boat skims over the grassy water, through a channel which has been artificially cleared, the amicable push-pull battle of the tarpaulin makes us feel like galley slaves — as if our efforts should be powering our progress.

Out on the water, speeding through shoulder-high grasses and thickets of pond cypress, the thrill of the ride is slightly dampened by the noise and the rain, but there are peaceful pauses when our 'captain' and guide, seated above us by the raised propeller, turns off the engine and points out a turtle or a water snake, an alligator or an ibis, with its striking white plumage, red face and elegant turned-down bill. The water in some places is less than twelve inches deep (airboats are the only craft other than canoes and skiffs which can navigate these channels), but the aquatic, almost other-worldly nature of the landscape creates a powerful impression that man can only ever be an interloper here, and that the Everglades's delicate, seasonally changing ecosystem should be protected at all cost.

On the road back to Miami, Dara finds that this trip and especially Florida's wilder expanses have refired her energies for the script she jokingly refers to as her 'trailer home/white trash' project. She is thinking of grafting German myths and legends onto the unsuspecting Florida landscape.

'I'd like to film *Tristram and Isolde* here!' she exclaims, turning from the wheel as she drives, looking for all the world as if she could take us right now to some Teutonic god-realm of rivers, lakes and mountains. 'This is the perfect setting for passion – the tension of what passion is about. My lovers can't get married, so they can't murder their passion.'

She mentions a book John Hood has previously recommended to me, Leopold von Sacher-Masoch's dark romance, *Venus in Furs* (it is from the author's name that the word 'masochism' was coined), and talks of combining it with *Lohengrin* and setting it in a Florida backwoods environment of drive-in movie theatres and alligator farms. 'The story is made for Florida,' she says. 'It's so simple: Girl meets boy. Girl whips boy. Boy loses girl. Girl loses whip. Boy gets girl back again.'

As the wetlands diminish behind us and US 41 becomes the western, gas station and liquor store-lined edge of Miami's Southwest Eighth Street, Dara quietly talks to me about her childhood, a classic confrontation between the Old World and the New.

'I always thought the boys in Florida were better looking,' she laughs. 'The German boys were really ugly! For my summers in Germany, I was deposited in a *kinderheim*, which is a home for children in the Black Forest, founded by my uncle for kids to get fat and healthy after the war – but I was still sent there long after the war was over. And I had to hang out with these Catholic nuns, who would weigh you every month, because you had to get fat. It's a little house, an old Benedictine-monk fishing cabin, a really small house, because the Benedictine monks in medieval times were as small as children.

'It's not until later that I really appreciated Germany,' she says. 'Florida was always – the kids knew more about sex, you could run around, you didn't have to wear clothes, you could do drugs, you could do all these things.'

'So which do you feel, American or German?'

She looks at me and smiles the healthy, tanned smile of, as she might say, a Florida babe. 'The Germans have no swear words. They don't know how to do it, they don't know how to get angry, they don't know how to be really free. But I guess, here in Florida, I feel more German, and there, I feel more American, so it's sort of in between both things. Like my films, too. In Germany, they think they're much too entertaining and frivolous, and here people sometimes see them as heavy and more difficult, so it's always between two worlds.

'But my imagination works here, which is really significant. I don't imagine stories in Germany, I imagine them here. It seems like this is a place of more possibility, because so much less has been done already. In Germany and older places, so many things have happened that you're restricted. There are limitations – there's taste and manners and all that sort of shit, and here there's none of that. It's bad taste and no manners, and you're free to create.'

I think of all the clumsy trash culture of Florida and America, and realize: '*Yes, it's ugly as hell sometimes – but I actually miss it when I'm away!*'

'It's primal here,' Dara says, 'it's still a swamp! It buzzes when it's hot, and it *is* hot, you have to give in to it, you can't control it. In Europe, people are

203

always controlling everything, and here you're completely controlled by the heat – it holds you in bondage, you just have to do what it says! And that's really nice, to be strapped down by it like that. You're really at its mercy. It's very sexy. The heat is sexy. The afternoons here are sexy.'

We are back in Miami proper now. The gas stations and liquor stores have given way to the *botánicos* and colourful fruit stands of Calle Ocho. As we pass Orlando Menes's chess park and the flaming-torch monument to the *exilio* 2506 Brigade, the Martyrs of Girón (the Bay of Pigs), Dara turns to me and admits, 'I know that how I see Florida isn't really at all how it is. I take it on romantically, and you can do that if you're seeing it from the outside. I love the way it's all constantly decaying. And history is so short here. Under the field, there is *nothing* there. There never was a house there, there never was a sidewalk, never a road!

'In Europe, you dig down and hit the Romans, there are all these layers of dead cultures. Here, it's pioneering. You can do anything, there's nobody stopping you. And there's a lot of death here – I think the death that is here is important.'

'How do you mean, a lot of death?' I ask, suspecting that she does not have slain Cubans in mind.

'Well, there's the heat, there's the old people, and it's the end of the line. It's one of the last places, one of the first places, but it's not a through place, it doesn't really feel like a place where people move on.' I glance at her, thinking about all the friends I have known here who have moved on, yet agreeing that there is something final about Miami. Up ahead, the downtown skyline is shooting blinding shafts of light at us, reflected from the sinking sun. Beyond, lies the Beach and home. 'It's an end place,' continues Dara, 'like in *Midnight Cowboy*, when he makes the journey down and dies in Miami Beach. That's OK. It's OK to die in Miami Beach, because it's the end.'

20

IT'S QUIET OUT HERE

Back home, I do what I always do after a trip: I take a swim in the sea. With the palm trees and neon-framed hotels of Ocean Drive backlit by the sun's dying glow, I float motionless in the water and feel its calming pull easing my weary bones.

I love the beach: I should not underestimate its influence in keeping me here. Far more so than the supposed hipness of 'SoBe' – of Ocean Drive and now Lincoln Road and the new development of a Mediterranean-style 'village' below Fifth Street – it is the accessible natural beauty of a stretch of sand, only a few blocks from my apartment, which binds me to this place. Where else can you swim in the warm rain with a tiny silver fish, perhaps an inch in length, circling you for an hour, no matter how fast you move, doubtless believing you are a rock? Or watch, at night, the silent streaks and flashes of lightning over a moonlit sea (or, on one occasion, the distant plume of flame from a space shuttle as it lifted off from Cape Canaveral, about two hundred miles up the coast)? Or go for a run in the morning and swim out with a school of tarpon, each one six or seven feet long – or witness the difficult landing of a ten-foot, three hundred and thirty-pound hammerhead shark, its jaws razor-sharp even in death, like the grin on a taxman's mailbox?

Late afternoon, when the sun's light softens and the heat diminishes a little, is a favourite time. But perhaps most seductive of all is early morning. Seven a.m. on a weekday is like an undiscovered gem. In summer, the Atlantic is usually mirror still at this hour. The sand is deserted, save for a few old folks up for a swim before the heat becomes lethal, and perhaps a police patrol car, dislodging – sometimes with surprising courtesy – the homeless who have slept on the beach. On a winter's morning, it might be eighty degrees Fahrenheit or it might be sixty, and cool days, when they come, are relished ('A chance to accessorize,' as one friend puts it). The light this early is always fine: either a clear, warm, low-elevated sunlight or a wash of cloud, like the fog of memory.

This is a good hour to run and swim, before the beach gets busy, while the Dade County earth-movers are raking over the sand and the line of seaweed at the water's edge to keep the beach in shape. Pelicans fly low over the ocean like clumsy antique seaplanes, eyes trained for fish with which to stuff their sagging bills. Tiny sandpipers make rapid, darting runs alongside the waves, abruptly turning and retracing their hurried steps. Gulls gather, searching as ever for food, their orange and black bills open in their strangely muted cry.

Andrew Kuncas is a lifeguard who, like so many in Miami, came to Florida from somewhere else – Pittsburgh, in his case. I've often wondered what lifeguards think about all day, stationed in their tiny huts. 'On days like today where it's overcast,' he says, 'not many people come out, it can get kind of boring. But on a regular day when you have a large crowd, the crowd itself is rather entertaining. And then there's a lot of minor problems – people who masturbate in public, people with dogs, lost children, people who are bothering other people by drinking or playing loud music or whatever, so the day goes by pretty fast. It's not numbing.' But when I try to draw him out on his feelings about the sea, on whether he shares the sense of inner peace it gives me, he says only, 'Yeah, it's quiet out here.'

We talk about body culture, which in Florida sometimes seems the only culture. (My best friend Spike, visiting from London, once told me, 'Here, the body has replaced personality.') On the beach, tourists aren't identified merely by their white or broiled-lobster skin, but by their obvious unfamiliarity with a gym. Andrew, who's in his thirties and well honed but not to the point of obsessiveness, says, 'Women here respond totally to body type. The more you work out, the better your body is, the more likely you are to be able to pick them up.' Although, as he admits, it's not always easy because 'women see lifeguards as promiscuous and untrustworthy. Sometimes I can go months without dating.'

Of another aspect of local body culture, Andrew is less accepting. Despite liberal views on the poor representation of women and minority groups among City of Miami Beach lifeguards (three Hispanic, three women and one African-American out of a total of fifty-five), Andrew is unhappy about what he sees as an overly dominant gay culture in the clubs and on the beach.

In the evenings, certainly, fantasy wear is the

norm for gay clubs such as Warsaw and Icon, and cross-dressers are not an uncommon sight on Washington Avenue. On the beach, G-strings for men are permitted – as they are for women, along with topless bathing, rare in the US (there is also a nude beach further up the coast) – and at two beaches in particular there's a definite emphasis on male physique.

'It affects living here,' says Andrew. 'Twelfth Street isn't so bad, that's the respectable gay beach, but at Twenty-first Street, which used to be the main gay beach, there's a lot of hustlers and Italian hairdresser types. I resent my tax going to Aids treatment.'

(A rather different line is taken by the Greater Miami Convention and Visitors Bureau, which aggressively courts gay and lesbian tourists, and the billions of dollars they spend nationwide each year. 'It's not an ideological or political thing at all,' says the Bureau's spokesman, José Lima. 'It's about hard dollars.')

For me, the beach in many ways defines Miami and Florida – even down to their absurdities. I still remember one of the earliest conversations I overheard on the sand, a month or two after I first arrived, as America was gearing up for the Gulf War. South Beach was just starting to peak as a location for fashion shoots, at times rivalling London, Paris and Milan as a supermodel lure, but more often providing the backdrop for somewhat less glitzy catalogue work.

As I lay in the sun one January afternoon in 1991, feeling more alienated than I might otherwise have done by the militaristic mood in the air and the 'Support Our Troops' and 'Kill Saddam!' stickers and T-shirts in the shops, I heard two male models standing at the ocean's edge, discussing the situation in the Gulf.

'Yeah,' I heard one of them say. 'It's getting serious. It's going to make working in Milan really difficult.'

But perhaps the time I liked the beach best was during another, more immediate crisis: the great cyclone of August 1992 – Hurricane Andrew.

Partly because, like Dara, I tend to romanticize even my worst experiences, or because most of my friends and I emerged relatively unscathed, I look back on Hurricane Andrew as a curiously halcyon period. Just as I have positive memories of the weeks immediately following the diagnosis of my son's cancer (we moved as a family into the hospital in London; it was unusually sunny and hot; early one morning on the children's ward I made a cup of tea and felt strangely alive, in the midst of despair), I recall embracing the hurricane and its attendant inconveniences – the evacuation, the lack of electricity and water – in a spirit of adventure. If anything it fulfilled my *Robinson Crusoe* fantasy of Florida, threw seaweed up on the beach, shut down the air-conditioning, stopped toilets from flushing, and made it wild again.

The damage was immense. Until the Los Angeles earthquake of 1994, Andrew was the worst natural disaster in US history. It left more than thirty-five dead, caused twenty billion dollars worth of damage, made one hundred and fifty thousand people homeless, and all but destroyed the town of Homestead (just south of Miami, on the approach to the Keys) and – crucial to the local economy – its neighbouring Air Force base.

Yet, only a day before Andrew struck, nothing seemed out of joint . . .

21

APOCALYPSE NOW

Saturday, 22 August: No sense today of impending trouble. In the evening, I try to watch a videotape of David Cronenberg's *Naked Lunch*, but the sound on the tape is bad, so I give up and instead catch a TV weather report about a hurricane in the Atlantic, gathering force and headed this way. The computer graphics of swirling cloud formations have little impact on me. In spite of the storm that hit southern England in 1987, felling virtually every tree in Brighton, where I lived, and wreaking havoc on the buildings, I give no thought to this one.

Sunday, 23 August: Woken from a deep sleep by the phone ringing at nine forty-seven a.m. By the time I answer, it has rung off. I lie there, drowsy, aware of activity in the alley behind my apartment: voices, car engines running, doors opening and closing. Somehow these are not the sounds of a normal Sunday morning. I reach for the TV remote and hit CNN. A map fills the screen. Hurricane Andrew, as this storm system has been named, is about to strike the Bahamas, moving directly west on the same latitude as Miami. I turn to WSVN7, the local Fox affiliate (Rupert Murdoch's TV network) and the most reliably sensational in its news coverage. A list of zip codes is rolling, together with the announcement, *'This is not a voluntary evacuation. This is mandatory.'* There is mine: Miami Beach, 33139. Andrew has attained wind speeds of one hundred and forty-five miles per hour. It is due to hit Miami at dawn tomorrow.

I lie there, tempted to go back to sleep, mulling it over. Like most of the neighbourhood, my apartment is a 1930s Art Deco construction. How resilient would it be in the face of a major storm? Finally I call my friends, Frank and Christina, and get their answering machine.

'I know it's early on a Sunday morning,' I say, 'but apparently they're evacuating the Beach. What are your plans?'

My problem is this: I have no car and nowhere to go outside the projected hurricane area – my friends all live directly in its path. But the TV is announcing a list of hurricane shelters. Evacuation buses will run along Route A1A all day.

Realizing I have only twenty-five dollars with which to weather the storm, I venture out on my bike in search of cash, water and food. The general mood is more of resignation than panic. The weather is calm and sunny, but there are lines at the cash machines, and they all run out of money before I can get to them. In the stores, everything non-perishable has disappeared from the shelves and bottled water is hard to come by. Many people I talk to remember the last major hurricane here, twenty years ago, when Miami Beach flooded, and simply want to get out.

Back home, I quickly search through my laundry and put a few T-shirts in the wash. To the accompaniment of Peter Gabriel's 'Passion' – a suitably disorientating soundtrack, its Moroccan-inspired drumming summoning images of the Sahara and vast, windswept dunes – I move my TV, fax and other electrical equipment into a closet, then take the pictures off the walls. I still haven't had breakfast, but as I sit down to eat, the phone rings. It's Andrew Douglas, my photographer friend, who has just landed in Los Angeles and seen the news.

'I'm jealous,' he says. 'You wanted to go through a major hurricane – and this one has my name on it! I wish I were there. We're both emotional junkies, aren't we? What are you going to do?'

'I'm torn,' I tell him. 'I'd like to see what the public shelters are like, but I'm tempted to tough it out on the Beach and surf the Big One.'

There's more than an element of bravura in this – aside from the fact that I can't actually surf – but also a grain of truth. I once read a description by a pilot who had flown his small plane right into the eye of a hurricane. His plane had dropped a thousand feet and at first he had been scared, but then he was struck by a sense of calm and beauty, surrounded as he was by an immense wall of water and light. Perhaps I might see the same? Perhaps this could take me closer to whatever it is I'm always searching for: the colours to burn more brightly; a transcendent experience, far outside everyday life. Or do I just want something to write home about?

Finally I reach Christina and Frank, and decide to join them at their apartment, a few blocks away. Frank is English and the same age as me (thirty-seven at this point in time). A club DJ and sometime

214

drug dealer, he's also one of the most honest men I know. Christina is Venezuelan, twenty-three, beautiful, bright, darkly funny and a wonderful friend.

Over a beer, we debate whether to go or stay. They don't have a car either, and are a good deal less intrigued by the prospect of the shelters than I am. Reluctantly we decide to move and set out around four p.m., like refugees, lugging bags of clothes, blankets and food through strangely silent streets.

'I feel like an idiot,' Frank complains, as we walk along in search of the bus.

'We'll all feel like idiots,' I say, 'if it doesn't hit. But if it does, we might not feel so stupid.'

Already the Beach has a post-holocaust feel to it. Parked cars stand abandoned. The whole area is deserted. Palm fronds rustle softly, but there's no real wind. The archetypal calm before the storm.

The first shelter we are taken to is full, but by six p.m. we're ensconced within Palm Springs North Elementary School, in a northwestern suburb of Miami. A mosaic on the entrance wall celebrates Mickey Mouse. There is also a framed copy of the Pledge of Allegiance – and a quotation from former US President James A. Garfield (assassinated in 1881):

Next in importance to Freedom and Justice is Education, without which neither Freedom nor Justice can be permanently maintained.

Inside the school auditorium, the floor is covered with mats on which we will sleep – or not. The three of us promptly stake out our territory in front of two TVs showing an advertisement for the Hearing Helpline featuring Ronald Reagan. A deaf President? To mark our arrival, we open some beers I have brought with me.

'There is to be no consumption of alcoholic beverages inside the school,' an amplified voice announces. 'Please drink outside.'

So we do, then take a walk to check out the neighbourhood and get another six-pack. There's not much to see: tract homes, playing fields, a park, a gas station. A few people are boarding up their houses. One has 'REPO' painted on its side.

'I'd go crazy living here,' Christina remarks. 'I'd like a house, but not here.'

Time passes slowly. A young Red Cross volunteer tells us he was at the Lollapalooza rock and rap festival yesterday in downtown Miami: 'Lush were awesome!' The constant news coverage on TV reports that Andrew is gathering strength. It is currently rated a category four hurricane, with wind speeds of between 150 and 155 miles per hour. A category four has the capacity to cause serious structural damage. But it's only five miles per hour off a category five. At that strength, its impact will be catastrophic − and Miami Beach is where Andrew's eye is expected to make landfall.

There are about 250 of us inside the school, a mixture of locals, French and American tourists, Red Cross volunteers and police. Fascinated by how out of place they seem, I watch a bird-like European couple on a mat directly across from mine. The woman is blonde and dressed in white: pretty but slightly drained − like a Russian movie star. The man has short hair and a serious face, far removed

216

from American ebullience. They seem to communicate with one another silently. In all the time we are in the shelter, I hear them utter only the briefest exchanges, in a language I cannot identify.

Closer to us is a French family, a husband, wife and the most beautiful little boy. I draw a Snoopy for him, write '*Bonjour!*' in the thought bubble, then realize it should be, '*Bonsoir!*' The child performs a perfect bedtime ritual, shaking his blanket and sheet and laying them carefully over the mat that will be his bed for the night. He hugs both his parents before he tucks down. He is full of life and quiet acceptance – no hint of nervousness or resentment or impatience.

Unlike a woman at the back of the hall, who is the first to crack. Ignoring the pleas of her ten-year-old daughter, she complains loudly that other people have better mattresses – failing to recognize that some people have brought their own. An argument breaks out and it takes a policewoman to calm her. Later, I find myself trapped in conversation with her, listening to a rehearsal of her woes.

'My husband's in Connecticut.' She stares intently at me. 'He's no good. My family's no good, either. I hate them all. That's why I'm in therapy – and why my daughter's so fucked up. She peed on me, here on the mat! Can you believe that? She peed on me . . .'

'I can believe it!' Christina says when I tell her. 'That woman's retarded. If she were my mother, I'd pee on her too!'

As night comes, Frank, Christina and I try to sleep, but the lights are kept on and the TV coverage is

217

relentless. There are reports of surfers and 'hurricane junkies' partying on the Beach. We wish we'd stayed there, the images are so spectacular: wild, windswept palms twisting in the rain and the fallout from the lashing surf; news reporters, their hair slicked to their scalps, their features bleached in the darkness by single spotlights, struggling to make themselves heard to the camera above the pounding of the sea and the roar of the wind.

'It's Eric!' cries Christina, as a grinning, dark-haired surfer dude appears on screen, waving at the camera as he lugs his board out into the foaming water.

'Nothing will stop Eric hitting those waves!' Frank laughs.

And in the fuzzy TV picture that tries to make sense of the darkness of the beach, we see Eric and other wet-suited maniacs riding the raging white surf, then wiping out in spectacular eruptions of spray.

The image cuts to Ocean Drive – more deserted than we have ever seen it. Everywhere windows are shuttered with wood or metal, already straining in the wind. Neon signs knock against walls as they shift on their mountings, and the few, amorphous, sand-coated cars and tortured palm trees seem Martian in their strangeness.

Next there's a report of a still more fatalistic party in Key West. Stuck right down at the southernmost tip of Florida, surrounded by ocean, there's nowhere to evacuate to: the authorities have closed US-1, the lone road linking the Keys to the mainland. As locals make the best of it, drinking on Duvall Street to a mixed soundtrack of booming music and a still-greater booming wind, some are old enough to remember the great Labor Day hurricane of 1935. Even stronger than Andrew now, it destroyed railway bridges and cut off whole areas of the Keys. (The Overseas Railroad was never rebuilt, but surviving sections were used to complete the Overseas Highway, US-1.) Ominously, a reporter points out that 480 people died in that storm.

Here in the school, the Red Cross volunteers, who are mostly in their teens, seem both excited and nervous. 'Have you ever been through a hurricane?' they keep asking. 'What's it like?' By one forty-five a.m., the TV is reporting all the shelters full; people are told to stay where they are.

At intervals we go outside to face the driving rain. There's a thrill in the air now. A school sign rattles on its screws, then is torn away by the wind to fly into the night. Lightning arcs silently, like the flares from distant bombs. Across the street a tree collapses against a house – but gradually, like someone very old sitting down. We watch as an American flag rips back and forth on its pole.

'Old Glory's holding up so far,' says a cop, with what I hope is a hint of irony.

Inside, we pray each time the power fails that the back-up generator will not kick in, that finally we might have darkness and silence in which to sleep. After TV reception is finally lost, two old Jewish men in the front row talk for the remainder of the night, so that we sleep fitfully and our first news of the hurricane's eye striking Miami around five a.m. is interspersed with a commentary on the Talmud, ethics, Confucius, Stalin:

'Stalin was an anti-Semite. He was as bad as Hitler.'

219

'What about Lenin?'

'Lenin was anti-Semite also, but not so bad. But then he got sick.'

'Where in Russia were you from?'

'Minsk.'

'Minsk? Is that in Poland?'

'No, not Poland. White Russia. I'm from White Russia.'

'Sweden used to own part of Poland. It had a northern part of Russia and part of Poland. My wife was Swedish. I know.'

Monday, 24 August: We wake to an air of uncertainty and a sense of anticlimax, as we realize the hurricane has come and gone.

We have power from the generator, but no TV and extremely low water pressure – the toilets aren't flushing and there's only a trickle from the taps. At least one Miami Beach-based TV station, WSVN7, is still broadcasting, but for some reason we can't receive the signal, only a relay on the radio.

The news is patchy. Apparently the Beach has been spared the worst of the damage: the major destruction is around Homestead, an hour south of Miami by road. There have been several deaths, no-one is sure of the number. The bridges and causeways leading to Miami Beach are closed until noon at the earliest, and a dusk to dawn curfew will be in force across Miami tonight, to limit looting.

Our immediate reaction is one of regret, that we're here and not home. We eat the breakfast that's provided – orange juice, cereal and bananas – and listen, rapt, as the volunteer supervising our shelter stays glued to his cellular phone to ensure that we're well stocked for lunch. He's a man of impressive girth, dressed in a dark blue shirt, jeans and a bandana, and our food situation seems to be his prime concern.

'Look at the size of him!' grins Frank. 'All he keeps saying is, *"Do we have enough food? Do we have enough food?"* There's no way we'll starve with Big Daddy in charge!'

After waiting in line for about thirty minutes at the school's payphones, I manage to make a collect call to my parents in England to let them know that I'm alive. At least the telephone lines are working. I quickly call a few friends in the southern suburbs, down towards Homestead where the damage is worst. One group of students I know got so drunk at their house, waiting for Andrew to strike, that at its peak their energies were devoted to crawling along the corridor to throw up in the bathroom. Another friend, Alison, spent the night sitting with her family on the edge of the bathtub of their house in Kendall, with the rain pouring in after their roof had blown off. 'We've lost everything,' she tells me. But everyone I reach is safe.

By mid-morning, we're all restless and eager to leave the shelter. The toilets stink and there's no water to wash our hands. Having opened my big mouth to propose that it might not be too difficult to unblock the toilets, I find myself performing this task, with the help of a policewoman holding a torch.

'You may have noticed the flood we just had,' Big Daddy announces grimly to the assembled throng. 'This was caused by someone placing a paper cup in the toilet. We have receptacles for cups and everything except toilet paper, which is the only thing that should be disposed of in the toilet bowl. Otherwise, it's not only insanitary, but time-consuming for our volunteers to clean up.'

Twelve hours in a shelter and we feel unclean, dehumanized. I think about the camps in Bosnia and other trouble spots. Someone said that prisoners arriving at one Serbian camp were shocked at the state of the people already there. 'How could they sink so low?' they asked. They thought the detainees had been there for months. In fact they had been there ten days.

With no officially organized transportation home, one of the evacuees brightly takes up a collection and succeeds in chartering private buses to take us back. We leave around five p.m., and the journey home is through a war zone: palm trees wrenched out of the earth, traffic lights hanging down across the streets, puddles the size of lakes, crushed cars, boarded-up buildings, roofs blown off.

On Indian Creek, a stretch of water alongside Collins Avenue on Miami Beach, houseboats have been torn from their moorings and dumped upside down, to sink or stand on end at weird angles. As we approach the Deco District and our own apartments, we fear the worst, but for some reason the damage here is minimal despite being marginally closer to where Andrew's eye hit. Frank and Christina's apartment is fine, and when I reach mine, not even a window-pane is broken.

My power is out, but there's still a little water in the taps. I fill the bath, fill every bucket and pot I have, aware that soon, as at the shelter, my toilet may not flush. Then I take my bike out and cycle around. Even with minimal damage, the Beach is almost unrecognizable. Trees and telephone poles are down everywhere. I have to manoeuvre to avoid broken glass.

On Ocean Drive, I realize that I'm starting to enjoy this. There is a layer of sand over everything, piles of kelp and seaweed line the shore, and the smells are incredible – a briny, fishy stink mixed with the lush green scent of freshly severed vegetation. Through a tangle of fallen palms, whose roots have left huge craters in the ground, I glimpse the damage to the hotels and restaurants which line Ocean Drive. Metal shutters have been torn open by the wind and the neon signs look as if they've been chewed up and spat out. Wooden lifeguard huts have been tossed two or three hundred metres from the beach to the street, where they lie in splinters.

Outside the Adrian Hotel at the corner of Ocean and Eleventh Street, I run into Frank and Christina, also out on their bikes. A small crowd has gathered by the bar at the front of the hotel, watching a TV balanced on a low wall, its cable strung back inside. The hotel must have its own generator: the rest of Ocean – the rest of Miami – is blacked out tonight.

The devastation on screen is the first evidence we've seen of Andrew's full effect. Photographed from the air, Kendall and Homestead look like the site of some nuclear strike. Yet the images of ravaged buildings hold little emotional impact. If anything, there's a certain thrill at the scale of the destruction.

'South Miami was ugly to start with,' says Frank. 'Just a little home improvement.'

Twenty minutes after curfew, we swim in the ocean. It's wild, the swell about five feet high, the water warm and foaming. We ride up on the waves, bobbing above the sand in a way that's impossible when the sea is its normal, calm self. The skyline of low-rise Deco hotels looks strange with no lights. I can almost taste the broken palm fronds, the salt in the seaweed.

As I cycle home, a squad car cruises by, its loudspeaker crackling: '*Get off the streets! The curfew is now in effect!*'

The sun is setting, the sky ahead a diorama – vivid reds and oranges, the palm trees set on fire by the rays, like the end of *Apocalypse Now*.

It's dark as I carry my bike up to my apartment. I bang my knee on the doorframe and curse as I hunt for matches in the gloom. I don't own a torch. I wouldn't even have candles, were it not for the fact that I love the *santería* votives in their glass jars decorated with saints and goddesses that cast weird shadows as the wax burns low. I find my favourite on the mantelpiece and light it. A crude drawing of a sturdy African woman comes to life beneath the legend:

Chango Macho
Luck Money Power Love
Espírito de buena suerte
vela de ofrenda

I boil water on my gas stove to make some tea, then negotiate the foreign masses and unfamiliar legs of my furniture – still upended as I left it in preparation for the storm – and sit on the floor in the dark, listening to the sounds outside.

Across the alley, someone has turned on a radio. A jolt of Spanish music (a rumba, a dance tune from the 1940s), another channel, then hurricane news, broadcasting twenty-four hours a day at the moment. The acoustics of the neighbourhood have changed. Usually there's a constant hum of air-conditioning units. With no power, the night sounds strangely flat. Because of the heat, everyone's windows are open. I hear snatches of conversation, a dog barking, a violent argument in the building across from mine. It feels as if it is after midnight. I think it's eight o'clock.

An hour later, the phone rings. It's Candace, a Jamaican friend who lives in Miami.

'My cousin died,' she tells me. 'He was just twenty-five, married, with a little boy.' Her voice is soft. She's not crying, simply in that state of curious numbness which comes when someone dies. 'It's so stupid,' she goes on. 'He was trying to hold a mattress to the window, to keep out the wind. A shard of glass pierced right through to his heart.'

Tuesday, 25 August: The day after the hurricane, strange stories start to circulate. Three hundred monkeys have escaped from a University of Miami research facility and are rumoured to have Aids. People are said to be shooting them on sight. As the radio continues to relay non-stop hurricane coverage, I hear this:

'We've just had word from the Federal Prison in South Dade that they've spotted at least two baboons which are on the loose from Metro Zoo.

225

They're hoping some of the Metro Zoo employees might be listening to this and tell them what to do. For the public, you should know that these baboons are considered dangerous. If you see them, holler, shout, but do not approach.'

As the great clear up begins, time seems suspended. Living in the apartment is like camping out. With ninety-five degrees Fahrenheit heat and no fridge, perishable foods and milk keep only a few hours. I eat lots of peanut butter-and-banana sandwiches. A tanker is parked outside a school on Sixth Street dispensing free drinking water. From the taps there's only a trickle, so I freshen up with a swim in the sea. Trees and other debris still block many roads throughout Miami and few people make unnecessary journeys. As a result the Beach is like a well-kept secret.

I relish this period, enjoying a sort of castaway existence, safe in the knowledge that it's only for a limited time. The roar of chainsaws is everywhere. President Bush visits South Florida and declares it a disaster area. Suddenly we have a local economy which has no banks open, no lights in stores, few goods, no electronic cash registers and limited means of checking credit cards.

Yet there is a sense of cooperation in the air, together with a gallows humour. Michael, the Israeli-born maintenance man of my building, whose own house was only slightly damaged by the storm, tells me:

'You see, God provides! There'll be many jobs now. You don't need wars to create jobs!'

I cycle around South Beach, feeling somehow fulfilled by the havoc, the sense of isolation. I was like this when my son was sick in hospital: it's as if I need my ordered world to be shattered, need the pain of real adversity, in order to find meaning. And yet this is not an addiction – I can be happy, very happy, with great meaninglessness.

As evening descends, the general smell of decay is increasing. On Washington Avenue, I stop for the sugary high of a *café con leche*, still available despite the lack of water and electricity. Cycling home, with police cars cruising the streets in search of curfew offenders, and Miami's evening temperature hovering around ninety degrees Fahrenheit, I feel as if I'm in some Latin American capital at dusk. I wait for a frightened white horse to run through the streets, pursued by an army jeep, as in Costa-Gavros's *Missing*.

Sunday, 30 August: This sense of a militarized, Third World country is heightened when I drive with Fran Brennan, a young reporter on the *Miami Herald*, to the site of Andrew's greatest devastation: Homestead.

The journey down is tortuous and strange, with heavy traffic and many military vehicles on the road. The rotting smell in the air is so strong that we have to roll up the windows, and long before we near Homestead the impact of the destruction on the senses is far beyond anything television or photographs can communicate.

Descriptions of structures you thought to be solid ripped open like paper cartons, or of cars tossed by the wind on top of one another, are mere words. It takes the scale of mile after mile of devastated, roofless buildings, together with the fetid stench of decaying food and vegetation – and possibly (rumours run rife on this) bodies still buried in the rubble – to bring home the full force a major hurricane can deliver.

Homestead is a circus, both media and military. Watched by a conglomeration of TV and newspaper reporters, the army runs around building 'tent cities' for the homeless, to accusations of poor organization and suggestions that no-one will want to live in them. Before Hurricane Andrew, Homestead's economy was built primarily around the local Air Force base, now 90 per cent destroyed. The surrounding area is largely agricultural, but the hurricane has left many of the farmers homeless – and wiped out the meagre jobs and homes of many more migrant farm workers from Mexico, Guatemala and other Latin American countries (some of them legal immigrants, the majority of them not). With the customary inequity of natural disasters, this one has made poor people poorer.

Besieged by mosquitoes, Fran and I cover ourselves in bug spray and dodge showers of rain. We are both wearing shorts, but Fran's legs are suffering more than mine. She grins at me as if to say she's been through worse in the past – and doubtless worse is yet to come.

With the constant, thrilling chop of military helicopters landing and taking off, we press through the throng of journalists to witness flying visits by the likes of the Reverend Jesse Jackson, a stirring man even in a polyester suit, and 'the preppy-looking guy', as Fran calls him – the President's son: Jeb (what-kind-of-name-is-that?) Bush.

228

Then, abandoning the madness of Homestead City Hall, we visit a shelter run by the Cuban American National Foundation – a political organization, founded and funded by exiled Cuban millionaire Jorge Mas Canosa, a man renowned for his vitriolic hatred of Fidel Castro and his ambition personally to replace him. But the shelter seems benign enough, offering medical care, food, water and assistance with housing and insurance claims, and we help unload a truck in puddles formed by the intermittent rain.

The lines of people waiting for help from any source are affecting. One of the biggest problems people have is a lack of information: with their homes and possessions destroyed, few have access even to a radio, and newspapers are almost impossible to get hold of. Many are frustrated, waiting long hours in the heat only to find that they are not eligible for a particular benefit or that they must come back tomorrow. Some speak little or no English. Their desperation shows in their faces and in the thrown together, often donated, T-shirts and shorts they wear. They have little option but to wait for other relief agencies to arrive, drinking the cups of water handed out by volunteers, their children enjoying an occasional free ice cream.

Around five p.m., a dust storm blows up and it starts to thunder. Dramatic arcs of lightning burn across the sky, one scoring a direct strike on the Homestead water tower. We retreat inside the *Miami Herald* trailer, which has been home to a clutch of journalists for the past few days – and has the garbage, scars and smells to prove it.

229

One of the reporters, Raul, is on the radio phone to the *Herald*'s downtown office as we enter. Like a soldier in the field frustrated by central command's failure to understand the on-the-spot situation, he turns to the others with a despairing shrug.

'They're asking for a physical description of the weather! What the hell do they mean, a physical description?'

He glances outside the trailer window, where a torrential rainstorm is in progress.

'*A ninety per cent chance of rain,*' he murmurs deadpan into the phone. Then, turning to his fellow hacks: 'A physical description? What's that – as opposed to a spiritual description?'

'The weather was sombre,' someone invents. 'Sombre, ethereal and eclectic.'

'Yeah, all three at once,' mutters a woman photographer, labelling her film at a dilapidated, fold-down trailer table.

'A physical description,' Raul grumbles. 'It's fucking raining!' Then, with mock concern for the editor sitting down the line in the comfort of his Miami office: 'Anything else?'

'Give 'em hell, Raul!' cheers one of his fellow troopers from the back of the trailer.

Due to continuing problems with looting, there is still a seven p.m. curfew in force in Homestead and South Dade, and journalists are no exception. As I'm driven home by a *Herald* reporter who has spent much of her life covering Mexico City, we are both struck by how alien South Miami seems at this moment, how impoverished and Third World, compared to the rest of the United States.

What puzzles me is that I seem to need this

foreignness. Even in Britain, much of my mental energy was devoted to transforming everyday experience into something not immediately recognizable – attempting to see my own homeland as if I were a stranger.

Back in my apartment, the heat is lethal. The couple in the next building are arguing violently again, and in the silences between their shouts and crashes I hear the crickets outside. I now have power in my bedroom but nowhere else, so I move everything through into there. With no food in my hothouse kitchen, I am delighted when Frank and Christina call to suggest we go out: there's an old Pedro Almodovar film, *Pepi, Luci, Bom and the Women at the Bottom of the Heap*, screening at the art house cinema on Lincoln Road.

'It has air-conditioning,' Christina points out.

'I'm there!' I tell her.

As I leave the apartment, a reporter is interviewing the Florida Insurance Commissioner on my newly restored TV.

'The scary thing is,' the Commissioner is saying, 'this is just the first hurricane of the season.'

22

THE CELESTIAL RAILROAD

During my first couple of months in Florida, on a hot and humid Christmas Day, I picked up an English friend from Miami's AmTrak railway station. She had been unable to get a direct flight from London (Christmas prompting an annual nightmare invasion of these balmy shores), and instead had been forced to travel via New York, then make the twenty-six-hour train journey down from there.

While waiting by AmTrak's singularly unromantic platform in the midst of a low-income wilderness, I spent some time walking around the worn metal tracks and chanced upon a gleaming, polished-bronze, private Pullman carriage from another era. It stood alone, unhitched to any engine or other rolling stock, blades of grass and weeds poking through the sleepers below it – but very obviously not abandoned. I mused for a while on what it might be like to travel America in this gem, to see the nation's expanses sweeping past from its step, and remembered a Broadway musical I had once enjoyed, *On The 20th Century*, which had captured some of the romance of crossing the country on one of the most glamorous trains of its day.

Perhaps I wondered briefly who owned this relic from another age, but soon my friend arrived and I forgot about it.

                    *   *   *

Later, much later, thinking about Florida's early
development – inextricably bound to the all-
consuming Henry Flagler and the growth of his East
Coast Railroad, first to Palm Beach in 1894, then
Miami in 1896, and finally Key West in 1912 – and
thinking, too, about my intended title for this book,
I called the Miami Public Library about a rumour I
had heard that there was once, somewhere around
Palm Beach, a railway station at a spot named
'Mars'.

Further research (in particular, an exhaustive article by Geoffrey Lynfield in the 1984 issue of
Tequesta, the journal of the Historical Association
of Southern Florida) showed that this in fact had
nothing to do with Flagler, but rather was part of a
narrow-gauge line, known as the Celestial Railroad,
which operated in the 1890s, north of Palm Beach,
between the still extant towns of Jupiter and Juno.
The evidence is a little sketchy, but it seems there
were two, or possibly three, stops on the line:
Neptune (which once housed a post office), Venus
and Mars.

The Jupiter and Lake Worth Railroad, which
operated the line, apparently had only one small,
wood-burning engine and no means of turning it
around, so that for the short, northward, Juno to
Jupiter run, it always had to shunt backwards.
Should it break down, all transportation ceased until
it could be repaired. The fare was ten cents per mile.

Captain T. M. Rickards, writing from Life Station
7, Biscayne, Florida, in 1892, offered this con-
temporary description:

                         233

The seven mile trip by rail from Jupiter (where the lighthouse looms majestically over the inlet) to Juno was through what appeared to me a rather barren waste, the monotony broken by the flag stations Mars and Venus (these latter planets, I can affirm confidently now, not withstanding the opinion of other eminent astronomers, are not inhabited) . . .

Other writers were more romantic in their accounts, mentioning shipments of pineapples, fish and turtles – and unscheduled stops along the line to enable tourists to pick flowers!

All that remains now, in the absence of even the tracks, is a cosmic suite of names. (I recall the distracting thrill of the fact that the woman in the William Kennedy Smith rape case came from Jupiter; transformed by court TV into soap opera the trial seemed suited for outer space.) There is the Celestial Dock, the railroad's old Jupiter terminus, now replaced by a modern jetty projecting into the Indian River at the Suni Sands Mobile Home Trailer Park; Jupiter Light, the old lighthouse; the town of Juno Beach, with its street names such as Saturn Lane, Venus Drive, Mars Way, Neptune Road and Starlight Lane; even a Celestial Building on Juno's Celestial Way, home to such local businesses as Celestial Realty and the Celestial Travel Agency (its slogan: 'For Service Out Of This World!').

It was in the weeks following Andrew's devastation that I heard of the destruction of an antique private railroad car belonging to 'millionaire-philanthropist' (a term more usefully applied to

Batman's duller, uncaped *alter ego*) Mitchell Wolfson, and realized that it must have been his carriage I had seen at the AmTrak station two years before, and that it might be fun to meet him – millionaire-philanthropists not ranking high on my list of friends.

I put in some calls to Wolfson's office, and with the help of a local journalist, Tom Austin, an interview was arranged. But before this could happen, Tom called early one Friday evening to tell me, with customary understatement: 'You're finally on the A-list! You've been invited to dinner tonight at Micky's club . . .'

This is not my usual speed. Seated around a long, central table in the quiet elegance of Micky Wolfson's private supper club, a few blocks away from the Friday night madness of Washington Avenue and Occan Drive, is a cast of characters literally too rich for any but the most success-driven, wish-fulfilling, Jeffrey Archer-type of novel.

Our host turns out to be a compact, bearded man in his mid-fifties, metal-rimmed spectacles perched on his nose, a challenging, very nearly malevolent undertow belying the genteel charm he at first exudes. Having inherited eighty-five million dollars twelve years ago from the family Wometco cinema chain, he has created two art museums (one here on Miami Beach, the other at a castle he bought in Genoa, Italy), founded an annual art magazine and endowed a foundation. Perhaps with good reason, people tend to view Micky as a Henry James figure, a sophisticated, intelligent man adrift in the wrong century and the most ridiculous place – *Miyaaami?*

The assorted guests gathered at the table include two elegant, cosmopolitan Italian women of a certain age and a younger American woman, flamboyantly dressed all in white (and later dismissed by one of her fellow guests as 'trash'), as well as Tom and my novelist friend, Brian, staunch survivor of our road trip to Florida's Arcadian heart.

At least my immediate dinner companion – one of the Italian divas – is not interested in the usual South Beach conversational diet of who's screwing who/who's building what/who's become a junkie, but after a time even her passionate accounts of novelist and painter friends have me reaching for the trigger of the Uzi secreted beneath my chair.

I glance at Micky, who – like a schoolboy bored with his own plate and keen to try what everyone else is eating – chooses this moment to join our discussion of Fellini's *Casanova*.

'Have you read the new, revisionist book about Casanova?' he asks, cool blue eyes twinkling like distant stars behind his glasses. 'I've only read the reviews . . .' He smiles, impishly. 'Now all of the bad people are good, and all the good people bad.'

Just which of these Micky considers himself to be remains a mystery, but the evening takes a livelier turn when, with dinner done, he whisks us outside to the striking luxury of his white 1962 Cadillac Fleetwood, complete with whitewall tyres, leather upholstery, streamlined dashboard and a stylish radio which sadly doesn't work but seems to promise a twilight zone of broadcasts from the early 1960s.

We take off in this monster, Micky at the wheel,

another six or seven of us crammed quite comfortably into its spacious interior. After a couple of brief stops at a nightclub and to admire the exterior of Micky's museum on Washington Avenue, he pauses outside another of his hovels, a former Southern Bell Telephone Company building with an exquisite Deco façade. 'The old cable to Havana still runs underneath!' he exclaims.

With *salsa* in the air, slowly we edge up South Beach's narrow, palm-lined Espanola Way, a large Cuban crowd spilling out from a tapas bar and surrounding the car. The Cadillac's windows are down, the night outside is hot. Drunken couples – Hispanic, white, black, gay, straight – spill across the street in a confusion of colours, sounds and smells: music; snatches of conversation in Spanish and English; sweat, perfume, liquor. Bodies thump against the almost stationary car; faces gaze in, eyes popping, mouths broadening in mostly generous smiles.

'Hey, beautiful car, man!' declares a Latin voice.

'This is just like Havana.' Micky turns to his guests.

'This *is* Havana!' says Brian.

Then an errant thought seems to cross Micky's brow. 'Dare we?' he wonders aloud. 'Is it too risky?' A mischievous gleam lights his eyes. 'No, let's do it!' And we are off on an Adventure, across the antique bridges of the Venetian Causeway, heading for the night-time netherworld of Overtown and Little Haiti – areas many Miamians tend not merely to avoid, but to deny the very existence of – in this most conspicuous of vehicles.

'Poor girls,' Micky proclaims with none too

convincing sympathy. It emerges that not only was the two Italian women's plane delayed, so that it took eight hours to reach Miami from New York, but they had been at Micky's house for only fifteen minutes when he gave them another fifteen to get ready for dinner!

But neither is complaining. Indeed, one has begun singing spiritedly in French. It falls to Brian, ever cynical (or at least wishing to appear so) and recently returned from a million-dollar private cruise as the guest of an Asian princess, to offer a note of ironic protest: 'I'm tired of being a plaything of the rich.'

Two a.m. is a memory by the time Micky drives us past his offices, located somewhat perversely in a block he owns opposite a former crack house on the fringes of Overtown. We sail through the derelict streets of Lemon City, past the old town hall and railroad workers' wood-frame housing ('This is how Miami used to look,' explains Micky excitedly), on to what one of the local guests describes, with a distinct lack of glee, as the 'senseless killing district' of Little Haiti.

But Micky is not just driving aimlessly. He is looking for a Haitian club called Obsession, and when he finds it closed, he stops his immaculate white machine on a quiet – an extremely quiet – street, rolls down his window and calls across to a group of young Haitians sitting on the kerb opposite.

'What happened to Obsession?' he shouts. 'Why isn't it open?'

The young men seem amused, perhaps even bemused, by the sight of this maniac in a Cadillac, but on the back seat, Tom and Brian are noticeably anxious.

'He's going to get us all shot!' mutters Tom.

The Haitians offer no opinion on the fate of Obsession, but one of them calls across – as he rises to his feet, the click of a semi-automatic weapon only a heartbeat away – 'Hey, can I buy your car?'

'I only just bought it myself,' Micky calls back with a chuckle, wisely pulling out onto the road and driving away. Then he turns to us all, still smiling, and asks, 'Don't you find this wonderfully sympathetic?'

At three a.m., we are out of the car, examining a commemorative marker at the heart of the tiny pocket neighbourhood of El Portal, northeast of Little Haiti, towards Biscayne Bay. Modest 1920s houses, their lights dimmed, are laid out on a quiet street, at one end of which is a small mound ('The only hill in Miami!' claims Micky) and the plaque.

'This is the most exclusive community in Miami,' he offers slyly, smiling all the while. 'Only seventeen hundred souls – and no-one ever moves, they just pass the houses down through the family. That's the town hall, the post office, and this mound marks the site of the Tequesta Indian Nation. There's a tunnel here leading under the street to this house . . .' Micky approaches the small dwelling opposite the mound and seems seriously to consider knocking on its door. 'The householder must allow you to see the tunnel, if you ask.' But it's three in the morning, two men are approaching from the shadows farther down the street, and thankfully he thinks better of it.

We return to South Beach, via Surfside and Bal Harbour, observing landmarks perhaps only Micky would choose to identify: the best adult bookstore in Miami, the best greasy spoon, a supermarket that was once a gambling den.

Encouraged by his exuberant mood, I inquire about the railway carriage which led me to him – a 1926 Pullman business car, The Hampton Roads, he informs me – and hear a description of how he would travel the length and breadth of North America in his two private carriages, until both were destroyed by the hurricane.

'That was a remarkable experience!' he exclaims. 'It was really one of the great adventures. I think we were the last to run it quite like that. Nobody took fifty-two-day, seventeen-thousand-mile trips, because they couldn't stay away for two months.'

'And you went to Mexico and to Canada?'

'Yes, yes.'

'And to South America?'

'No, because the rails don't go there. We went as far as we could go . . .'

But when I ask about the Celestial Railroad, he knows no more than I do.

By now, one of the Italians has dozed off, but Micky seems tireless. As dawn approaches, we close the evening with a nightcap and a tale he tells of once passing out at the Victor Hotel on Ocean Drive and Twelfth Street – and waking up, two days later, in the same room.

With sleep fast approaching, one of the group waxes philosophical and offers this passing thought: 'In the end, we all just want somebody to love us for five minutes. And usually, five minutes is enough.'

23

WHY THEY HAVE TO SHOOT A MAN?

Most of my friends spend most of their time trying
to stay well away from the Miami police – sometimes with good reason, often simply because
they're not looking for trouble, which when it
comes may be only the worse for a flashing red-and-
blue escort. So what in God's name am I doing now,
riding shotgun on the front passenger seat of a
Miami P.D. patrol vehicle, when, the world being
what it is, I should probably be handcuffed, trussed
and busted in the back?

I have something of a mixed attitude towards cops
myself. I've seen the beatings, seen the videos,
watched the TV shows, the movies, even smiled
uncertainly at a T-shirt I saw a hefty black man
wearing on Miami Beach: 'L.A.P.D. – We Treat You
Like A King!' (Remember Rodney . . .)

I know how bad they can be, but I've also never had
a run-in with a cop in all the time I've spent in
America. Hell, the one occasion they were called to
my apartment by neighbours complaining about the
noise from a party I was throwing, they practically
ordered me to continue – with the volume turned
down a notch – when I was tired and ready to quit. Of
course, I'm white, English, reasonably articulate even
when less than sober, and doubtless perceived as
another nugget in South Florida's goldmine: a *tourist*.

But now, sitting next to one of Miami's finest, I feel distinctly uncomfortable. If lines were drawn, this is not the side I'd be on – though we all say that till we need help! I simply wanted to find out what it was like to police Miami's most notoriously violent area, Liberty City, and with the help of some old press credentials, I'm doing just that, riding along with Officer David Chang, a twenty-nine-year-old patrolman who's been on the force for four years, on his full ten-hour shift. And all it took was my autograph on a waiver which stated, among other things, 'I further understand and have full knowledge of the basic nature of law enforcement work and fully realize the possibility that dangerous situations may arise which could result in my being physically harmed or injured, as well as fatally injured . . . I NEVERTHELESS, FREELY AND VOLUNTARILY ASSUME THESE RISKS' – plus a warning from a cop downtown that my most dangerous moments would come driving in my own rented car to and from Liberty City Police Station in Miami's Sector 10.

Which was perhaps overstating the case, since I have driven through the area on other occasions without feeling that at any moment I would be shot at. However, given the murders in South Florida, three or four years back, of ten foreign tourists in twelve months – mostly within the jurisdiction of the Miami P.D. – they are understandably wary of anyone from outside the neighbourhood driving through.

Friday, three p.m.: There's a strange sense of invulnerability that comes with walking into an inner-city police station with nothing to report and little to hide, but now that I've found Lieutenant Skumanich, my contact at the Liberty City post on North West Sixty-second Street, and been shown into a small-ish, nondescript room which reminds me more of school than hard-core police territory, I find I'm uneasy. How will the cops feel about me, a white-Limey-liberal-pinko writer, sitting in with them as they ready themselves for their long shift out there in the 'hood? How will the officer I'm assigned to deal with ten hours in my company: will we get on, or will he take an instant dislike to my snotty British accent, run a make on me and come up with that unpaid parking ticket from 1992, the incident out-side the high school a year earlier, or that time in L.A. when Hugh Grant and I . . .? It wasn't easy even dressing for this gig. What do you wear to go riding with a cop – do you try for a formal look or dress for the streets? (In the end, I wore what I always wear: black 501s and a T-shirt.)

As fresh-faced young officers – male, female, black, white, Hispanic – file into the room, they take only cursory glances in my direction. I guess a lot of people go riding with the Miami P.D. This pre-dominantly black neighbourhood is by any measure a danger zone, a noted guns'n'crack territory sprawl-ing around the optimistically named Martin Luther King Boulevard, yet here in the briefing room the cops are joking with all the mixed sarcasm and bonhomie of *N.Y.P.D. Blue*. Someone has given the telephone beeper number of a female officer to a man she doesn't know, and two of her female colleagues are ribbing her about it.

'He's OK,' says one. 'He's a public prosecutor. He's cute.'

'I'm not interested in "*cute*",' says the first officer, an attractive black woman with a hungry gleam in her eyes. 'Are we talking "*cute*" or "*handsome*"? I like big men . . . *something I can climb on!*'

Meanwhile, on a desk at the front, alongside more innocent fliers promoting 'Pig Bowl Charity Fund' events, 'wanted' sheets are laid out for the taking. Xeroxed photographs of suspected offenders, mostly young black males, stare up at anyone who cares to look – some with a weary, troubled expression which belies their years and suggests a short lifetime of little ease; others cold as ice. The charges are a numbing catalogue of aggravated battery, aggravated assault and homicide. The victims are often girlfriends or wives or someone known to the suspect – underlining the fact that it's the people who live here, rather than tourists or day-trippers, who are most at risk:

WANTED: B/M – **THOMAS DUBARI** – AKA **'WINKY'**. DOB: 04-27-72. HAS DE LA SOLS, GOLD TEETH. POSSIBLE DRUG DEALER. SUSPECT STABBED HIS EX-GIRLFRIEND WITH A TYRE JACK, CAUSING A THREE-INCH LACERATION. SUBJECT IS VIOLENT. ARREST ON PROBABLE CAUSE.

WANTED: FOR QUESTIONING ONLY IN REFERENCE TO THE HOMICIDE OF LARRY MATTOX. B/M – **AARON COOPER JR**. DOB: 12-08-71. SUBJECT FREQUENTS THE AREA OF N.W. 15 AVE. AND 64 ST. ALSO SUGAR HILL PROJECTS (N.W. 15 AVE. AND 71 ST.). SUBJECT IS ARMED AND DANGEROUS,

INFORMATION SUGGESTED SUBJECT MAY
SHOOT IT OUT.

Roll-call is just as it looks on TV – a senior officer
briefing, in this case, eleven men and five women
on their duties in the upcoming shift – though there
are no *Miami Vice* Armani suits in evidence here.
Nor is it quite as homey as it used to be on *Hill
Street Blues*, although there's a groan when the shit
task of the day is assigned ('The back gate', the dull
job of security here at the station), and David Chang
probably offers up a silent cry of despair himself,
dumped with babysitting me while I take my out-
sider's glance at Miami Blue in action.

Three forty-five p.m.: We're on the road in a beat-up
blue-and-white Chevrolet Caprice patrol car which
Chang – as his friends call him – has given a brief,
mandatory inspection before leaving the pound, and
already I'm feeling the buzz, the automatic sense of
authority, that comes with riding in one of these
things. We're going to be all right, Chang and me, I
think we're going to get along just fine.

A large, not entirely athletic individual who
nonetheless seems younger than his twenty-nine
years, Chang is practically a one-man map of
Miami's ethnic diversity. Born in Bangladesh, of a
Chinese father and a Spanish mother, he was raised
in Venezuela before moving first to New Jersey, then
to Miami. With short, dark hair and a roundish face,
he looks Chinese, speaks Spanish – and English
with a broken Spanish idiom – and likes his work.
He has a wife and a nine-year-old stepdaughter,
whom he has helped care for since she was three

and loves as if she were his own.

With the exchange of personal details behind us, we roll out onto Martin Luther King Boulevard, into a zone of run-down convenience stores and liquor marts. This is not the kind of area most tourists would knowingly head for, but one wrong turn off US-1 or I-95, the major coastal interstate highway, and you could find yourself staring at a pastel pink grocery store decorated with a huge painted portrait of America's lost messiah of racial tolerance, the Reverend Dr King – or, if luck deserts you, down the wrong end of a gun.

Which is what happened, south of here, to German tourist Barbara Meller Jenson, who got lost driving a rental car from Miami International Airport to Miami Beach in April 1993, and who then fell victim to Miami's 'bump and rob' technique, and was shot to death when she stopped her car. Months later, in September of the same year, another German tourist, Uwe-Wilhelm Rakebrand, was wise enough to keep moving when a yellow Ryder truck repeatedly bumped his rental car on the airport expressway – but still died at the wheel from a single shot which hit him in the back and sent his car spinning out of control into oncoming traffic. His pregnant wife successfully struggled to avoid a major collision and save her own life.

When, only a week later, a British tourist, Gary Colley, was shot to death, and his girlfriend, Margaret Anne Jagger, injured at a roadside rest stop near Monticello, in north Florida, it sealed the state's image as one big shooting range, with open season on foreigners and a flak jacket part of the

246

required dress code. The world's media had a field day. ('*How's business?*' ... '*Booming!*' cracked a Florida tourism official in a *Guardian* cartoon which showed guns blasting and bullets flying from every direction on a palm tree-lined street.) Florida's thirty-one billion-dollar tourist industry seemed in a state of cardiac arrest, and the police and car rental companies were forced to come up with all sorts of initiatives, such as dissuading visitors from renting at the airport, removing identifying stickers and licence plates from rental cars and sending undercover cops out on the streets posing as tourists – presumably clad in Mickey Mouse T-shirts, loud floral shorts and fake sunburn.

While these isolated incidents (and clearly ten in a year isn't isolated enough) were very sad, the resulting outrage had much to do with the fact that the victims were white and in the wrong place at the wrong time. For those in the wrong place *all* the time – the people who make their lives here in Liberty City, or in Overtown, or in other inner-city ghettoes across America – death is one more statistic. Local young black males, aged between fifteen and twenty-five, are more likely to be shot to death on the streets than was the average Marine fighting in Vietnam. It takes the shooting of a child – if the victim is black or Hispanic – to make news, and even then a long media attention span is hardly guaranteed. Not when, in Miami and surrounding Dade County, a child dies from a bullet every twelve days.

Four-twenty p.m.: I'd be happy to report that our first destination, as Chang's shift began, was a donut

247

shop, but instead we have been driving through the neighbourhood immediately north of N.W. Sixty-second Street, past single-storey clapboard houses of a simple construction, some newly painted, most fairly dilapidated, and each with small front yards of tangled, yellowing tropical growth.

Donuts might actually have been more exciting than our first call, which was to check out an abandoned, possibly stolen Toyota minivan. Now we're sitting in the patrol car on the corner of N.E. Seventy-sixth Street and N.E. Third Court, while Chang writes it up – in the shadow of a huge silver water tower which looms over us on its spindly legs, like one of the Martians in H. G. Wells's *The War of the Worlds.* Hawks circle overhead, and there's a remarkable sense of calm for a few minutes as people walk by or stand chatting with neighbours outside their houses. But this is a crack zone, David tells me, and he points out several young Blacks he says are crack dealers.

'They don't like me!' he says in his musical, heavily Spanish-accented English. He laughs. 'I hassle them! They'd be doing drug deals now, if I wasn't here. If I see someone white here, in a nice car, they're here to buy drugs – or they're lost.'

As we sit, waiting for a tow truck to haul the minivan away, a man walks up to us and announces through the open window of the patrol car that he has just been robbed, crossing the railroad tracks a few metres behind us.

'Four black kids, one with a gun!' gasps the man, who's Hispanic, in his mid-thirties, in an ill-fitting jacket, and sweating profusely as he talks. 'About ten minutes ago – they took my wallet!' He glances back in the direction of the tracks, still agitated.

'OK,' says Chang, trying to calm him.

'I heard footsteps,' the man goes on, 'and I said to myself, "*If I run, maybe it's bad!* " When the kid got next to me, he was nervous, he was very nervous, and he said, "*Don't move, or I'll kill you!*" '

'Did he touch you?' asks Chang, still seated beside me in the patrol car.

'Yeah, yeah,' says the man, leaning down towards the window. 'That's when he pulled out an envelope I had from a bank in Coral Gables, with five single bills in it, and my wallet – all it have is just a Medicaid card.'

'OK,' says Chang.

'The gun was small,' the man says, 'like a Saturday night special. Maybe I should have done something – I took four years of karate – but I didn't know if the gun was real or not!'

'That's a smart thing you do,' Chang tells him, smiling as he starts to call the incident in on the portable police radio at his side. 'You maybe know kung fu, but the bullet go a lot faster, believe me!'

Chang gets a brief description of the attacker, then calls it in, along with our location. The woman at the other end of Chang's police radio relays the call – 'Four black males, first subject: sixteen to seventeen years of age, actual offender about five foot three, dark complexion, short hair, blue jeans, carrying a .38 Smith and Wesson special' – then blurts out such a rapid-fire succession of police codes that she sounds like an auctioneer selling a prize pig: 'One-eleven, one-twelve, one-thirteen, one-sixteen, one-twenty-five, one-twenty-eight, oh-six, fifteen, sixteen, one-eleven!'

And yet something about the man's story doesn't quite ring true, although it could be that he's simply in shock. As he goes over the details again and again, he continues to sweat though the temperature is not high by Miami's more than generous standards. He is overweight and nervous, and through the patrol car window our main view is of the brown sleeves of his jacket, which are too short for his arms. He'd been sent out, he says, to buy groceries for his wife.

'I didn't even think I was going to make it out of there!' he exclaims. 'One of the kids, the youngest, he must have been about twelve years old! I said to the one with the gun, *"Man, I got this jacket in the flea market. I'm poor like you!" "Turn your face and keep walking, or I shoot you!"* he says. I'm not about to turn around and look – not with all the shit you see on TV . . .'

'It's not worth it,' Chang agrees, still trying to calm him down. 'Not for a few dollars.'

He tells the man to go home and we drive across the rusting railroad tracks and down a few desolate streets, looking for the kids, whom Chang thinks he would probably know. But he doesn't expect to find them: 'They're out of here,' he says. 'They're not going to be on the street now. And maybe it didn't happen exactly how the man say. You know, maybe he was going to buy crack from them and something happen, the kid pull a gun and say, *"Give me the money!"* There's a lot of stuff like that happen around here – if you want to become a cop, here is where you learn. When you work here, anywhere else is nothing!'

Six-ten p.m.: We visit a convenience store, the Food Spot, run by Habib, a friend of Chang's, also from Bangladesh, who jokes about Chang's weight, likening him to a Sumo wrestler. I ask Chang if he remembers Bangladesh, but he says, 'Only from pictures.' I'm impressed in the store that Habib seems to know all his customers by name. Despite the nature of the neighbourhood, there's still a sense of community here.

Seven p.m.: Next Chang and I sit for a while in the stationary patrol car on Biscayne Boulevard, or US-1, which along with I-95, is one of Miami's two busiest north-south routes. While this stretch, around N.E. Seventy-second Street, is a lot safer than it used to be, thanks to increased policing, it still isn't the best place for a family night out.

'Mostly here, it's prostitution,' says Chang, as we watch a weary-looking black woman in a tight green dress and a wig strut her stuff outside a tawdry motel. She might be a transvestite, it's hard to tell from this distance, but whatever she is, she seems a world apart from Julia Roberts in *Pretty Woman*. 'Most of the hookers are doing crack.' Chang nods in the woman's direction and she seems to sense this, turning and glancing our way, then hesitating before moving round a corner, out of sight. 'She sell her body for five, ten, twenty dollars. Maybe if she can find an idiot who pay fifty dollars, that's her money for the day! But mostly they do rock – which cost ten dollars – then she's back on the street in twenty minutes.'

This stretch of Biscayne is curious, because it's lined with strip clubs and tacky-looking, neon-lit motels with exotic, adventure-promising names like The Sinbad or The Seven Seas – offering exotic, adventure-filled extras, such as 'T.V.' (*yes!*) – yet it's hard to imagine many travellers, in their right minds, stopping here. Not surprisingly, Chang says that much of the business is done by the hour.

I ask if he's ever had to deal with any of the highly publicized tourist attacks in Miami, and he tells me that in October 1992, when he was working a different sector, out by the airport, he was the first on the scene of one of the earliest incidents involving a German visitor. Renate Morlock had been sitting with her husband and two daughters in a car outside a McDonald's at the corner of N.W. Thirty-sixth Street and Twenty-second Avenue, when three black youths, all sixteen or younger, approached her car. One of them, Antwan Brown, then aged fourteen and carrying a gun, opened the passenger door and tried to grab Morlock's handbag, but in a reflex action, she refused to let go.

'What happened,' explains Chang, 'was they went to rob the lady. The kid really didn't want to shoot her, but because the lady was fighting with him, he got nervous and he shot her.'

Hearing him describe it, as the lights of cars flash by on Biscayne, it all seems quite reasonable – but it's not hard to imagine Morlock's fear and confusion, nor even perhaps the mixture of stupidity, bravado and anxiety on Antwan Brown's part.

'At the time I arrived,' says Chang, 'I tried to talk to the lady and the husband and to the girls. The only big problem – they don't know English, and I don't know German! So it was a big barrier. We no can get description, no nothing. I went with the lady to the hospital. We stayed like five or six hours, she was in surgery, in emergency care. The next day, I meet with the investigators, they tell me that the lady got paralyzed, because the bullet went straight to the spinal column. One shot, right through the armpit. There wasn't much blood, a little spot. That's why we thought she was OK, but I feel bad. She had to go back to Germany in a wheelchair.'

Brown and his two friends were finally caught, following a re-enactment of the crime. Brown plea bargained a charge of attempted first degree murder, and was sentenced to twenty years, out of which he will probably serve nine. His defence attorney, Larry Sparks, thought the sentence unduly harsh, reflecting a view here, especially among African-Americans, that crimes against tourists receive special attention, while crimes against local people – which are obviously far more numerous – carry less weight.

'This boy is really a sacrifice to the tourism industry,' Sparks said. 'If this case didn't involve a tourist, it would have been handled in juvenile court. This would have been a five- or six-year sentence.' All the same, Renate Morlock will never walk again.

Seven-twenty p.m.: As I ride with Chang, I find it hard to get to grips with my own feelings about these attacks – and about violence in Miami generally. I know the city's reputation, but in the five years I've been here, I've never felt at threat. I've been at nightclubs, on the streets, and on the beach, at all hours of the day and night, and the only even halfway violent incident I've witnessed or been involved in was when I took a couple of punches outside a camera store – from one of the store managers – after an argument over a camera I had bought escalated when, to make a point, I walked out with the store's own cellular phone. The only guns I've seen drawn were in my first week here, by the woman I bought most of my furniture from, and by someone I was dating, who playfully held a small pistol to my head. I often feel more anxious on the London Underground at night than I do anywhere in Miami – but to be fair, I wouldn't plan on visiting Overtown or Liberty City on foot at night, although I wish that I could.

And now, bouncing around the battered interior of a police car, red-and-blue lights flashing and siren wailing, as Chang speeds through darkened streets to answer a call to a break-in at an elementary school, I feel the adrenalin rush cops must at first love and then get weary of. I *know* this is real, and I *know* real people get hurt out there and die, leaving family and friends as devastated as I was when I lost my son, yet still it feels like a movie, and I wonder if that's part of the problem. Not that in America everything seems like a movie sometimes, and so violence seems glamorous; but that violence *is* glamorous, in the sense that it scares and excites, it sends hormones pumping and emotions rushing, and makes everything more immediate even as it makes it somehow removed . . . less real . . . like a movie.

This isn't just a twentieth-century phenomenon, either; it's not movies that are to blame. I remember, in Flaubert's *Sentimental Education*, Frédéric walks through the bloodshed and riotous upheaval of mid-nineteenth-century Paris and is struck by how

254

unreal the suffering seems – how like a masque you might see at the theatre.

Certainly tonight seems quite fantastic as we arrive at the Little River Elementary School, in the company of three other patrol cars. I'm sure that by the standards of this sector, a possible break-in at a school is literally child's play – and in England, I can't imagine the police would feel particularly stressed at all – but in the dark shadows of Little River's clustered buildings, Chang feels prompted to snap open the trunk of the car and retrieve the pump-action, Remington A-70 Express Magnum shotgun he carries, in addition to the handgun in his holster. Maybe this is partly for effect – because I'm here. The other cops seem fairly relaxed as they spread out around the grounds, flashlights in hand, the school's alarm system blinking soundlessly above us, but as with anything in America, and especially in this part of Miami, there is a small but real risk that someone will shoot at you.

In the event, nothing happens, and when we are joined by the school superintendent – who walks up, booming, '*All right, all right!*' in an accent that sounds Jamaican but is actually Nicaraguan – I sense that, on a Friday night, an alarm call at a school is decidedly routine.

Eight-twenty p.m.: The light from an illuminated sign outside the King Motel, back on Biscayne, fills the patrol car.

GOD BLESS YOU NICE ROOMS, reads the neon – so that you can't be sure whether it's the customer or the rooms that will be blessed. PHONE AVAILABLE BEST RATES.

There don't seem to be many customers around to be blessed, not even a transvestite crackhead hooker in sight, so when Chang has finished writing his report on the elementary school call-out (paperwork, I am coming to understand, is an overwhelming part of any cop's working hours), I ask if I can handle his gun. I try to explain how alien it is, coming from a non-gun culture such as Britain, even to *see* guns at close range, but it all feels very odd – almost intimate: like asking for a first kiss.

Carefully Chang takes his gun and removes the magazine clip and a bullet from the chamber, before passing it to me.

'It's a Glock,' he says. 'Nine millimetre. Made in Austria.'

He shows me how to cock it, letting me pull the slide back with a satisfying click. And he shows me how you can get your finger caught: 'Believe me, a lot of people get a big chunk of meat out!'

'It's all plastic, except for the chamber?'

'The chamber and the slide, that's metal. All the rest, the handle, the grip, all that's plastic. Even the magazines are plastic. They do it that way because it's very light weight and it's comfortable. They went through a lot of stuff. When we test this gun, they put it through mud, through sand, they shoot it under the water, everything! It's very good, this gun.'

He talks about it enthusiastically, even affectionately, and I can see how he might feel that way – this gun could save his life. But more than that, there's an undeniable thrill in holding a gun, no matter that it could take a life – or take nineteen lives, given the clip of bullets beside me.

Holding it, I'm thrown back to a gun show I went to in Coconut Grove, during my first months in Miami. I went with my friend, Jodi, who had grown up on a farm in Pennsylvania and was very comfortable around firearms, but for me the fact that I could walk into the show and, with a Florida driver's licence and eight hundred dollars, or an American Express card, walk out carrying an Uzi, came as a surprise.

'What do you *do* with an Uzi?' I asked the gentleman selling them, as I slammed an empty magazine into the weapon in my hands. 'I can see how, if you're a drug dealer or something, one might come in handy – but who uses them otherwise?'

'Well, *I* have one,' the man responded, sounding a little affronted. 'I go into a field and fire it off.' He grinned, catching the gleam in my eye as I waved my empty Uzi this way and that around the convention centre, only a block or two away from all those tourists out there. 'Of course, they're expensive to use,' he said. 'You get through a lot of shells.' Happiness, I thought, is a warm gun.

When I tell Chang that I was surprised at how easy it is to buy an Uzi, he reminds me that the law has changed – there's now a mandatory seven-day waiting period. An Uzi, he tells me, can be semi-automatic or automatic.

'Semi-automatic is like the Glock,' he says. 'Every time you want to shoot, you have to press once the trigger.' He mimes doing it with his gun: '*Pop one! Pop two! Pop three!* That's semi-automatic. Automatic, once you press the trigger, it go *brrrrrrrrrr*, until you finish all the magazine.' I feel

as if we are kids again, talking about toy guns –
except that these are real: they kill. The sense of
innocence is only enhanced by the way Chang
pronounces 'trigger', which makes it sound like
'*tiger*'. He smiles at me in the cool glow from the
motel's sign.

'That's why the Uzis, any full automatic machine
gun, is illegal in this country. The only way you can
have one is you're a collector and you have to get a
special permit and all this stuff. Those Uzis you saw
in Coconut Grove are semi-automatic.' Now he
looks at me slyly. 'But those Uzis, I know how to do
it. You get a file and take the firing pin, the spring,
and you file it down and make it full automatic!'

Chang hasn't had anyone shoot at him with a full
automatic, but his friends on the force have: 'We
have a big shooting, like five, six months ago. The
guy was using a full automatic Uzi, full of bullets.'

I ask him the same question I asked at the gun
show: 'Why would anyone buy an Uzi, except to
commit a crime?'

'People like it,' he says. 'Like me, I'm a gun
collector. I love guns! I even do my own bullets. The
little head, I do myself. The case, I buy, they come
from the factory, but I drill all my bullets, I put my
own powder, to go practising. There's a lot of people
like that. And especially if you're a hunter and like
to go hunting once in a while. But no, I don't know
why people want to buy Uzis.' He grins. 'To protect
your house, it's really not convenient. You're better
with a shotgun than an Uzi.'

Still no-one has gone into the motel, and I'm surprised at how quiet Chang's radio has been: it's

258

almost nine o'clock on a Friday night and nothing much is happening. But perhaps perversely, I feel that talking about guns has brought us closer – even if, despite my evident pleasure in handling them, nothing will shift my not entirely unique belief that they lie at the heart of America's problem with violence and should be banned. Gun supporters can endlessly rehearse all the usual arguments about the constitutional right to bear arms (wilfully misinterpreted, opponents say), or the fact that criminals will always find a way to get hold of weapons, or – a particularly annoying chestnut – that '*Guns don't kill people, people do!*' The figures speak for themselves: thirty-three thousand gun-related deaths in a single year in the US, as opposed to twenty-five (deaths, not thousand) in Britain, and even fewer in Australia. Thirty-three thousand. As a British friend, Robert Elms, once observed: 'That's not a crime statistic, that's civil war!'

At the same time, I would not suggest, at any point in the near future, sending police officers like Chang out on the streets without protection. When I ask if he's ever had to shoot anyone, he says, 'Not yet,' but admits that the closest he came was at a domestic incident.

'One time, I have a call,' he sighs, as we make a U-turn on Biscayne in search of food. 'Like a boyfriend-girlfriend fight. And when we get there, the girlfriend tell us that the boyfriend have a machete and was cutting her face and arm. She have lacerations, she was bleeding! And she tell us he just left, like two minutes ago, and was probably going to the grocery store around the corner.

'So myself and my partner went that way. I got

259

there first, and I saw the black guy with the same description, with the machete in his hand, full of blood! I pull out my gun and I say, *"Stop! Drop the machete!"* Then I say in Spanish, *"Bota el machete!"* We give warnings in languages – if I know five languages, I give it in five languages!

'He keep coming to me. I say, *"If you no stop and drop the machete, I have to shoot you!"* The guy keep coming at me, I already was pulling my trigger to shoot the guy. But – maybe let's say, less than a second – my partner arrived there, the guy saw my partner and he dropped the machete. But if my partner was, let's say, five seconds late, I would shoot the guy.'

It's because of situations like this that officers are required to request backup before intervening in potentially violent situations. Chang says he didn't feel nervous. 'But that's with a machete. Maybe with a knife, that's a different situation – because a knife, he can throw it at you, and if he's a good knife-thrower, he can kill you!'

Nine p.m.: Meal break, and as we sit in a Wendy's hamburger joint on US-1, opposite the Pussycat All-Nude Show, I feel that I'm starting to get the rhythm of Chang's wearying, ten-hour shift. Certainly I notice that cops tend to get good service, wherever they go.

It's been a quiet night so far partly because we're covering Sector 20, which is east of Sector 10 and Liberty City proper. But Chang has talked to a fellow officer in Sector 10, and even he has had only three calls so far, this shift.

Chang tells me a story of how, when he was just

starting out at the Police Academy (you remember the movies), some kids stole his car – his own car, not a police vehicle. 'It took seven days to find it, where they dump it in a river in Opa Locka! They wrote "Cop" and "Pig" all over the car. They break the stereo, they cut my shirts in pieces, they even steal a jacket!' But worse, it cost him three hundred and twenty-five dollars to have it towed out of the water.

Perhaps because of this tale, I don't feel as critical as I might when we run into a little obstruction as Chang tries to reverse the patrol car out of its spot in the Wendy's parking-lot. Another car is blocking our path, while its driver, a young black guy, waits for his girlfriend to buy take-out from the restaurant. The driver has seen us get into the patrol car and has made no effort to move. Chang starts the engine and turns on his lights. Still the driver doesn't budge. 'He knows,' says Chang. 'He's fucking with us. Now I'm going to fuck with him!'

He turns on his red-and-blue lights and briefly sounds the siren, to let the driver know he's being pulled over. 'Even if he have only a parking ticket due,' Chang says, 'I'm going to make him look bad in front of his girlfriend.'

So he has the driver get out of the car and stand and wait while Chang checks *everything* – his driver's licence, the papers for the car, whether it's been reported stolen, whether there are any out-standing charges against the driver, whether he ever took another kid's hamburger bun at school . . .

By now, of course, the driver knows he pushed things too far. Sharply dressed and perhaps usually a little cocky, he glumly sits on the boot of his car, waiting for the ordeal to be over. His girlfriend, who emerged some time back with their food, is clearly pissed off with Chang, but looks as if she might give her boyfriend a hard time about this later, too.

Nine-thirty p.m.: A more sympathetic side to Chang emerges as we check out a minor burglary at a low-income apartment house on the edge of Lemon City, just east of – and indistinguishable from – Liberty City.

A dignified but somewhat dishevelled man of about forty, who introduces himself as Mr Jackson, has reported the theft of four bottles of cologne from the single, padlocked room he rents. He estimates their value at about twenty dollars. Through the gravity of his tone and the rich Caribbean accent with which he tells of his loss, he paints this as a tragedy on a scale unimagined by Dostoievsky, and Chang seems moved by Mr Jackson's concern – as I am by the small details of others' lives which police officers must witness every day.

Mr Jackson is wearing a baseball cap, a personal stereo, trousers but no shirt, and I try not to stare at the scars graffitied across the dark flesh of his back – the result of severe burns or maybe a car wreck. I glance around his room – gloomy and cluttered with books, yet otherwise almost empty – as he explains that the crime occurred after he had padlocked the door, while he was walking down the street, drinking a beer with his friend, Fred. He thinks it was the people upstairs who did it, and he tries to persuade Chang to have the room dusted for fingerprints.

'I read a lot,' he says. 'I have a disability. I know the law. I know that if you leave a pack of cigarettes in your car and the window is open, and someone puts their arm in and takes them, it's still theft!'

As we leave, I ask Chang how cheap a room like Mr Jackson's would be to rent. 'Not so cheap,' Chang says. 'He might pay two hundred and fifty, three hundred dollars for a room like that.' (By comparison, you can find a decent, one-bedroom apartment on trendy South Beach for six or seven hundred dollars a month.) 'The landlord, he have five rooms in the house – maybe he makes the same on all the rooms. It leads to a lot of unpaid rent, a lot of fights.'

Ten p.m.: We answer a call to another apartment house about a missing thirteen-year-old Haitian girl, Erliette, who hasn't been seen since she went to the grocery store at four o'clock. The old, red-tile roofed apartment building stretches a surprising distance back from the street and as we walk along its side, even in the darkness it seems more welcoming than many of the places we've visited tonight. We hear the murmur of a TV from inside, see the lights of a plane passing silently overhead – and find the girl's family outside on the stoop which leads to their home.

The girl's mother speaks Creole, but barely any English, so the girl's stepfather translates. A brother stands on the steps, while we hear another child playing inside. Everyone looks stern-faced, standing with arms folded but not much emotion in evidence – except for the mother, who seems as angry as she is anxious. She tells Chang that Erliette was born in Haiti, 'but she coming small': she came to Miami when she was little.

Chang asks for a picture of Erliette. The photo that's produced makes her look like any other

263

schoolgirl – bright eyed but slightly bored. Erliette's mother becomes agitated again, speaking rapidly and angrily in Creole, but the stepfather silences her with a single, '*Tsssssk!*' sound.

'OK, Papa,' Chang tells him, sounding reassuring as we leave them and walk back, past a few curious neighbours, to the police car.

Outside on the street, sitting in the patrol car while Chang radios in the details then writes out yet another report, he doesn't seem too concerned by the girl's disappearance.

'If she is four or five,' he says, 'then we would go to the store and start checking, maybe have ten or twenty men out looking. But thirteen – she probably go somewhere with her friends.'

Chang's police radio is busier now than it has been all evening, crackling with disjointed words and endless police code numbers: 'nineteen', a traffic violation; 'thirty-one', a homicide ('Somebody already got killed,' says Chang); 'thirty-two', a possible homicide or aggravated battery.

Erliette's street is dark and quiet. I think about how it must feel to be a parent in Liberty City or Little Haiti or any of the more dangerous areas. I know plenty of people who have grown up in Miami without a constant fear of violence, but they're mostly from the suburbs. In these less affluent streets, a parent's usual anxieties must be vastly multiplied. And the children themselves must also live with the shadow of the gun. Recently a three-year-old Haitian child was killed in the crossfire of a 'gang' incident – but the gangs themselves are children, often no more than twelve or fourteen years old. I remember reading a *Miami Herald* article about growing up in Liberty City, which quoted one black, thirteen-year-old boy, Duncan, as saying, '*I don't walk around because I'd be scared that someone might pull a gun.*' Marquena, a little girl of nine, said: '*If we be in the street, one day we might be in somebody's business and they might shoot.*' When people see crime as divided by race, they must accept the consequences of not putting an enormous effort into ensuring that the Duncans and Marquenas live in a better environment.

Ten-thirty p.m.: As we're about to drive away from Erliette's block, two young Haitian girls appear by the patrol car window, a little sheepishly peering inside.

Chang looks at me. '*Ha!* Don't tell me that's her!' He turns to them and asks, 'Who are you?'

'Me?' one of the girls replies. 'Did a lady call the police?'

'Yeah,' Chang tells her, smiling warmly. 'Any of you are the lady that is missing from the house?'

'It was her,' the first girl says.

'It was me,' the other girl agrees, flashing an awkward smile.

'No!' Chang laughs. 'You don't look like your little picture.'

And it turns out that Erliette was, as Chang predicted, safe all the time – with her cousin, the first girl, 'doing her hair'.

'You made me do all this paperwork, and you're here now?' Chang asks in mock consternation. Then, more seriously: 'How's your stepfather with you? He's OK?'

The little girl shakes her head. 'My stepfather? Oh, no, he's going to scream at me!'

'What about your mother?'

'I think she's going to beat me,' Erliette says, worriedly. 'She's going to start hitting me right here!'

'Well, I would beat you, too, if you're going to the store and you never come back, and you never even call the house!'

But Chang is still smiling at her, and when the parents join us on the street and Erliette's mother, after a brief display of relief, starts berating her in Creole, Chang takes the mother aside and delivers a polite warning. 'Do what you have to do,' he tells her, 'but don't do it too much – otherwise I come back and arrest you for abusing your daughter!'

He turns to the stepfather, who's been translating, and who seems the more benign influence in the household. 'OK, Papa,' he says again, leaving Erliette's fate in his hands.

After we've left, Chang worries that the girl is going to be punished too severely. He says Haitian families are big on discipline. 'The mother going to hit her hard, I know! She going to get something and hit her good. The father, I doubt it. But the mother will. That's why I tell her, "*Don't do it much*," because she hit her too much, I can take the mother to jail, that's abuse. One is punishment and one is abuse.'

Eleven p.m.: We answer a call of a shooting, back in the neighbourhood where we were almost eight hours ago, this afternoon. 'It's quiet tonight,' Chang says, despite the unending jabber and static from the police radio. 'Maybe there's a lot of stuff going on in Sector 10, but if there's too much, they call me, so it have to be very quiet.'

The shooting is nothing major, simply a report of a few gunshots heard in the street. Five black youths, aged between sixteen and eighteen, have already been stopped by other officers and are standing by a white Chevrolet, parked at the side of the street. Other kids stand around watching, laughing and joking, not taking any of this too seriously.

'Any guns in the car?' one of the officers asks.

'Yeah, but I got papers for it,' a kid dressed in a green T-shirt replies calmly, as if he's been through this before.

'All right, do me a favour,' the officer says. 'Everybody get on that side of the car!'

And everybody moves round, as if it's a game of musical chairs, while the officer retrieves the gun from the back floor of the car.

'It's a little .22, eh?' Chang asks.

'No, it's a .25,' the kid in the green shirt tells him.

'Have you ever been arrested before?' the officer asks.

'Yeah, about a year ago,' the kid replies smartly.

'Have you ever been arrested?' the officer asks another boy in a woollen cap.

'Yeah. Auto theft.' No attitude, no defiance, but cool, as though he knows the ropes.

'How old are you?'

'Eighteen.'

Because the gun is in the car – where no doubt one of the kids dropped it – rather than on their persons, they won't be charged with carrying a concealed weapon, which is a felony. In fact, because

267

the papers for the gun look OK, and it isn't really possible to prove that it has been fired tonight, the officer merely puts the gun, clip and bullets separately in the Chevy's trunk and tells the kids, 'Wait till we leave to open it up.'

As we drive away, I'm surprised to hear that Chang, as a gun collector, nonetheless favours stronger gun control.

'School is a big problem now,' he says. 'Those eleven- and twelve-year-old kids have got guns and they are killing each other, shooting each other. The kid in school, he have friends around the neighbourhood or maybe from the same school, they are dealing with drugs, they know more than him. So he's drafted: *"Oh, here, you want to be cool, you come with us! We give you guns, we get money!"* That's how it's going, step by step. So they give him the gun, so he wants to show off. So that's a problem. The gun control here has to be strongly enforced, because there's too much guns, too much.'

Eleven-fifty p.m.: On our way downtown, to the main Miami Police Station, to refuel the car and stock up on stationery for the eternity of paperwork police business entails, Chang drives me through Overtown, which he used to patrol.

Miami's other most notoriously violent neighbourhood, Overtown, like Liberty City, is predominantly black and poor. Near-derelict houses spill out onto the streets. Abandoned stores and other businesses rot in the shadow of the elevated Metrorail and the web of elevated highways which tore this once thriving area apart. There's a powerful sense of dislocation. Pockets of poor young Blacks gather at the lighted doors of shacks which serve as all-night liquor marts, or in an open-fronted pool hall which, with thriving tropical weeds slowly strangling the adjacent, vacant lot, might be buried in the heart of Jamaica or St Vincent – not here beneath Florida's constantly moving, often suspect night traffic.

From the perspective of a car, especially a police car, again everything seems unreal, the detail lit by streetlamps or our headlights; faces turning, hostile or guarded at the sight of a patrol car, giving nothing away.

'You see this, this is like the movie, *Zombie*!' Chang declares and laughs. 'All these people in the street! These are bad people. This is a bad area.' He points to a group of kids clustered in the shadows around a low wall. 'You see, those are typical *roberes*!' The word comes out like a tortured cross between Spanish and English. 'They're staying in their corner to check out people with car, with stuff in the back, so they make their little signal, and the people down there, maybe they're waiting – *pah!* – they get them.'

But I wonder, looking at the people hanging out, gathered in groups, drinking, talking and listening to music, just how bad they are. A black woman in her twenties cycles past on a bike. A young Rastafarian couple walk with their daughter, a little girl of about three with dreadlocks. The mood is so strongly Caribbean that I wish I could come down here alone and drink. I'm sure I'd be fine, but there's just that tiny chance that I'd choose the wrong night or the wrong street.

I think about a homeless man I talked to one night, around this time, at the bus stop by

269

Government Centre in downtown Miami – which is certainly more deserted than Overtown at night, and sometimes seems more desolate.

James was Black, probably about thirty and from Orlando, though he hadn't been back there for two years. He had a sister there, he told me, but he no longer had any contact with the rest of his family. 'We've all got to look out for ourselves.'

He wanted a dollar at first and I gave him the change I had, maybe seventy-five cents, maybe a little more, but mostly he wanted to talk. One old man had just brushed him away. 'Maybe he's been mugged before,' said James.

He asked if I liked Miami. Said he couldn't find a job, he'd been looking all last week. He had such a quiet earnestness, I wanted to believe him. 'I'm not prejudiced,' he said, 'but it's difficult getting a job here if you don't speak Spanish.'

He asked if I'd ever been to Germany. He'd been there for eighteen months, in the army. He talked about the '*poof*' houses, the brothels. He pointed to Miami's old courthouse windows and said the '*poof*' houses were like that, women in all the windows.

I said it was so quiet downtown at night. He told me there were strange people around. A man last week, walking down Flagler, downtown's main shopping street, totally naked. The police arrested him. Another man who came up to James and said, 'Do you know the Devil?'

'I know of him,' James replied.

'Do you like to play games with the Devil?'

James walked away from him fast.

We shook hands a couple of times and I gave him

the two slices of pizza I was taking home in a box. I'd thought about taking a taxi from the Metrorail, instead of waiting ten or fifteen minutes for the bus – downtown always seems so bleak at night – but I was glad we'd talked instead. James seemed grateful for the company, the contact. Then I remembered Mariel Hemingway's line at the end of *Manhattan*, which had been much on my mind that night:

'*You have to have a little faith in people.*'

Twelve-ten a.m.: Chang's shift ends at one a.m., but the officers on the night shift have been on call since nine p.m., putting double the manpower on the streets during the crucial late evening hours. Which is probably just as well, since Chang admits he's tired, and I'm getting that end-of-a-long-haul blurriness that makes the crackle and fizz of Chang's police radio increasingly weird.

'It has to be a white knight for me, twenty, over,' reports a male officer across the airwaves.

'We're on twenty-five, open,' responds the female dispatcher, then her voice bobs up and down on a sea of static. 'You might pop a lee... might pee on me... or carry things in for personal-many-stops... for my love, echo three six delta.'

'Yo, biggee,' the officer replies – or I think he does. 'More bad on the vehicle!'

As we drive back towards Liberty City, Chang spots a friend of his in another patrol car. '*Conyo Mendes!*' he cries, rolling down his window. The other cop, Mendes, shouts something back. Chang looks at me and laughs. '*Mi* observer!' he calls through the window to Mendes. 'He's a writer! So he's . . . you know, he want somebody throw a rock

271

at me, so I can shoot him!' Now I'm laughing, too. 'He want some action,' Chang cries out, 'but there's no action in Liberty City!'

Twelve-twenty a.m.: But ten minutes later, there is. Just as he's winding down, ready to go home and sleep, Chang receives a call that a man has been shot in the head outside an apartment building on the fringes of Sector 10. It's not his call, but Chang knows that, vulture-like, this is the sort of thing I expected to see.

When we arrive, the area is already cordoned off with police tape and several patrol cars and two ambulances are on the scene. The victim, a grey-haired, gentle-faced African-American man in his fifties, is lying where he was shot, on a patch of dirt under a canopy in the front yard of the low-rent apartment complex. Neighbours gather around, mostly black, mostly middle-aged. As we approach, another black man who seems as if he might have been the victim's friend, stands by one of the ambulances, weeping.

'Why they have to shoot a man like that?' he asks. 'Why they have to shoot a man?'

The victim's name is John. We watch as paramedics ease him onto a stretcher. He has been shot just above his right ear. Blood is everywhere, and some vaguely solid matter is protruding from the wound, which holds a special fascination: it seems unreal, like prosthetics, special effects. More so than at any other point tonight, I have the sense of a movie. Isolated in pools of light, the onlookers might be extras, or a film crew. I hear crickets in the grass, snatches of dialogue, bursts of static from police radios – it sounds as if it's dubbed. The softly enveloping night heat only heightens my disbelief that a man may be dying in front of me. Why don't I feel more?

I stare at John's face as he's carried to an ambulance, trying to intuit some sense of who he is behind his weary, lined skin and short, matted hair. He looks peaceful but dazed, as if he's already one step removed from everything around him. No-one knows quite what happened, except that there may have been an argument. He has two gunshot wounds, the other in his body.

Chang and I mount the steps of the ambulance to peer inside. Across the road is a Jewish home for the elderly. A young policewoman joins us and asks, with compassion rather than callousness: '*Did you see his brains coming out of his head?*' There is an excitement, an agitation, to her manner which suggests that inwardly she's having a hard time dealing with this.

We watch the paramedics as they try to cut open John's shirt and hook up an IV bag, but in some reflex action beyond consciousness, he struggles with them, his arms flailing as he tries to hold them off.

'Don't fight us, Charlie!' they shout, battling to save him. In the background, I hear the crickets again. A plane flies overhead.

Twelve-fifty a.m.: We return to the Liberty City station, where I ask Chang how he feels, watching someone close to death.

'You get used to it,' he says. 'The harder part is the first look, all the blood, the guts and the smell.' His

273

most haunting memory is of a traffic accident victim who died in his arms – a woman who had been crushed by a car. This may be in part because he considers many of the victims of violence he comes across in Liberty City 'bad people', or it might simply be that it is the most intimate and moving experience he has had of death itself.

I thank Chang for his time and consideration, say good night and shut myself in the solitude of my rented car. I happen to have with me a tape of an old rap track, 'Follow The Leader', by Erik B and Rakim, that I used to play to numb the pain after my son died. I slide it into the car's cassette player now and turn up the volume. Whatever Erik B and Rakim intended, the lyrics always seemed to me to apply universally; we are all slaves in different ways:

> But remember – you're not a slave
> Because we was put here to be much more than that
> But we couldn't see because our mind was trapped
> But I'm here to
> Break away the chains
> Take away the pain . . .

As I speed back along the elevated concrete snake of I-95, Miami is wide open before me, drawing me on along this strangely deserted expressway: the troubled streets of Liberty City to my right, the dark mass of Biscayne Bay and the Beach to my left, the lights of the downtown skyline ahead, each one like a crisply burning dollar bill.

I feel charged, I can feel my emotions racing – that sense of invulnerability again that comes from ten hours spent riding in a cop car, but also its opposite:

the struggle I've just witnessed between life and death. There *is* violence out there, but it grows only greater unless we treat all of its victims with equal concern – unless we refuse to let it blind us or divide us.

I don't believe in 'bad people', only bad acts.

John died from his bullet wounds.

24

UNBELIEVABLE, DAD

I'm not sure why, but the clock is ticking. With a definite sense of time running out, I'm thrilled when my best pal from London, the nefarious Spike Denton, arrives in Miami with a Scottish friend, Hamish Renfrew, in tow.

Hamish is a pilot and, like all true Scots, a madman, whom I first heard about a few months before, when Spike called and babbled down the phone that he had just had one of the most incredible days of his life. Hamish had turned forty, and to celebrate his birthday, had flown five or six friends, including Spike, across the Channel to Paris for lunch. More than that, he had let each of them take a turn at the controls.

'It was unbelievable, Dad!' Spike told me, using the shared nickname all of us who know Spike use – for no known reason – for each other. 'I flew the fucker for about twenty minutes! Hamish would say, "*Head for that cloud over there*," I'd touch the controls and we'd fly straight at the cloud. It's the most incredible high. You've got to try it!'

Which is the plan now. We stand, Spike, Hamish, my girlfriend, Charong, and I, on a peaceful suburban airfield, under the warm blue heavens of a South Florida Sunday morning so perfect it could almost be a dream. Here I am, with people I love, about to take the controls of a plane for the first time in my life and fly north, up the coast, to a tiny island for lunch. Even the heat god is with us, the air temperature balmy and in no mood yet to slap us around.

Hamish has made all the arrangements, renting the plane for the day, telling us pilot jokes ('What does LUFTHANSA stand for? "*Let Us Fuck The Hostess And Not Say Anything!*" '), staying sober for the twenty-four hours before the flight – no mean feat on South Beach – even helping us *find* Tamiami Airport in the car, with the aid of his trusty GPS, an almost pocket-sized, digital 'Global Positioning System' which locks on to a signal from the control tower and, on a tiny screen, shows you your position on, or relative to, the ground.

Now, as we climb up via the wing into the surprisingly small, blue and white, four-seater Trinidad TB-20 aircraft we're to fly in, loading a few cold drinks and sweatshirts into the rear (it can get chilly up there, Hamish has warned), I feel in good hands. Hamish may be a madman and a Scot, but he's also very serious about flying. I sit up front, next to him, with Charong and Spike directly behind us. There are only two radio headsets in the cockpit, so for the moment, Hamish and I put them on. Once we're airborne, we'll be able to communicate with the others only by shouting above the engine noise.

Hamish runs me through a few basics, the most important being that the control stick currently lodged in my sweaty palm is ultra-sensitive and responds best to a gentle touch. If I move it too far, the plane will lurch accordingly.

'Just imagine it's a woman's nipple you're

holding,' urges our captain over my radio headset, his confident manner matching his tanned, rather sporty features, 'and not your dick!'

I will take off, he tells me, under his guidance – but only one of us will have control at any one time. (There is a second control stick on his side of the aircraft.) 'When I tell you, "*You have control*," ' he says, 'you acknowledge it by replying, "*I have control.*" When you pass control back over to me, you tell me, "*You have control*," and I'll then acknowledge it back.' He's very firm about this, and since our lives may depend on it, I'm in no mood to argue.

As the Trinidad's engine kicks into gear and Hamish clears us for departure with the Tamiami Tower controller, the reality of this little adventure suddenly strikes me. I'm not so much nervous as wary – that I'll cock something up and either Hamish will have to pull us out of a nosedive, or we'll never make it off the ground and I'll simply run the plane into a tree.

I glance behind at Charong and Spike, who both seem remarkably cheery. Browner than an Aztec, his tan set off by a spiky short blond coiff, Denton grins enthusiastically and gives me a wink. Charong, dark-haired and glowing despite a slight summer cold, beams a smile at me and thankfully voices no thoughts along the lines of, '*We're all going to die!* '

We taxi onto the runway and I take hold of the stick. I concentrate, thankful that I have no fear of flying – I have a fear of *falling*, especially from a great height at night into a cold, dark, shark-infested sea, but that's another story.

With final clearance from the tower, Hamish tells me to pull back gently on the control as we throttle forward. Suddenly, miraculously, I feel a lift in my body and know we've left the ground. The plane seems surprisingly frail – less solid than a car – yet as I pull harder on the stick, urged on by Hamish, and we climb farther above the earth, I feel safe, cocooned within this little contraption of metal, glass and plastic in a way that I can only compare to childhood fantasies of 'sailing', while riding a home-made wooden go-cart.

The airport vanishes below us and we pass over toy houses and trees, wisps of cloud drifting by the windows as we steadily climb. I glimpse the glistening water of Biscayne Bay to one side, the strangely distinct islands of Key Biscayne and Miami Beach, and beyond those the big blue of the Atlantic Ocean, but right now I'm concentrating on a bigger blue – the sky – as we reach five thousand feet and Hamish tells me to ease the stick forward and level out.

I spend a few minutes practising keeping the wing-tips in line with a hopefully reliable horizon of clouds, but then Hamish assumes control in order to navigate us around the fiendishly busy airspace that blankets Miami International Airport. I'm glad for the break. The take-off was a joy to experience, but I would hardly say I'm a natural, and the concentration involved – not least my rather forced efforts to keep my movements gentle, which instead resulted in a marked jerkiness at times – has left me feeling a little wired. I relax, finally able to gaze out of the cockpit at the vast sprawl of Miami below, amazed at the detail I can see from this height: the sun glinting off car windows, teardrop-sized swimming pools in suburban gardens, the coin I lost a month ago in Little Havana . . . I turn again to Spike and Charong, expecting to be met by pale, ghostly reflections of their former selves – and instead find them shouting conversation at each other and staring at the view.

I take back control, a little north of Miami, but the spot we're headed for, Jekyll Island, is just over Florida's border into Georgia, three and a half hours' flying time away, so for much of the trip Hamish leaves the plane on autopilot, pausing only to demonstrate a few tricks. At one point, he flies us straight into a cloud – not unlike slamming into a brick wall or taking one of the faster rides at Disney World, only a good deal more mysterious. Shortly after, he tilts the Trinidad on its side, wings to the ground at a ninety degree angle, which provides enough of a rush to prompt a unanimous decision *not* to loop the loop this trip.

As we journey up Florida's east coast, we're tempted to try buzzing the Kennedy Space Centre, but the prospect of an F-111 shooting us out of the sky quickly loses its appeal and, anyway, Cape Canaveral is shrouded in such a haze that we'd probably ram straight into the space shuttle.

A little further north, we're just able to make out the creamy-grey fortress of St Augustine below. The oldest continuously occupied settlement in the United States, founded in 1565 by Don Pedro Menéndez de Avilés, a Spanish admiral, it was for centuries a stronghold against the pirates who plundered the galleons bearing the treasures the *conquistadores* in turn had stolen from Mexico and Peru. (Farther up is Amelia Island, once a hideout for premiere league pirates such as Blackbeard and

Captain Kidd.) Now a tourist trap, St Augustine is also close to where old Ponce de Leon first landed, which has led to a handy local industry promoting a supposed fountain – in fact, a none too inspiring well – of youth.

From our eagle's eye viewpoint, Florida looks flatter than a roadkill and, at times, about as inviting. Jacksonville, especially, seems resistible: the largest city in the state, it appears to go on for ever. I am Miami-based and Miami-biased. I love Miami's mood, its ethnic mix, its light, its transience, its position between north and south, between First World and Third, its occasional nickname: the Capital of the Caribbean. I'll have none of this north Florida hogwash.

What strikes me most, however, from up here, is how undeveloped much of the state is – still great swathes of green, giving the illusion (when you're down amongst it) that paradise is possible. I try to imagine how it must have seemed to the Spanish when they first arrived; or to the British, who governed Florida for two decades after the Spanish traded it for Havana in 1763, only to swap it back, like a ping-pong ball, this time for the Bahamas, in 1783. Or perhaps more importantly how Florida's original, indigenous people must have seen it, as many as three thousand years earlier.

When finally Hamish touches down at Jekyll Island – landings requiring just a little more practice than take-offs – we find history of a different sort. A largely unspoilt strip of forests, salt-marshes, dunes and beaches, the island's focal point is the Jekyll Island Club, an imposing Victorian hotel built in the late 1880s as a clubhouse and cottages for New York's wealthy élite (J. P. Morgan, Joseph Pulitzer, William Rockefeller, William K. Vanderbilt, an Astor or two).

With a reservation for lunch, we stride into the Grand Dining Room wearing a motley assortment of shorts, cut-off jeans and T-shirts, and carrying a *Pilot's Handbook* I've brought in order to check out such reassuringly named problems as 'Graveyard Spin', 'Carbon Monoxide Poisoning in Flight' and 'Illusions Leading to Landing Errors'.

'Where are the slaves?' inquires Charong, in a not so *sotto voce* – and of course they're still here, only now some of them are white and called waiters.

'Where are my golf shoes?' demands Spike. 'We're not leaving till we get out there on those greens.'

But we do. Following an afternoon spent navigating a small motorboat around the Jekyll River and marshes, and investigating the older cottages (including the 'Brown Cottage Chimney' – all that remains of the house millionaire Bayard Brown built, then abandoned, in 1888, sailing for England at the age of thirty-seven to become the self-exiled Hermit of the Essex Coast', self-exiled reputedly as the result of unrequited love), we return to the island's small airstrip.

Charong manages a much more impressive take-off than mine, banking the plane sharply under Hamish's instruction as we climb. We cross back into Florida, then follow the coast south as night falls. Isolated within our tiny craft, the stars seemingly close enough to touch, I recall a man I once met in New York, named Gardner, who with enormous passion told me of the beauty of flying seaplanes in the Pacific during the Second World War. He described how they would fly a large triangle from the islands up to Japan, drop their bombs (not so beautiful), then return, all in total darkness, since any kind of navigational light might attract the wrong sort of attention. It was difficult finding the islands again on the way back, and they were usually perilously low on fuel, but Gardner said that touching down on the ocean in the starlight was the most extraordinary experience.

'It was like touching down on velvet,' he said. 'Like the most incredible sex you've ever had . . .'

As the lights of Miami fan out before us like a computer graphic, our landing isn't quite as orgasmic as that, but at least we suffer no Illusions Leading to Landing Errors, and we get there. Having secured the plane for the night – literally tying its wings and tail to hooks in the tarmac – we head for South Beach and a welcoming bar.

25

THE END OF AMERICA

The clock *is* ticking, but not for me. First I hear it
from someone else – John Hood is on the 'Ten Most
Wanted' poster of the Miami Beach Police. Then I
hear it from John: he has to leave town, *fast*!

'What happened?' I ask him.

'I'm not quite on the list,' he laughs. 'But my picture's up. We're not just talking probation any
more.'

We have a farewell dinner. Charong can't make it
and Spike's no longer in town – so it's just me, John
and about ten of his friends.

We eat on Ocean Drive. John wants to treat me.
He's dressed, as ever, in a spiffy suit and hat. It's like
eating with Humphrey Bogart on speed. John orders
steak au poivre for us both and a particularly fine
red wine. He gets up to make a call. Our food
arrives. Partly because I'm in conversation with
someone else, I don't touch my plate. Hood comes
back.

'That's what I love about you, Alex,' he says, smiling the smile that seems like a tough-guy gesture but
actually betrays his big heart. 'Good manners! You
wait until I'm back to start eating. *No-one* on South
Beach does that! Here, they can't even spell "good
manners" . . .'

A night breeze is blowing, rustling the palms along the sidewalk. I stare at John. Despite his outward cool, he seems tense. I know he's wired. Uptown or downtown: the drugs of the Beach. Coke and dope.

He asks what he should do. 'Should I stay, take my lumps, or go?' His Monday night club, the Fat Black Pussycat, has started up again. There's a guy interested in franchising it in six cities across America. 'Two grand a week for doing nothing,' Hood says, 'just for keeping the concept fresh. You know, maybe Chicago one week, Atlanta the next.'

'How serious is it?' I ask, meaning his problem with the law. 'Do you think maybe you should stay and sort it out, rather than have it hanging over you?' But I know as I say it that that's not what he will do. He's going to skip town – and I'm sorry he's leaving.

I think about David Chang, the cop I went riding with, and wonder what he'd think of Hood. They might even get on. John says he has friends on the force who look out for him; certainly when he used to work club doors, the cops always seemed happy to talk to him.

'Just don't rush anything,' I say. 'Think about it.' And then, 'How well could you disappear?'

'*Huhnh!*' John laughs and snaps his fingers. 'Maybe I should go to London? London's a cool town.'

'I think they'd like you there,' I tell him. 'You could get back to writing.' My friend, Brian Antoni, who is not always entirely sympathetic when it comes to John's problems, nonetheless believes he has incredible talent as a writer – which he's wasting on South Beach.

'Yeah,' says Hood. 'London . . .' Then another of his friends says something to him, and he's off, racing in a different direction. It's late. I need sleep. I thank him for dinner and say good night. I tell him I hope that I'll see him again before he goes.

And I do. The following Monday, Charong and I call in at his club for a few moments – early, just before midnight – and he's there, different suit, same hat. He hugs us. We have a drink. 'Are you still in trouble?' I ask. 'I'm leaving,' he says. 'I just have to settle some business with the club, then I'm gone!'

'We'll miss you,' I say. And we lose him in the crowd a minute later.

A couple of weeks go by. I ask friends if they've seen John, they say no. Was he at Fat Black last week? They don't know.

I'm putting some photographs into an album, when I come across a Polaroid of him taken at my fortieth birthday party. Suit, hat, same old B-movie gangster Hood – maybe illusional, maybe self-delusional, but a good guy to have at your birthday. In the picture, we're boxing with each other. Both poseurs: we'd crumple in an instant against Tyson. Or Benn. Or Beau Jack, at seventy.

Maybe I see something of myself in Hood. I have more focus, but he has more fun . . . or so it seems. His is a different kind of intellect: faster, more fact and quote orientated. But I know he respects my work. I could never fault his behaviour towards me since we met, nor would I want to. And I have the very generous inscription he wrote in my birthday gift, a facsimile first edition of Hemingway's *For*

Whom The Bell Tolls:

> Alexander,
>   May your books, too, be reissued in rare,
> first edition facsimiles. And be collected & read
> the world over.
>
> Best, & more,
> Hood

Then one night, I get a call.

'It's Hood.'

'Hey! Where are you?'

A pause. 'You went to Cuba, right?'

'Twice. I loved it.'

'You think I should go to Havana? Or farther – to Tierra del Fuego?'

'To visit, or to stay?'

'Either. Both.'

I try to picture John Hood in Havana's old town . . . and realize it's not difficult. Hood and Havana were made for each other! John can walk those mean streets and fit right in. The old 1950s cars, the old 1940s rumba tunes. Hell, he might even run into George Raft and the boys at the casinos.

And then more seriously: 'Why not?' I tell him. 'It's starting to feel like South Beach did five years ago. There are trendy new restaurants – some of them even have food! And some people think that's where the next big club scene is going to be . . .'

He listens.

'Where are you?' I ask again.

'Key West,' he says. And for a moment, despite the hour, I wonder if he's calling from Hemingway's house.

*　*　*

I want to see him before he leaves. Charong and I have been thinking of taking a trip to the Keys – it's been a while – and this seems a good reason to go. I love the drive down, I love the drive back, and I like Key West – but a day and a night there, and I start to go stir-crazy. If South Beach sometimes feels like a small town, Key West is a hamlet by comparison. With Hood there, it will feel more like home.

We decide to rent a convertible, rather than take Charong's car. The best deal is at the airport, but this involves a ghoulish scene, waiting in line with stocky families in Bermuda shorts and 'Life's A Beach' T-shirts, while their children try to start World War Three.

Finally, at about eleven on a Thursday morning, we're in the car and ready to go. It takes only five minutes on MacArthur Causeway for me to learn that I've been in Florida long enough to understand that riding in a convertible in the middle of the day in the middle of July is *not* a good idea. You want the top down, you want to feel the wind blowing through your hair, but the vicious midday sun takes no prisoners. As you baste in your own juices, it's either put up or fry up.

We take the turnpike, the toll road that's a faster route towards Homestead and the Keys than following US-1 through South Miami. We've brought a selection of tapes along, but don't feel like listening to anything but Marvin Gaye, *What's Going On?*

After an hour or less, we hit Florida City – small enough to give Key West nationhood. The scenery starts to change, and as green stuff on either side replaces endless hoardings and discount malls, we

288

can *smell* that we're close to the Everglades – and ready for the Keys.

The top of the Keys has never much interested me. The names are great – Lake Surprise, Key Largo (Bogie again, and Betty and Edward G.) – but there are too many tacky shell shops and trailer parks, too much evidence, after the brief promise of mother nature, of gross commercialization. Maybe in a different mood, we could appreciate the consistency of style, the shift from Miami tack, which is of another hue.

'THE FUN STARTS HERE AT LARGO LODGE,' reads a sign. 'WELCOME TO THE FLORIDA KEYS,' reads another – this one wed to a huge mural of an ugly green mermaid, surrounded by seashells. 'The Seatrail Motel,' we pass. 'Flea Largo' – a flea market. 'Squid Row.' I like that. Then a large, hanging, artificial dead shark.

Prompted perhaps by the endless array of churches along the roadside – big, small, ugly, ugly – I start babbling about how the old churches in Europe were always sited in positions of power: sometimes literally strategic power, but also with regard to ley lines and the 'vibrations' of the land.

'Here, it's gas stations,' Charong argues. 'The oil companies choose very carefully where they'll site a new station – how busy the road is, how strong the competition is, whether it's a major intersection . . .' She grins at me.

And we decide perhaps gas stations *are* the true churches of America – where you can bow down to Exxon or Texaco or Shell and offer up a prayer of thanks for the freedom ('free' may be putting it a little strongly) to move across this great land.

We pass Islamorada, where I once swam with

289

dolphins at the Theatre of the Sea. It was an organized, group experience (seventy-five bucks per person at the time), but none the less remarkable for that. I remember the twenty-minute 'dolphin orientation' session before the swim, at which we were told that dolphins respond best to active participation, to diving and play – and gently warned that (a) 'Although they don't bite, they do have sharp teeth, so don't stick your hand in their mouth!' and (b) 'Male dolphins sometimes get horny and may exhibit unusual interest in women swimmers!' (I also recall the tale of a group of dolphins who became completely obsessed with one male visitor – it turned out the man had a pacemaker, whose pulse they clearly enjoyed.)

But mostly I remember the swim itself as one of the more pleasurable experiences of my life. I wish it could have been in the wild, and I feel guilty at the dolphins' incarceration, but at least it was a natural lagoon and the joy of swimming with creatures of equal size and certainly greater grace was immense. They did seem genuinely playful, nudging their heads against us when we dove, and even the 'party tricks' – when a pair of dolphins would catch our outstretched arms with their dorsal fins and tug us at speed through the water, or propel us by our feet with their noses – felt less forced or exploitative than they might sound. I resisted, however, the opportunity to buy a 'Flipper Rules!' bumper sticker.

We zip past a sign announcing Lower Matecumbe Key and turn the music up. Now the road is starting to feel as it should – wide open and exposed. The highway that links the thirty or so larger islands that form the Florida Keys is for much of its length either a bridge or a causeway, with dazzling expanses of water, space and light on all sides.

Driving along it is a dream – unless, as one friend explained after a torturous roundtrip, you have a pathological fear of bridges. There are long stretches where the old bridge, built for Henry Flagler's Overseas Railroad, runs parallel to the road, the hulking metal girders on their concrete platforms seeming less an intrusion on an idyllic natural landscape than a soulful marker of an era long departed. The old bridges (some of which are now local pathways and roads) start and stop, often ending abruptly over open water – as if a giant had taken great chunks out of them with his teeth. The giant was the calamitous 1935 hurricane which put paid to the Overseas Railroad; and the sudden breaks, with their concrete barriers, sometimes prove a fatal surprise (especially at night) to motorists, looking for adventure, who ignore the warning signs and take their cars where they're not meant to go.

Most spectacular of all is the Seven Mile Bridge between Marathon and Bahia Honda Key, a feat of engineering which you tend to take for granted as you speed across it, feeling at times closer to flying than to driving. Water has never looked bluer than the ocean does here, and as Marvin sings and we suck on the warm beer we have opened, nirvana seems perilously close.

When we reach Bahia Honda, we stop for a swim off the beaches of the State Park, which not only look exceptionally beautiful, surrounded by stands of satinwood, silver palm and gumbo limbo trees, but

291

also *smell* incredibly funky – a powerful, sulphurous, bad-egg perfume, caused by the rotting of the seagrass on the sand, with an added contribution from the tiny crustacea which hang out on the seagrass.

Somewhere around here, I was once swimming – or rather, peeing – in the shallow water, when a stranger on the bank called out, in a curious tone of voice, '*Ahm, there's a fish behind you!*'

I glanced at him and knew instantly what he meant, then looked behind me and saw a baby shark fin about thirty feet away, moving slowly in my direction. With no hesitation, I made for the beach at all speed. The shark was probably no more than three feet long, but that was three feet too much for me.

By the time we roll into Key West, the heat has dipped enough to permit us finally to lower our car's top. The sun is still fairly high in the sky, and we actually get to enjoy for an hour or two the pleasure of riding around in a convertible.

We check into an hotel, the Eden House, then set about finding Hood. He's not at the number he left, and there's no-one there to take a message, so we venture out on the streets with no particular plan in mind.

This town always surprises me with how different it is from Miami. It's far more Southern and Victorian in style, dotted with balconies and porches, but it's also more islandy – right off Duvall Street, the main drag, is Bahama Village, an area housing a mix of descendants from Civil War-era Bahamian immigrants and newer hippie/arty types. Once considered too dangerous for tourists, now it's virtually the only place left that feels like Key West used to, before its gross commercialization.

At least here, we think, not everything will have Papa's name and image on it – Hemingway dominates Key West, as if no-one else had ever lived here. Then suddenly I remember a marvellous old man I met on a previous trip, who claimed he had sparred with the Great One himself.

In a grocery store opposite a part-Caribbean, part-1960s-acidhead crafts gallery, I try a long shot and tell the owner behind the counter: 'I remember, one time when I was down here, I drove past this tiny house with all this stuff outside – shells, dolls, all kinds of things. And the guy invited me in, I can't remember his name, but he was an old black guy who told me he used to spar with Hemingway. His family even cooked me and my friend some food . . .'

'That'll be Shine!' says the owner straightaway. 'You go down this street, right to the bottom, take a right, Shine's house is right there.'

So Charong and I take the car to the small, wood-frame house on Fort Street, and sure enough the outside is decorated with a sign which reads 'Ponderosa', and a whole confusion of objects, like a kind of folk-art shrine: dolls, dolls' heads, shells, model ships, bottles, paintings, hanging beads, Christmas lights, bits of old machinery, even old baseball caps – much of the stuff laid out on the worn sidewalk or standing, propped against walls, piled or balanced on top of one another, and exposed to the elements, come rain or shine.

Having got this far, I'm somewhat hesitant to

knock on the door, but when I do, a warm and wel-coming black woman, perhaps in her thirties and wearing a T-shirt which reads, 'I Always Get My Man!' opens the screen and says hello.

I ask for Shine and she laughs and says, 'That's my father. His real name is Kermit Forbes – but every-one calls him "Shine"!'

'He does all this stuff?' asks Charong.

'Shine, he's always done this, putting things together, long as I remember,' the woman says. 'But he ain't here. That man don't tell me where he's going!'

'What's your name?'

'Kim,' she says. 'Kim Forbes.'

'I like your T-shirt,' I say.

'So do I!' she says and laughs again.

I explain about visiting before, and how hos-pitable Shine had been, and she says she's sure he'd like to talk to me, he'll be back in about an hour – but they're getting ready to go to a funeral.

I feel immediately awkward, but she doesn't seem too fussed, and when a neighbour – a large black woman on a bicycle – cycles past and calls out, 'Where's your father?', Kim laughs some more and says, 'That's what they want to know!'

She suggests maybe we can come back later, and I tell her it depends on whether we can find the friend we're looking for, and thank her for her time.

We say goodbye, then suddenly I wonder: 'Did your father really box with Hemingway?'

She looks at me. 'Well, I don't know if they *box*, but I think they had their picture taken together when he was younger. My father have his picture taken with everyone . . .'

*   *   *

In the evening, as we're having dinner in a little place off Duvall Street, I hear a voice: 'Hey!'

I feel a hand on my shoulder. Charong sees him before I do, but he speaks first:

'It's Hood . . .'

I turn and see him smiling down at us. He looks fine. A sharp brown suit, a different hat. His face puckers into a Bogie-style frown.

'You trying to avoid me?'

Then he laughs and sits at the table. He tells us, as soon as we've finished eating, we must join him in the bar across the street. It's his last night in town and he's going to perform a song — with an incredible, two-tone, black and white, 1960s guitar he bought in a thrift store.

'Did you decide where you're going?' asks Charong.

'*Mañana*, I'm on a slow boat to Cuba,' he replies.

'You're going to Cuba by boat?' I say. 'I don't think they'll like that!'

'I'm reversing the drift,' says Hood. 'I'll be their first Republican refugee. Then I'll introduce them to Iceberg Slim, Ernest Tidyman. Do you think they're ready for *Shaft* and *Superfly*?'

'I'm not sure if they're ready for you,' I tell him.

The bar on Green Street, which has its own Hemingway connection, is filled as much with locals as with tourists when Hood comes on to perform. Clearly he has already found some supporters in this town, though their number is not legion. He appears to scattered applause, after a perfunctory introduction by one of the barmen, a Southern-sounding Marine Corps type with perhaps a suggestion of something more at work inside his head.

John sits on a stool in a single spotlight and waits for silence – as much as he's going to get – before announcing surprisingly softly into the microphone that he will sing a song written by the Brothers Gibb. Even speaking, there's a heartfelt, melancholy quality to his voice that commands attention.

Slowly he starts fingering a few chords and then eases his voice around the wavering, plaintive vocal. I've heard him perform before on Miami Beach – once, Radiohead's 'Creep', the second time, a Sinatra number – but this is different.

'*I started a joke, which started the whole world crying . . .*'

John enunciates each word with a bizarre, early Bowie-ish twist, but making them painful, not camp, dragging every last drop of emotion from the song.

'*But I didn't see, that the joke was on me . . .*'

It's not the kind of upbeat tune most people in Key West for a good and a wild time want to hear – and by about halfway through, John's audience is decidedly restive. But he toughs it out, and by the end has won a fair amount of applause from the crowd.

Charong shoots me a little smile, and when John comes over we tell him how much we liked it. But already his mind is moving on elsewhere, uncomfortable with praise, and unwilling to accept defeat. We finish our drinks, then on an impulse, take John out to the car and drive to the corner of South Street, where the 'Conch Republic', as Key West once briefly declared itself, has a large, stone monument, shaped like a buoy and coloured like a channel marker, set at the Atlantic's edge to identify, 'The Southernmost Point of the Continental USA'.

Above that are the more telling words – at least to John: '90 Miles to Cuba'.

We sit in the darkness for a time, our thoughts interrupted by other tourists walking by and the occasional flash from a camera. As the water laps at the jetty's shadowy stone walls, Hood lights a cigarette, briefly smokes it, then flicks it out over the ocean, its tiny red eye dying in the night.

'The end of America!' John says, and laughs. 'Where's the beginning?'

He drives back with us to our hotel and comes in for a while. The Eden House is pretty in a wood-deck kind of way, and our modest suite is comfortable, but John's mood seems very final, and I think we know that we won't see him for some considerable time.

We hug each other goodbye – and then Hood is gone.

I ask Charong if she's tired, and she says, 'Not yet,' so we go out by the pool and skinny-dip, then immerse ourselves in the jacuzzi, letting it ease away our aches as we stare up at the stars.

We return to the room and still can't sleep. Nothing on TV feels right, so we have a drink, then go back outside. It's much later than we thought: a pale orange glow is already eating at the night.

We climb in the car, put the top down and drive through near-silent streets, back past the 'southernmost' marker, and on, to stop by a paved boat ramp. The sun is starting to rise above the island, backlighting the trees and houses of Key West and sending a brilliant crack out over the ocean.

I look at Charong and try, dangerously, to see the future. I think about Hood, about Cuba and Miami. Here, next to the ramp, on a patch of sand barely large enough to call a beach, a young man of about twenty is building the most extraordinary sand-castle I have ever seen: a Gaudi-like palace of crenellated towers and terraces, intricate bridges and domes, which seem to defy gravity.

We watch him as he works with a fierce, quiet concentration. He sees us and says nothing, just continues to dampen tiny balls of sand from a half-filled bucket of water at his feet.

When finally he speaks, his gaunt Hispanic face is finely streaked with sweat and his eyes seem on fire. He's been up all night, building without a break. Yes, he's studied architecture. Yes, he's made other castles in the past. When the sea or the rain or strangers destroy them, he simply starts again.

He goes back to his building. It seems the clearest image of Florida you could have – of transience and rebirth. The Overseas Railroad. *Boom!* Build again. Hurricane Andrew. *Boom!* Build again.

The sun climbs the sky, cranking the heat up a notch, even at this hour. We get in the car and drive.

ACKNOWLEDGEMENTS

My first and deepest debt is to Charong Chow, for making me happy and, especially in the final months of the book, enduring my manic moods.

I must also thank Michael VerMeulen and Philip Watson of *GQ*, without whom this book would not exist. They sent me to Miami in 1990 to interview Nigel Benn, and I never quite left. In death, as in life, I hope Michael has found a good restaurant and bar.

Too many friends in Florida have contributed to the book in too many ways for me to name them all, but I would especially like to thank the following: Jeremy Jackson, Alison Blackwell, Patricia Romero, Steve, Bob and Brian Antoni and their parents, Anabella and Fernando Paiz and their children, Eliza Johnson, Jennifer and Jason Rubell, Dara Friedman and Mark Handforth, Gundula Friedman, Paul and Judy Lazarus, Tom and Lisa Austin, Claudia Hale, Michele Comerford, Adam Kuczynski, Cathy Steele, Dina Knapp, Mitchell Kaplan, Scott Price, Jeff, Cathy Leff, Michael Capponi, Greg and Nicole at Groove Jet, Garrick and Carla Edwards, Linda Smith, Laura Morgan, Cara, Laura and Jim Quinlan, Tery Valina, Jessica Probst, Daniela and Paulina Urrutia,

Veronica, Jemma Gura, Lorraine Rivera and of course John Hood. Thanks, too, to my earliest friends here: Shana Robbins, Stephanie Kerlin, Billie Speer, Carl Sheusi, Chris, Elissa, Tom, Jay, Michaela, and Carlos and Jodi Saybe.

Specifically, I owe thanks to Elizabeth Freire and Greg Aunapu, for information concerning *santería*; to everyone I talked to for the book, but especially Nigel Benn, Mitchell Wolfson, Danilo de la Torre, David Chang of the Miami Police Department and my Weeki Wachee mermaid, Deena; to John Imboden, for permission to reproduce his poem, *Happy Trails*; to Andy Rees at BMG Music Publishing; to Fran Brennan at the *Miami Herald*; and to the ever helpful Florida Section of the Miami Public Library.

Finally, I'd like to thank my friend and agent, Charles Walker, and my editor, Marianne Velmans, for keeping me on course and remaining calm even when I suddenly vanished to Australasia; my English friends, Frances Coady, Andrew and Stuart Douglas, Liz Jobey, Danny Boyle, Andrew and Kevin Macdonald, Robert Elms, John Simmonds, Hamish Renfrew and Spike 'Dad' Denton; and Ana Jornet for providing such a fine finale to the writing.

And much love to my sister and brother-in-law, Lynne and Peter Hayes, and to my parents, Eileen and Fred Stuart.

NOTES FROM A SMALL ISLAND
Bill Bryson

'NOT A BOOK THAT SHOULD BE READ IN PUBLIC, FOR
FEAR OF EMITTING LOUD SNORTS'
The Times

After nearly two decades in Britain, Bill Bryson took the
decision to move back to the States for a while, to let his kids
experience life in another country, to give his wife the chance
to shop until 10 p.m. seven nights a week, and, most of all,
because he had read that 3.7 million Americans believed that
they had been abducted by aliens at one time or another, and
it was thus clear to him that his people needed him.

But before leaving his much-loved home in North Yorkshire,
Bryson insisted on taking one last trip around Britain, a sort of
valedictory tour of the green and kindly island that had so
long been his home. His aim was to take stock of the nation's
public face and private parts (as it were), and to analyse what
precisely it was he loved so much about a country that had
produced Marmite, a military hero whose dying wish was to
be kissed by a fellow named Hardy, place names like Farleigh
Wallop, Titsey and Shellow Bowells, people who said
'Mustn't grumble', and *Gardeners' Question Time.*

'Splendid . . . What's enjoyable is that there's as much of
Bryson in here as there is of Britain'
Sunday Telegraph

'Bryson is funny because ie is not afraid to give completely of
himself'
Daily Express

'Laugh-out-loud funny'
Good Book Guide

'Always strikes a balance between entertainment and
information... his book is suffused with the sheer joy
of being alive'
Sunday Express

0 552 99600 9

BLACK SWAN

TOUCH THE DRAGON
Karen Connelly

'We will treat like a daughter, and you will treat us like father'

So begins Karen Connelly's year-long sojourn in Denchai, a small farming and merchant community in Northern Thailand at the age of seventeen. *Touch the Dragon* is the story of that year, of living with a Thai family and having the curiosity value of being the only non-Thai in town, of having to learn the language, customs and idiosyncrasies of the people whilst absorbing the extraordinary sights, sound and smells of a different culture.

Written with startling wisdom and perceptiveness, *Touch the Dragon* is a powerful and honest evocation of another culture. Not only is this the exciting response of a articulate imagination to a new environment but the thrilling début of a supremely gifted writer.

'A TRAVEL MEMOIR EXTRAORDINAIRE...ILLUMINATING, POIGNANT AND FUNNY'
Winnipeg Free Press

'FILLED WITH A STRING OF POWERFUL ENRICHING MOMENTS BEAUTIFULLY AND CLEARLY ILLUSTRATED IN CONNELLY'S POETIC LANGUAGE, WHICH SEEM AS FRESH IN THE READER'S MIND AS THEY MUST BE IN HER MEMORY'
Toronto Globe and Mail

'A LOVINGLY CRAFTED PIECE OF WRITING. THE IMMEDIACY OF CONNELLY'S LANGUAGE KEEPS THE NARRATIVE HUMMING'
Montreal Gazette

Winner of the Governor General's Award for Non-Fiction.

0 552 99690 4

BLACK SWAN

THE MAZE
Lucy Rees

An extraordinary quest for enlightenment in a barren desert.

One summer, Lucy Rees and her companion, Rick, rode on horseback through the breath-taking beauty of Arizona's painted desert in the shadow of its vast horizons, red rock canyons and diamond blue skies.

Their journey takes them from Tintagel on a windswept Cornish coast to the searing heat of America's hottest desert; from a small sevenfold maze carved in ancient stone to a barren hillside in North East Arizona where the same Cretan maze can be found on a rock not far from the dwellings of America's last surviving Hopi indians...

Part travel book, part spiritual enlightenment, *The Maze* describes with compassion and wit a journey of understanding through a beautiful and majestic landscape.

'THE COMBINATION OF TRAVEL, HORSES AND 'THE MEANING OF LIFE' MADE A FASCINATING COMBINATION – I WAS REALLY SAD TO FINISH IT'
Rachel Billington

'LUCY REES CHARTS CLEARLY AND TOUCHINGLY THE CONNECTIONS OF INNER AND OUTER JOURNEYS. SHE IS A WONDERFUL GUIDE TO ARIZONA AND AN EVEN BETTER ONE TO THE INTRICATE MAZES OF THE HUMAN HEART'
Jill Paton Walsh

'THE BOOK SURPRISED ME AND MOVED ME AND AT THE END OF IT I FELT THAT I TOO HAD MADE A CATHARTIC JOURNEY'
Maureen Lipman

0 552 14322 7

BLACK SWAN

A SELECTED LIST OF FINE WRITING
AVAILABLE FROM BLACK SWAN

99600 9	NOTES FROM A SMALL ISLAND	*Bill Bryson*	£6.99
99572 X	STRANGE ANGELS	*Andy Bull*	£5.99
99690 4	TOUCH THE DRAGON	*Karen Connelly*	£6.99
99707 2	ONE ROOM IN A CASTLE	*Karen Connelly*	£6.99
99482 0	MILLENNIUM	*Felipe Fernández-Armesto*	£14.99
99530 4	H. G.: THE HISTORY OF MR WELLS	*Michael Foot*	£7.99
99479 0	PERFUME FROM PROVENCE	*Lady Fortescue*	£6.99
99557 6	SUNSET HOUSE	*Lady Fortescue*	£6.99
12555 5	IN SEARCH OF SCHRÖDINGER'S CAT	*John Gribbin*	£7.99
99621 1	LAST GO ROUND	*Ken Kesey & Ken Babbs*	£6.99
99637 8	MISS McKIRDY'S DAUGHTERS WILL NOW DANCE THE HIGHLAND FLING	*Barbara Kinghorn*	£6.99
14433 9	INVISIBLE CRYING TREE	*Christopher Morgan & Tom Shannon*	£6.99
99504 5	LILA	*Robert Pirsig*	£6.99
14322 7	THE MAZE	*Lucy Rees*	£6.99
99579 7	THE HOUSE OF BLUE LIGHTS	*Joe Roberts*	£6.99
99658 0	THE BOTTLEBRUSH TREE	*Hugh Seymour-Davies*	£6.99
99638 6	BETTER THAN SEX	*Hunter S. Thompson*	£6.99
99601 7	JOGGING ROUND MAJORCA	*Gordon West*	£5.99
99666 1	BY BUS TO THE SAHARA	*Gordon West*	£5.99
99366 2	THE ELECTRIC KOOL AID ACID TEST	*Tom Wolfe*	£7.99

All Transworld titles are available by post from:
Book Service By Post, PO Box 29, Douglas, Isle of Man, IM99 1BQ
Credit cards accepted. Please telephone 01624 675137, fax 01624
670923, Internet http://www.bookpost.co.uk
or e-mail: bookshop@enterprise.net for details.
Free postage and packing in the UK. Overseas customers allow
£1 per book (paperbacks) and £3 per book (hardbacks).